PUBLIC RECORD OFFICE HANDBOOKS

No. 14

Records of Interest to Social Scientists

1919 to 1939

Introduction

Brenda Swann, Ph.D.
Maureen Turnbull, B.A.

Research Associates of the
University of Kent at Canterbury

LONDON

HER MAJESTY'S STATIONERY OFFICE

1971

PREFACE

An archive is to the social scientist a tool as important as the laboratory is to the natural scientist. It is where the records of social experience are assembled in an organised fashion. Given the paucity of opportunities for controlled experiment in the social sciences, we must exploit to the fullest extent possible the data that are the by-product of other people's purposes. Very commonly these purposes are administrative. And that means that the documents become available already organised according to some more or less intelligible principle. But if, as is normal, the interests of the researcher are widely different from those of the administrator, a process of translation and systematic interpretation of the latter's aims and ambience is necessary if the search for relevant information about underlying social processes is to be effectively pursued.

It is this need which the present booklet is intended to serve. It is, so to say, a prolegomenon to the series of guides through the mass of new material that has recently been opened at the Public Record Office, as a result of the welcome liberalisation of some of the rules governing the confidentiality of official documents. It is our belief at the Social Science Research Council that this new cache of documentary data probably contains matter of great potential importance to social scientists. We were therefore pleased to make a research grant to the University of Kent for systematic analysis and description of these Public Record Office documents with the aim of accelerating their use for scientific purposes.

The Council is grateful to the Public Record Office and Her Majesty's Stationery Office for allowing this Guide to be published in the Public Record Office series of Handbooks.

7 July 1971   ANDREW SHONFIELD

CONTENTS

CONTENTS BY CODING

INTRODUCTION

The public records are the archives, ancient and modern, of the central government of this country. The main repository is the Public Record Office in Chancery Lane, London, WC2A 1LR, with additional search rooms at the Land Registry, Lincoln's Inn Fields (entrance in Portugal Street). The search rooms are open from 9.30 a.m. to 5.0 p.m. on Monday to Friday, and at Chancery Lane only from 9.30 a.m. to 1.0 p.m. on Saturdays (when all documents must be ordered in advance).

To consult the public records a Reader's Ticket is required. A Temporary Permit, valid for one week and not renewable, may be obtained at the Enquiry Rooms at Chancery Lane or the Land Registry. A full Reader's Ticket, valid for three years and renewable thereafter, requires a recommendation from someone of recognised position to whom the applicant is known personally or from a recognised institution (*e.g.* Embassy, University). Application forms for a full Reader's Ticket may be obtained in advance by post from the Public Record Office.

Not all official or public records are kept at the Public Record Office. A few government departments because of special circumstances have been appointed places of deposit by the Lord Chancellor under powers given to him by the Public Records Act 1958, s.4. These include the Charity Commissioners, the Post Office, the India Office Records (now a part of the Foreign and Commonwealth Office) and the Board of Customs and Excise which retains its own records for 100 years. Under these same powers public records of local origin and interest, such as quarter sessions, colliery, and hospital records, have been deposited in local record offices. A list of such places of deposit was published as Appendix D to *The 5th Annual Report of the Keeper of Public Records* (for 1963), with amendments notified in subsequent *Reports*.

The Public Records Act 1958 specifically exempted from its operations records emanating from Scottish departments (which are kept at the Scottish Record Office, Edinburgh), registers kept in the General Register Office, and records of the Public Trustee relating to individual trusts. In addition certain types of records whose status was not clear before 1958 have sometimes escaped from official custody. This has been especially true of private office papers of ministers, which in some departments were formerly permitted to depart with the minister on his retirement. This was most likely to happen with non-departmental ministers such as the Chancellor of the Duchy of Lancaster and the Paymaster General. Such papers, where they survive, are with the private papers of individual ministers, or reach the Public Record Office as gifts or deposits, or are given to libraries. Records are normally transferred to the Public Record Office when they are between 25 and 30 years old, but exceptionally where they are required for continuing administrative purposes, they may, with the consent of the Lord Chancellor under s.3(4) of the 1958 Act, be retained for a longer period. For example, the service departments retain twentieth century records of service of members of the armed forces.

ACCESS

Access to the public records is governed by the Public Records Act 1958, s.5 as amended by the Public Records Act 1967. Records are normally open to public inspection on 1 January of the year after that in which they become 30 years old.

However, the Lord Chancellor, at the request of the transferring department, may prescribe a longer or shorter period of closure.

Some classes of records are, therefore, open on transfer to the Public Record Office, even though they are less than 30 years old. In other cases classes of records or individual records may be closed for 50, 75, or 100 years. Records closed for periods longer than 30 years fall into three categories: (i) exceptionally sensitive papers, the disclosure of which would be contrary to the public interest, whether on security or other grounds (including the need to safeguard the revenue); (ii) documents containing information supplied in confidence, the disclosure of which would or might constitute a breach of good faith; and (iii) documents containing information about individuals, the disclosure of which would cause distress or embarrassment to living persons or their immediate descendants. Lists of classes which do not conform to the 30-year rule are displayed in the search rooms. Where a file, volume, or other assemblage of papers covers more than one year, it is the date of the latest paper which determines when the 30-year period begins to run.

ARRANGEMENT OF RECORDS

The records at the P.R.O. are received from various government departments and are kept in the form in which they are received. The documents are arranged in groups, indicated by code letters. In the past these corresponded to the departments from which the documents were transferred, but more recently it has been necessary to use these code letters in a much more flexible manner, otherwise the frequent reorganisation of the machinery of government would have resulted in a multiplicity of codes and the fragmentation of series of records. Now the same code continues in use after the department to which it originally related has been wound up, has changed its name, lost the function concerned, or been merged in another department; continuing classes are not interrupted and new classes are given the same code letters as related classes dealing with the same function. For example, records of most research boards will continue to be placed in the DSIR group although the Department of Scientific and Industrial Research has been absorbed by the Ministry of Technology, which in turn has merged with the Board of Trade, and some research boards have been transferred to other departments.

Within each group the documents are arranged in classes, each class corresponding to a function or some aspect of the work which produced the records, or, as in the case of Miscellanea, a class may be a collection of documents brought together for convenience of reference or storage. A class may contain very few documents or several thousands.

The documents within a class are listed by the transferring department and are arranged as so many pieces. Each piece is numbered and may consist of an individual file, a box containing many files, or a bound book of papers.

P.R.O. GUIDE AND SUMMARY

Copies of the official P.R.O. *Guide* and Summary of Records are in each search room. The published *Guide* is in three volumes: Volume I describes records of the mediaeval courts for the whole of their period of existence and modern legal records; Volume II describes State Papers and departmental records which had reached the P.R.O. by 1960; and Volume III describes records transferred between 1960 and 1966. The search room copies of the *Guide* are kept up to date in manuscript. There is also an unpublished Supplement describing new classes transferred since 1966 and existing classes for which the *Guide* entry has been substantially amended.

The Summary of Records is in two parts, the first part relating to the groups described in Volume I of the *Guide*, and the second to the remaining groups.

The *Guide* gives a history of each department which has a corresponding group and attempts to arrange the classes within groups according to their nature, origin, or subject. For each class it gives the title, covering dates, number and nature of pieces, and a description of the contents. The Summary lists the classes in numerical order within each group, giving covering dates, class title, and number of pieces. The inclusion of classes in the *Guide* and Summary does not necessarily mean they are open to public inspection. A new form of *Guide* is in preparation which will replace the existing Volumes II and III, the Supplement, and the Summary.

CLASS LISTS

Class Lists, describing individual pieces, which may be files, volumes, or even single documents, are normally prepared by the transferring department and reach the P.R.O. together with the records to which they relate. Where a class covers a short span of time and the whole class can be transferred at one time, the correspond-ing list will be complete. But it is more usual for classes to be the subject of a succes-sion of transfers, each adding a further number of pieces to the class, with a corresponding addition to the class list. This can result in problems of arrangement within the class list. Where lists are arranged in chronological order the sequence may be disturbed by transfers out of order, especially where there are individual pieces with a wide time-span, and the chronological order may start again with each transfer. Similarly where lists are in alphabetical order of subjects, persons, or places, each new transfer is added as a new alphabetical series. Where lists are arranged on a classified subject basis, new additions are normally interpolated into the existing lists. These interpolations may be on separate sheets, even though the last existing sheet for that subject is not filled, so that a partly filled page need not mean the end of a section. Sub-headings in a class list may refer only to one file and do not necessarily extend to the next sub-heading.

It should be remembered that the administrative circumstances of a wide range of scattered and different departments dictate not only the arrangement of the records but also the form which lists and other finding aids take and no single standard form of list, however convenient for the searcher, would meet those circumstances. Therefore, if material which is sought is not in what appears to the outsider to be the most likely place, this does not mean that it is not available. It may, however, be necessary to search carefully through the rest of the class list, in other related classes, even in classes in other groups. Anyone making a search in the public records will find at least an outline administrative history of help; it is often more profitable to approach the records from the point of view of the administration which created them than from that of their subject.

Where files are arranged in sections or subject indexes are provided, care must be taken in looking for a reference to a particular country. In some classes, such as Treasury Finance and Supply, all countries are put together under 'C'. England sometimes includes Wales; Hampshire is often listed under its correct name of Southampton. All countries belonging to the Commonwealth are usually in sections called 'colonies and protectorates'. Countries which have or had two names may be found under either or both, for example, Iraq and Mesopotamia. Places which are not independent but which changed their status or were in dispute may be found under their own name and not that of the country in which they belong, for example, Upper Silesia and Wei-hai-wei.

SEARCH ROOMS

In addition to the *Guide* and Summaries, each search room has lists of records which are produced at the Land Registry and of those which are stored at Ashridge, Hertfordshire, and a selection of class lists and other research aids relating to the records which are produced in that room.

The class lists of the records for the inter-war period, 1919 to 1939, which are of interest to the social scientist are to be found in the Round Room and the Long Room on the ground floor at Chancery Lane, and in the East and West Rooms on the second floor at the Land Registry. Class lists of the Cabinet Office and Prime Minister's Office records are in the East Room, and those of the Air Ministry and Colonial Office are in the West Room. The Rolls Room, on the first floor at Chancery Lane immediately above the Long Room, through which it is reached, contains some service department class lists. Foreign Office class lists and indexes are divided between the Enquiry Rooms at Chancery Lane and at the Land Registry.

Some class lists are found in two or more search rooms, some only in one. The card index of class lists kept between the doors in the Round Room, should be consulted in order to locate a particular list. Each volume of class lists is identified by a number or letter or a combination of both at the top of the spine to indicate the room and the press (a vertical section of shelving) to which it belongs and by a number at the bottom, to indicate its position in the press. These identifications are not regarded as permanent and are subject to change from time to time to take account of the addition of new volumes and the splitting of existing ones. The removal of volumes may also on occasion affect the numbering.

In the Round Room the presses are numbered; presses 1 to 4 being to the right of the entrance, press 5 between the two entrance doors and presses 6 onwards to the left. Presses at present containing class lists and other research aids likely to be of interest to the social scientist are:

Press 2: State Papers Domestic and Foreign; Home Office
Press 4: Colonial Office (and Commonwealth Relations Office); Treasury
Press 5: Card index of class lists and reference works
Press 6: Service Departments
Presses 7 and 8: Public Departments
Press 13: Courts of Law
Presses 20 to 22: Reference works

Similar systems, with an alphabetical prefix to indicate the room, apply in the Rolls, East, and West Rooms. In the Long Room the presses are lettered; presses A, B, and C, each of which covers two divisions, contain the class lists of departmental records.

Tickets of a different colour are used in each search room for ordering documents. Supplies of these are kept in boxes in the respective search rooms; tickets for use in other rooms may be obtained from the officers in charge or from the Enquiry Rooms.

In the Land Registry records are stored close to the search rooms and records can be produced in about ten minutes. At Chancery Lane storage may be more remote and some time may elapse before documents are produced. Delay can be reduced by ordering documents in advance by post or telephone (this is essential for documents required on Saturdays). Documents stored at Ashridge require three days notice for their production at Chancery Lane; they can be seen in the search room at Ashridge.

SCOPE OF THIS GUIDE

In this guide, the groups which contain inter-war material have been arranged under the headings of Finance, Foreign Affairs, Industry and Trade, Social Services, etc.; and the Cabinet, Prime Minister's Office, and others which deal with the whole range of government activities have been put together at the beginning. The groups whose records are of direct interest to social scientists have been dealt with more fully than others whose records may be of marginal interest. But because it is difficult to think of any records which are quite without any interest to the political scientist, economist, economic historian, or sociologist, all groups with inter-war material have been included, except some judicial classes consisting solely of formal records of court proceedings.

For each group, a brief history of the department from which the records reached the P.R.O. is given, together with the main transfers of function to and from the department. It is hoped this will enable the searcher to find relevant documents which may have remained with other departments and so reached the P.R.O. under other groups. The section dealing with the social service ministries has a general introductory note and list of transfers of function in order to clarify the numerous administrative changes that have taken place since 1919.

Within each group the classes with inter-war material are listed in numerical order unless otherwise stated. Where appropriate a description of the class and its contents is given and, when the arrangement allows, the piece numbers of the inter-war material are given, and sometimes the piece numbers of records of special interest, or pieces which might not be looked for in the class. Unless otherwise stated, the class lists contain descriptive titles and dates of the pieces. The basic particulars of a class are set out as follows:

GROUP CODE and
CLASS NUMBER Name of Class
                  Time span. No. of pieces. [P.R.O. *Guide* Access if not
                                             reference].   30 years.

The number of pieces and the time span should give some idea of the amount of inter-war material. If no P.R.O. *Guide* reference is given particulars of the class will be found in the Supplement.

The information showing the number of pieces and the time span of each class is correct for early summer, 1971; new classes may reach the P.R.O. at any time, or new pieces be added to existing classes. The total number of pieces given in this guide can be checked against the total shown in the Summary to see whether new pieces have been added. Most records of the war years, 1939–1945, will be open on 1st January, 1972, and these will contain some pre-war records. Some new classes which are being transferred to the Public Record Office during 1971 have been listed in this guide without detail.

Some cross references have been given, but these are not exhaustive. It should be remembered that the Treasury deals with almost everything, and its class lists should always be consulted, particularly Finance (T 160), Supply (T 161), and the Chancellor of the Exchequer's Office, miscellaneous papers (T 172). Most subjects can be found among the Cabinet Papers, particularly CAB 21 and CAB 24. Other classes which cover a wide range of activities are the correspondence and papers of the Prime Minister's Office (PREMIER 1), the Commercial Department of the Board of Trade (BT 11), and the correspondence and papers of the Development Commission (D 4). For any study of the beginning of this period the records of the Ministry of Reconstruction should be looked at, and for the years 1929 to 1932, the papers of the Chief Industrial Adviser (BT 56). When looking for material on a particular topic, it is useful to remember that the title of a piece does not always describe everything contained therein, and that papers are often added to later files dealing with the same subject.

Some records which are not open for inspection are included in this guide, either because they will soon be open, or so that their whereabouts are known and time is not wasted looking for them elsewhere.

Since this Handbook was written a decision has been made to limit the code letters of all classes of records to a maximum of four characters to enable them to be used in computer processing.

The authors who are research associates of the University of Kent wish to thank the Keeper and other officers of the Public Record Office who have given them every assistance in the preparation of this handbook.

CENTRAL DIRECTION

CABINET OFFICE

The Cabinet Office before 1916 had no secretariat. No secretary attended meetings of the Cabinet and no minutes were taken. The King was kept informed by the Prime Minister who sent him after each meeting a private and personal letter giving an account of the proceedings.

The Cabinet Office grew out of the secretariat attached to the Committee of Imperial Defence. This Committee began as the Defence Committee of the Cabinet in 1895, it was reorganised and called the Committee of Imperial Defence in 1902, and given a small secretariat in 1904.

In November 1914 the Committee of Imperial Defence (C.I.D.) was absorbed by the War Council, consisting of five ministers, the Leader of the Opposition, and two Chiefs of Staff. This was replaced by a Cabinet Committee that was originally formed to conduct the Dardanelles Campaign. In November, 1915, a new War Committee was set up. In December, 1916, Lloyd George, on becoming Prime Minister, discarded the traditional large cabinet and the War Committee, and set up a War Cabinet of five ministers. The secretariat of the C.I.D. had served the War Council, the Dardenelles Committee, and the War Committee; it was now attached to the War Cabinet and its mainly Service personnel was augmented by civilians.

When the War Cabinet ended in November, 1919, the C.I.D. was re-established, and the secretariat continued to serve both the Cabinet and the C.I.D. It is strictly a secretarial organisation with the function of assisting the Cabinet by recording decisions and by the collection and distribution of papers.

The more important Cabinet papers are indexed, and there is a comprehensive guide to the early records called *The Records of the Cabinet Office to 1922* (P.R.O. Handbooks, no. 11, H.M.S.O., 1966). Therefore the classes in this group are not as fully described here as others. The classes are listed in two sections, classes containing records of the War Cabinet or Cabinet, and classes containing records of the Committee of Imperial Defence.

A complete set of class lists and indexes will be found in the East Room of the Land Registry where the records are produced. It should be remembered that usually the title of the document is used in indexing and this may not adequately describe all the contents.

CAB 1 MISCELLANEOUS RECORDS.
1866–1934. 41 pieces. [III 17]

28–30 1919–1922. The papers deal mainly with foreign policy but there are files on the Special Industries Committee, the proposed Ministry of Ways and Communications, and civil unrest in Great Britain.

31–34 1909–1920. Papers of Sir James Masterton-Smith who worked at the Admiralty and in the Ministry of Munitions.

35–41 1905–1934. Miscellaneous papers of the Cabinet and Committee of Imperial Defence, recently transferred. Some are first drafts of papers filed elsewhere, others are additional pages of documents filed elsewhere, and others are new material. Each piece is a box or envelope containing papers packed at random. Handlist is available in the search rooms.

CAB 21   REGISTERED FILES.
          1916–1939.   768 pieces.   [III 17].   Various files are closed for
                                                    50 years.

124–768   1919–1939. These are selected files on various matters considered by the War Cabinet and the Cabinet.

CAB 23   MINUTES.
          1916–1939.   101 pieces.   [III 17].   Various items are closed
                                                    for 50 or 100 years.

This class contains minutes of meetings of the War Cabinet, including those withheld from circulated minutes on grounds of secrecy, and also from November, 1919, Cabinet Conclusions, which are briefer than minutes being mainly records of decisions taken. The minutes and conclusions are indexed, and photocopies of the conclusions are available on the open shelves in the East Room.

CAB 24   MEMORANDA.
          1915–1939.   288 pieces.   [III 17].   Various items are closed
                                                    for 50 years.

These are the papers circulated to the War Cabinet (GT series) and the Cabinet (CP series). There is an index for each year of the CP series.

CAB 26   HOME AFFAIRS COMMITTEE.
          1918–1939.   24 pieces.   [III 18]

This class contains minutes of meetings and papers circulated. There is usually one volume per year, each volume is indexed.

CAB 27   COMMITTEES: GENERAL SERIES.
          1915–1939.   663 pieces.   [III 18]

The minutes and papers of various committees are arranged chronologically.

CAB 28   ALLIED (WAR) CONFERENCES.
          1915–1920.   9 pieces.   [III 22]

CAB 29   INTERNATIONAL CONFERENCES.
          1916–1939.   162 pieces.   [III 22–23]

1–102   1916–1922. Memoranda of the Peace Conference, proceedings of the British Empire Delegation, Council of Heads of Government, Council of Ambassadors, Heads of Delegations of the Five Powers, Allied and International Conferences on the Terms of Peace and Related Subjects, British Empire Delegation to the League of Nations, and meetings of the Allied Prime Ministers in London, 1922.

103–106   1924. London Reparation Conference.

107–116   1929–1930. The Hague Conference.

117–135	1929–1930. London Naval Conference.
136–137	1931. The London Conference.
138	1932. Conference on the Situation in the Danubian States, London.
139	1932. Lausanne Conference.
140–145	1933. League of Nations, Monetary and Economic Conference, London.
146	1935. Anglo-French Conversations, London.
147–158	1935–1936. London Naval Conference.
159–162	1939. Anglo-French Staff Conversations.

CAB 30   WASHINGTON (DISARMAMENT) CONFERENCE.
          1921–1922.   33 pieces.   [III 23]

CAB 31   GENOA (INTERNATIONAL ECONOMIC) CONFERENCE.
          1922.   13 pieces.   [III 23]

CAB 32   IMPERIAL CONFERENCES.
          1917–1937.   137 pieces.   [III 23]

This class contains papers of the Imperial Conferences held in 1921, 1923, 1926, 1930, and 1937, and of the following:

Imperial Wireless and Cable Conference, London, 1928.

Committee on the Organisation of Communications Services, 1928–1929.

Conference on the Operation of Dominion Legislation, 1929.

Imperial Economic Conference, Ottawa, 1932.

Committee on Economic Consultation and Co-operation, London, 1933.

Economic Discussions with Australian Ministers, 1935.

Commonwealth Prime Ministers' Meetings, London, 1935.

Economic Discussions between United Kingdom and Dominion Ministers, London, 1935.

CAB 33   POST-WAR PRIORITY AND DEMOBILISATION COMMITTEES.
          1918–1919.   26 pieces.   [III 18]

CAB 40   WAR PRIORITIES COMMITTEE.
          1917–1919.   171 pieces.   [III 19]

CAB 43   CONFERENCES ON IRELAND.
          1921–1922.   7 pieces.   [III 23]

CAB 44   OFFICIAL WAR HISTORIES: NARRATIVES (MILITARY).
          1914–1965.   45 pieces.

This class contains draft chapters of unpublished volumes prepared by the Cabinet Office Historical Section. Most papers deal with the wars, the inter-war material concerns relations between Great Britain, Italy, and the Sennussi, 1912–1924, the occupation of the Rhineland, 1918–1929, and the occupation of Constantinople, 1918–1923.

CAB 45   OFFICIAL WAR HISTORIES: UNREGISTERED CORRESPONDENCE AND
PAPERS.
1904–1957.   291 pieces.

These are miscellaneous documents used in the compilation of the official War
Histories.

CAB 58   ECONOMIC ADVISORY COUNCIL.
1925–1939.   208 pieces.

A Committee of Civil Research was set up in 1925 as 'a standing committee
reporting to the Cabinet, analogous in principle to the Committee of Imperial
Defence'. It was re-formed in 1930 as the Economic Advisory Council. This class
contains the minutes and memoranda of the Committee and Council and of the
numerous committees and sub-committees which were set up. Piece 16 contains a
history of both the Committee and Council.
    Subject index is available in search rooms.

CAB 61   IRISH BOUNDARY COMMISSION.
1924–1925.   168 pieces.

CAB 62   INTERNATIONAL COMMITTEE FOR THE APPLICATION OF THE AGREE-
MENT REGARDING NON-INTERVENTION IN SPAIN.
1936–1945.   89 pieces.
See also FO 849.

CAB 63   PRIVATE COLLECTIONS: HANKEY PAPERS.
1908–1944.   191 pieces.   Various files are closed for 50 years.

Lord Hankey after service in the Royal Marine Artillery became Assistant
Secretary to the Committee of Imperial Defence in 1908, and Secretary in 1912.
He served the War Council, the Dardanelles Committee, and the War Committee,
and was appointed Secretary to the War Cabinet in 1916. After the war, Lord Hankey
served the Cabinet and the Committee of Imperial Defence until he retired in 1938.
During the Second World War, he became Minister without Portfolio, Chancellor
of the Duchy of Lancaster, and Paymaster General, and served on many Government committees.

15–53	1919–1938. Copies of memoranda prepared for the Cabinet, to-gether with correspondence.
54–65	1926–1937. Engagement diaries.
66–82	1932–1935. Papers concerning visits to South Africa, Australia, New Zealand, and Canada.

CAB 64   MINISTER FOR THE CO-ORDINATION OF DEFENCE: REGISTERED FILES.
1924–1939.   36 pieces.

CAB 103   HISTORICAL SECTION: REGISTERED FILES.
1918–1959.   148 pieces.

These files contain progress reports, estimates, and correspondence on various
subjects; little inter-war material.

CAB 104   Registered Files: Supplementary.
         1923–1939.   164 pieces.   Closed for 50 years.

COMMITTEE OF IMPERIAL DEFENCE

In the following classes, some items are closed for 50 years. The first eighteen classes are described in the *Guide,* Part III pp. 19–22:

CAB 2   Minutes. 1902–1939.   9 pieces.

CAB 3   Memoranda. Home Defence. 1901–1939.   8 pieces.

CAB 4   Memoranda. Miscellaneous. 1903–1939.   30 pieces.

CAB 5   Memoranda. Colonial Defence. 1902–1916; 1919–1939. 9 pieces.

CAB 6   Memoranda. Defence of India. 1901–1939.   6 pieces.

CAB 7   Colonial/Oversea Defence Committee: Minutes. 1877–1939.   18 pieces.

CAB 8   Colonial/Oversea Defence Committee: Memoranda. 1885–1939.   56 pieces.

CAB 9   Colonial/Oversea Defence Committee: Remarks. 1887–1914; 1919–1939.   21 pieces.

CAB 10   Colonial/Oversea Defence Committee: Minutes by the Committee. 1912–1914; 1919–1939.   10 pieces.

CAB 11   Colonial/Oversea Defence Committee: Defence Schemes. 1863–1922; 1925–1939.   216 pieces.

CAB 12   Home (Ports) Defence Committee: Minutes. 1909–1939. 6 pieces.

CAB 13   Home (Ports) Defence Committee: Memoranda. 1909–1939. 29 pieces.

CAB 15   Committee on the Co-ordination of Departmental Action. 1911–1939.   39 pieces.

CAB 16   Ad Hoc Sub-committees of Enquiry. 1905–1939.   231 pieces.

CAB 18   Miscellaneous Volumes. 1875–1919.   99 pieces.

CAB 34   Standing Sub-committee. 1921–1922.   1 piece.

CAB 35   Imperial Communications Committee. 1919–1939.   45 pieces.

CAB 36   Joint Oversea and Home Defence Committee. 1920–1939. 23 pieces.

CAB 46   Air Raid Precaution Committees. 1924–1939.   32 pieces.

CAB 47   Advisory Committee on Trade Questions in Time of War. 1924–1939.   15 pieces.

CAB 48   Industrial Intelligence in Foreign Countries. 1924–1939. 10 pieces.

CAB 49   STANDING INTER-DEPARTMENTAL COMMITTEE ON CENSORSHIP. 1924–1939. 20 pieces.

CAB 50   THE OIL BOARD. 1925–1939. 19 pieces.

CAB 51   MIDDLE EAST QUESTIONS. 1930–1939. 11 pieces.

CAB 52   WAR LEGISLATION COMMITTEES. 1924–1929. 8 pieces.

CAB 53   CHIEFS OF STAFF COMMITTEE. 1923–1939. 55 pieces.

CAB 54   DEPUTY CHIEFS OF STAFF COMMITTEE. 1932–1939. 13 pieces.

CAB 55   JOINT PLANNING COMMITTEE. 1927–1939. 19 pieces.

CAB 56   JOINT INTELLIGENCE COMMITTEE. 1936–1939. 6 pieces.

CAB 57   MANPOWER COMMITTEE. 1923–1939. 30 pieces.

CAB 60   PRINCIPAL SUPPLY OFFICERS' COMMITTEE. 1924–1939. 73 pieces.

PRIME MINISTER'S OFFICE

During the nineteenth century, the Prime Minister's official staff consisted of two or three private secretaries, and an unpaid parliamentary private secretary. When Lloyd George became Prime Minister in 1916 he supplemented his staff by a bureau of experts drawn from outside the civil service. This was abolished when the Coalition Government ended in 1922.

The Prime Minister's office now consists of private secretaries seconded from departments and a small permanent staff.

Prime ministers and other ministers on relinquishing office usually take their private and party political papers with them. The documents in this class are therefore the remaining official papers.

PREMIER 1   CORRESPONDENCE AND PAPERS.
       1916–1940.   443 pieces.   Various files are closed for 50 years.

These papers cover a wide range of subjects. There are many papers dealing with economic affairs and unemployment, foreign policy, proposals for reorganisation of government machinery, and reports of deputations. Subject index is available in the search rooms.

PREMIER 2   HONOURS: LISTS AND PAPERS.
       1916–1938.   99 pieces.

These papers relate to New Year and Birthday Honours, etc., lists of names with official citations.

PREMIER 5   APPOINTMENTS.
       1907–1967.   174 pieces.   Various files are closed for 50 or 75 years.

The papers are concerned with ministerial and ecclesiastical appointments, also appointments to the Civil List, to Boards of Museums and Galleries, to Royal Commissions, and miscellaneous appointments, e.g. Astronomer Royal, Constable of the Tower. Files dealing with ecclesiastical appointments are closed for 75 years, those dealing with trustee and miscellaneous appointments are closed for 50 years, the remainder are open after 30 years. The files headed 'Ministerial Appointments' contain some papers on procedure.

PRIVY COUNCIL OFFICE

The Privy Council was originally the King's body of advisers. Its place in the formulation of policy has been taken by the Cabinet, and the main function of the Council is now the transaction of certain formal acts of state. It also grants charters to boroughs and institutions of all kinds, for example universities, colleges, and the institutes which govern many of the professions. The Privy Council has held powers since the Medical Act, 1886, and the Dentists Act, 1878, to supervise these professions, and under Pharmacy Acts has control over chemists and the dispensing of poisons. Its powers under the Midwives Acts were transferred to the Ministry of Health in 1919. Much of the work of the Privy Council in the past has been done through committees, some of which developed into separate departments of state, e.g. the Board of Trade, the Ministry of Education, the Ministry of Agriculture and Fisheries.

During the inter-war period committees of the Privy Council were responsible for state sponsorship of scientific research. A committee of the Council for Scientific and Industrial Research was set up in 1915; its records have been transferred to the P.R.O. as a separate group, DSIR. A Medical Research Committee was formed in 1913 with funds provided by the National Insurance Act, 1911, and answerable to the Minister responsible for National Health Insurance. In 1920, it was made responsible to a Committee of the Privy Council, and became the Medical Research Council, incorporated by charter. Agricultural research was sponsored by the two Boards of Agriculture, and by the Development Commission which in 1911 began to plan the research needed. In 1930 it was decided to form an Agricultural Research Council similar to the Medical Research Council, and this was incorporated in 1931. In the cases of the A.R.C. and the M.R.C., a Committee of the Privy Council is responsible for them and makes appointments to the Councils, but they are considered to be non-departmental authorities, and their records have not been transferred to the P.R.O.

In 1949, the scope of the Agricultural Research Council was widened to cover nature conservation, and in 1956 the Nature Conservancy was set up as a separate body responsible to a committee of the Privy Council.

In 1959, a new Committee on Overseas Research was formed to deal with scientific research in or for overseas territories and to co-operate with international agencies in promoting such research.

A new Minister of Science was appointed in 1959 who took over responsibility for the five research committees of the Privy Council. This office was combined with that of the Minister of Education in 1964; for most of the five years that it existed the office of Minister of Science was held by the Lord President of the Council.

Between 1954 and 1957, the Lord President of the Council was responsible for the Atomic Energy Authority. In 1957 the Lord President's powers were transferred to the Prime Minister; they later went to the Minister of Science, and in 1965 to the Minister of Technology.

The Judicial Committee of the Privy Council acts as the Supreme Court of Appeal for the Commonwealth, except Great Britain and those countries which have abolished the right of appeal to it. The earlier work of the Judicial Committee is described in Part I of the *Guide*, p. 165; no twentieth century records have as yet been transferred to the P.R.O.

PC 1   PAPERS, MAINLY UNBOUND.
        1481–1946.   4,570 pieces.   [II 233–234]

The few inter-war papers deal with the granting of charters to boroughs and colleges.

PC 2   REGISTERS.
        1540–1957.   748 pieces.   [II 234]

The Registers of the Privy Council contain minutes of its proceedings, orders, reports of committees, copies of King's Regulations and Admiralty Instructions, maps concerned with the granting of charters to boroughs showing division into wards, and maps showing approved changes in parish boundaries.

PC 3   SHERIFFS' ROLLS.
        1844–1935.   92 pieces.   [II 235]

76–92   1919–1935. One roll per year. Rolls contain the names of three nominations for the office of sheriff in each county of England and Wales, except Cornwall and Lancashire.

PC 4   MINUTES.
        1670–1928.   27 pieces.   [II 234]

27   1906–1928. Minute book, indexed.

PC 8   ORIGINAL CORRESPONDENCE.
        1860–1936.   1,269 pieces.   [II 234]

845–1269   1919–1936. The correspondence is arranged chronologically and is concerned with all aspects of the work of the Privy Council. There are papers on the granting of charters of all kinds, of the various committees of the Privy Council, their constitution and work, special references to the Judicial Committee, and consideration of various parliamentary bills dealing with matters such as pharmacy, architects, and dentists, and correspondence with the Channel Islands.

PC 9   CORRESPONDENCE, REGISTERS.
        1860–1935.   78 pieces.   [II 234]

62–78   1919–1935. One register per year, each volume is indexed.

PC 10   COMMISSIONS AND COMMITTEES.
        1899–1937.   83 pieces.   [III 108]

21–49   1923–1926. Statutory Commission for Oxford University; papers and report.

50–80   1924–1929. Statutory Commission for London University; papers, including those of Joint Committee for Promoting the Higher Education of Working People.

83   1936–1937. Court of Claims; to consider petitions to perform services at the coronation.

MINISTRY OF RECONSTRUCTION

Two Reconstruction Committees were appointed during the First World War; the first by Asquith in March, 1916, was re-formed by Lloyd George in March, 1917. Both Committees appointed sub-committees. The second Committee consisted of fourteen members with specialised knowledge and was divided into six panels. This Committee was dissolved when the Ministry of Reconstruction was formed and this took over most of the sub-committees.

Addison was appointed Minister of Reconstruction in August, 1917, and was succeeded by Sir Auckland Geddes in January, 1919. Sir Auckland Geddes was also Minister of National Service; some files in this group are stamped Ministry of National Service and Reconstruction but the two ministries were not amalgamated though for a time they shared the same minister, permanent secretary, and building.

The one class in this group contains some of the reports and some of the papers of the numerous committees and sub-committees set up; but many others that originated in the work of the Ministry were passed to other departments when the Ministry of Reconstruction was abolished in June, 1919.

Papers of the Ministry of Reconstruction can be found in the following:

AIR 2/121/B. 8979.   Report on the Mode of Entry and Training of Regular Officers in R.A.F. 1919.

BT 55/24.   Engineering Trades (New Industries) Committee, reports of seven branch committees.

BT 67.   Six papers of the Ministry.

LAB 2/213   Papers of Machinery of Government sub-committee, and papers on war pledges.

LAB 2/264   Standing Joint Industrial Council for Heavy Leather Goods.

LCO 2/508–509   Land Transfer Committee of Acquisition and Valuation of Land Committee.

LCO 3.   Acquisition and Valuation of Land Committee.

MH 55/517–518   Public health: subsidiary health and kindred services for women.

MT 39/30   Papers on transport, road construction, etc.

PC 8/835   Report of sub-committee on the Acquisition of Parliamentary Powers, and correspondence dealing with matters concerning the health of the population.

T 1/12205/38481   Reports of Demobilisation sub-committee.

RECON 1   MINISTRY OF RECONSTRUCTION.
1906–1920.   90 pieces.   [II 257]

This class contains many papers arranged in no particular order. They include the following:

General questions of industrial development after the war: consideration of supplies of materials, disposal of surplus government stores, and particular industries: cotton, engineering, forestry, iron and steel, public utilities, and wool.

Shipping; particularly German shipping, post-war trade, and shipbuilding.

Consideration of the civil service and local government.

Education: position of natural science and modern languages in education and adult education.

Financial questions: new issues of capital, currency and foreign exchange, and financial risks attached to holding trading stocks.

Housing: supply of materials, rents, and proposals for special housing banks run by county or municipal authorities.

Labour problems: effect of termination of the war on wages, emigration, employment of women, demobilisation and resettlement of ex-service men, juvenile labour and physical training, unemployment, and vagrancy.

Reform of legal and parliamentary procedure.

The following files are of particular interest:

40   1916–1917. Reconstruction Committees. Two files on the first committee with minutes of meeting on 24.3.1916. File on setting up of second committee with list of all sub-committees and personnel, advisory council and list of members and sections. 1917 progress report, and description of 125 papers.

41   Papers produced for the Reconstruction Committee, resolutions, etc. Handlist in search rooms.

70   Reconstruction problems and general questions relating thereto: organisation of lecture tours, pamphlets sent to the Ministry, Local Reconstruction Organisation Committee, minutes of first meeting, 11.12.1918. Reconstruction in Scotland, Wales, Ireland, and abroad.

89   Printed report of work of Ministry, 1919, Cmd. 9231, containing lists of all committees appointed by Asquith, Lloyd George, and the Minister, members of committees, terms of reference and whether report was published, and a list of all papers and other documents issued by the Ministry. File on arrangements for dissolution of the Ministry.

90   Miscellaneous papers mostly dealing with various committees include those of the 1916 Reconstruction Committee, also memoranda sent in by outsiders.

FINANCE

TREASURY

The Treasurer in mediaeval times was the presiding officer of the Exchequer, but since 1714 this office has been in commission. The Lords Commissioners met as a body until the middle of the 19th century, the Prime Minister being the First Lord, but the Treasury is now under the control of the Chancellor of the Exchequer. Formal acts, however, are still done in the name of the Lords Commissioners. The Treasury is a prerogative department, and many of its functions are not derived from statutes.

The Treasury has a central position in the structure of government. It is responsible for financial policy, for controlling public expenditure, and for economic co-ordination. It is responsible to Parliament for the imposition and regulation of taxation, for monetary policy, and overseas finance. It also controlled all matters connected with the management, pay, and conditions, of the Civil Service until 1968 when this function was transferred to the new Civil Service Department.

The main financial powers of the central government are entrusted to the Chancellor of the Exchequer and, while the Treasury is his main department, much of the work of raising and controlling public money is done through other departments. These are responsible to the Chancellor and work in close touch with the Treasury but are separate departments. In the inter-war period the main departments, apart from the Treasury, under the control of the Chancellor of the Exchequer were as follows:

Board of Customs and Excise.
Board of Inland Revenue.
Development Commission.
Forestry Commission.
Friendly Societies' Registry.
Government Actuary.
Import Duties Advisory Committee.
Mint.
National Debt Office.
National Savings Committee.
Office of Parliamentary Counsel.
Paymaster General's Office.
Stationery Office.
Treasury Solicitor.
University Grants Committee.

Most Treasury papers were filed in T 1 until 1920 when they were divided into five classes T 160–164. There are two classes for papers belonging to the Office of the Chancellor of the Exchequer, others for private office papers, and many other classes for out-letters, accounts, warrants, and special commissions. Most of these classes ceased to accrue before the inter-war period.

For this group the arrangement here is not in numerical order. It begins with T 1 and the classes into which it divides; other classes follow in order except for out-letters which are placed together at the end of the group.

T 1   TREASURY BOARD PAPERS.
       1557–1920.   12,626 pieces.   [II 284].   Various files are closed for
                                                    100 years.

Until June, 1920, most Treasury papers were filed chronologically in this one
class. T 2, T 3, and T 108 are means of reference to these papers, but are
difficult to use. A descriptive list of selected documents thought to be of interest to
social scientists has been made for the period autumn 1918 to June 1920 and is
available in the search rooms.

In July, 1920, a new classification was introduced and accruing Treasury Board
Papers were divided into the following classes:

T 160   FINANCE FILES.

T 161   SUPPLY FILES.

T 162   ESTABLISHMENT FILES.

T 163   GENERAL FILES.

T 164   PENSION SERIES (SUPERANNUATION FILES).

An account of the new registration system can be found in the Round Room.
The first annexe to this account gives in columns lists of subjects and the main
headings under which each subject was filed. The third column no longer corresponds to present arrangements, but the main headings can be helpful in trying to
locate a file.

In theory, papers dealing with the raising of money were filed under Finance,
T 160, and those concerned with spending money under Supply, T 161. In practice,
the division was difficult to maintain. General, T 163, contains subjects not assign-
able to Finance, Supply, or Establishment, subjects of interest to several Treasury
divisions, and Parliamentary bills on which several Treasury divisions might
wish to comment. Searchers should look through both Finance and Supply, and
then try General and Establishment.

For each of the five new classes, the files which ended in the period 1920-1930
are arranged in sections and there are yearly additions. The main headings of the
sections are given below and subsidiary headings where relevant. Within each
section in the 1920-1930 period the arrangement is often haphazard, being neither
alphabetical nor chronological.

T 160   FINANCE FILES.
         1890–1942.   1,165 pieces.   [II 284].   Various files are closed for
                                                     50 years.

1920–1930   Section Headings   *Class List*
                                                                Page

   Accommodation   1
   Agriculture; Credits Scheme (Agriculture Credits Act)   2
   Arbitration (international disputes)   4
   Charities   4
   Civil unrest   4
   Committees (and Commissions):   5
      general   5
      abroad (set up under Peace Treaties)   5

1931–1942

Indexes to files which ended in the years 1931 to 1942 are set out under each year under similar headings to those given above for the period 1920–1930. Extra headings may be used, *e.g.* in 1931 and 1934–7 there is a heading for 'Treasury'.

T 161   SUPPLY FILES.

1913–1942.   1,137 pieces.   [II 284].   Various files are closed for 50 years.

1931–1942

Similar headings, yearly additions.

T 162   ESTABLISHMENT FILES.
      1903–1942.   693 pieces.   [II 284].   Some files are closed for 50 or 100 years.

This class contains, apart from strictly establishment matters, files dealing with Treasury control, departmental functions and transfer of functions, a report on the cost of equal pay for women teachers, and several files on employment of women.

1920–1930   Section Headings
Accommodation
Art
Charities
Civil unrest (police strike, 1919)
Committees
Communications
Compensation
Contracts
Correspondence
Countries
Crown Estates
Departmental functions (including transfer of functions and accounting methods of government departments)
Ecclesiastical
Education
Elections (including papers of the Ullswater Committee on Electoral Reform)
Electricity
Entertainment
Escheat, general and disposal of individual estates
Establishment, general and all government departments arranged alphabetically
Exhibitions
Fighting Services (including civil employment, pay and allowances, and training

Finance
Fires
Friendly Societies
Funerals
Institutes and societies
Insurance
Labour
Land
Law
League of Nations
Libraries
Losses
Materials
Medical
Monuments
Museums and galleries
Parliament
Pensions
Photography
Police (including papers of Chalmers Committee, 1927–1930, and Lee Committee, 1925, and Home Office comments on Geddes Committee recommendations, 1922–1925)
Publicity
Records
Recreation
Refreshments
Registration
Rewards and gifts
Royal Family
Shorthand writing
Stationery
Statistics
Treasury
Witnesses

1931–1942
Similar headings, yearly additions.

T 163   GENERAL FILES.
      1920–1940.   130 pieces.   [II 284]

1920–1930 Section Headings
Civil unrest
Committees:
   abroad
   England
Communications:
   shipping
   vessels
Countries:
   Ireland, general

Ireland, northern
Irish Free State
Departmental functions
Development Fund
Electricity
Establishment
Finance:
    general (reduction of public expenditure, various votes, 1922–3)
    accounts
    banking
    estimates, 1922
    loans
    securities
    taxation
    taxation rates
Forestry
Insurance, health
Lunacy
Monuments
Parliamentary bills, alphabetical
Prisons
Recreation
Royal Family
War

1931–1940
Similar headings, yearly additions.

T 164   PENSIONS SERIES (SUPERANNUATION FILES).
        1917–1938; 1940.   220 pieces.   [II 284]

This class contains individual pension or injury compensation awards, and policy papers connected with the provisions of the various superannuation acts.

T 80   EXPIRED COMMISSIONS: WAR COMPENSATION PAPERS.
        1915–1928.   10 pieces.   [II 300]

    1–4   1915–1920. Defence of the Realm Losses Commission, minutes. (Out-letters in T 114).

    5   1916–1918. Defence of the Realm (Licensed Trade Claims) Commission, minutes and reports.

    6–9   1920–1928. War Compensation Court, minutes and reports.

    10   1923–1927. Irish Deportees (Compensation) Tribunal: awards and notes.

        1927. Admiralty Transport Arbitration Board, report.

T 105   EXPIRED COMMISSIONS: ROYAL COMMISSION ON NATIONAL MUSEUMS AND GALLERIES.
        1927–1930.   53 pieces.   [II 298]

The Commission was set up under Lord D'Abernon to report on institutions containing national collections in London and Edinburgh. There are files on each institution, on similar institutions abroad, reports of sub-committees, interim and final reports and other papers. It is an example of an 'unweeded' class, all records having been preserved. *See also* HO 45.

T 165   BLUE NOTES.
      1880–1934.   61 pieces.   [III 123]

Notes on government departments, with brief history of formation of each, and how financed; frequently revised. Contents of each volume are given in full in the class list.

    46–61   1920–1934. Volumes from 1916–1919 are missing.

T 169   EXPIRED COMMISSIONS: ROYAL COMMISSION ON THE CIVIL SERVICE (TOMLIN).
      1929–1931.   21 pieces.   [III 123]

    1–15   Memoranda of evidence and minutes of meetings.

    16–20   Minutes of evidence.

    21   Sub-Committee on Superannuation and Bonuses; papers.

See also HO 45.

T 170   BRADBURY PAPERS.
      1870–1922.   143 pieces.   [III 125]

Sir John Bradbury became Joint Permanent Secretary to the Treasury in 1913 and in 1919 was appointed principal British delegate to the Reparation Commission. This class contains his working papers.

    130–143   1919–1922. The papers for these years cover many of the topics of concern to the Treasury, including: financial dealings with the United States, taxation, unemployment, and papers on particular industries such as cotton, petroleum, and railways.

T 171   CHANCELLOR OF EXCHEQUER'S OFFICE: BUDGET AND FINANCE BILL PAPERS.
      1859–1937.   339 pieces.   [III 125]

The class contains papers dealing with proposals for the budget, new taxes, memoranda and statistical material from the Boards of Customs and Excise and Inland Revenue. The files are named and dated and the arrangement is roughly chronological.

    155–339   1919–1937. In addition to the above, the papers in this period deal with bills which would entail considerable expenditure, *e.g.* Pension Bills, Special Areas, Reconstruction (Agreement) Bill, and bills dealing with financial policy, *e.g.* Gold Standard Bill, 1925, Currency and Bank Notes Bill, 1928.

There is considerable overlap between this class and T 172 below. For example, the budget statement for 1924–5 is T 172/1374.

T 172 CHANCELLOR OF EXCHEQUER'S OFFICE: MISCELLANEOUS PAPERS.
       1792–1937.   1,858 pieces.   [III 125]

These papers deal with a wide variety of subjects. 1918–1919 papers begin at
piece 903, but there are some earlier files with post 1918 material, as follows:

251   1915–1924. Wasteful expenditure in government departments:
           question by A. J. Wakeford.

420–460   1917–1920. Papers belonging to Sir Hardman Lever during his
           appointment as Assistant Commissioner for Finance in the United
           States. (Later papers in T 186.)

655   1917–1919. Select Committee on National Expenditure.

675   1917–1920. Mr. Gibson Bowles: requisitioning of Royal Dutch
           Petroleum Shares under Defence of the Realm Act.

Between 1912 and 1924 the files are arranged yearly, with miscellaneous files
followed by reports of deputations and conferences. This section ends at piece 1374.
A new set of records was then added to the class. Pieces 1375–1386 contain files
covering the period 1898–1933. 1387–1439 are additional files for the period
1920–1924. Files from 1440 onward are roughly chronological, starting in 1924–5,
but many files contain material for a longer period for example:

1447–9   1924–1933. Land Value Tax.

1450–1   1924–1933. Taxation of road vehicles and road tax.

1452   1924–1937. Widows, orphans, and old age pensions.

1504–12   1925–1933. Inter-Allied Debts.

1520–9   1925–1937. Chancellor of Exchequer's speeches.

Subject index available in search rooms.

T 173 ROYAL COMMISSION ON AWARDS TO INVENTORS.
       1919–1937.   830 pieces.   [III 123]

1–34   General files, including papers leading to the seven reports of the
           Commission.

72–542   Claims files, giving date, name of claimant, and nature of invention,
           arranged alphabetically.

543–830   Transcripts of proceedings, giving date, name of claimant, and
           nature of invention, arranged alphabetically.

T 175 HOPKINS PAPERS.
       1914–1942.   124 pieces.   [III 125]

Sir Richard Hopkins joined the Board of Inland Revenue in 1902 and became
its chairman in 1922. He transferred to the Treasury in 1927 as Controller of Finance
and Supply Services, becoming Second Secretary in 1928 and Permanent Secretary
in 1942.

1–115   1914–1939. The class contains papers kept by Sir Richard Hopkins.

The following volumes of collected papers are indexed:

1	1914–1932. Miscellaneous papers.
47	1930–1934. Home defence policy.
48	1930–1935. Colonial and foreign defence.
50	1930–1939. Briefs on Cabinet papers.
52	1931. Miscellaneous correspondence on tariffs, etc.
56–58	1931–1932. General financial policy.
86	1933–1934. Miscellaneous correspondence.
88	1935. Miscellaneous papers on the Budget and the National Debt.
92	1935–1938. Inland Revenue.

There are other papers dealing with the above subjects, and with most topics of concern to the Treasury, especially Britain's financial relations with other countries, overseas trade, unemployment, and, towards the end of the period, topics that were becoming important such as profiteering on armament orders, price control, and the cost of living.

T 176 NIEMEYER PAPERS.
1916–1930. 33 pieces. [III 125]

Sir Otto Niemeyer became Assistant Secretary at the Treasury in 1919, Principal Assistant Secretary in 1920, Deputy Controller of Finance in 1922, and was Controller of Finance from 1922–1927. There are two volumes of collected papers which are indexed:

5	1920–1929. Monetary policy.
13	1923–1930. Bank Rate.

Other volumes deal with allied debts, taxation, gold standard, imperial economic conferences, financial agreement with the Irish Free State, the Royal Commission on Indian Currency, 1925–27, etc.

T 177 PHILLIPS PAPERS.
1922–1940. 52 pieces. [III 125]

Sir Frederick Phillips became Assistant Secretary at the Treasury in 1919, Principal Assistant Secretary in 1927, Deputy Controller in 1931, Under Secretary in 1932, and Joint Third Secretary in 1939. The following volumes of collected papers are indexed:

1	1922–1926. Estimates and national expenditure.
4	1925–1939. Miscellaneous papers.
12	1932–1933. World Economic and Financial Conference.
18	1933. Dollar depreciation; general papers.

There are other papers dealing with international monetary policy, budget papers, etc.

T 181 ROYAL COMMISSION ON THE PRIVATE MANUFACTURE OF AND TRADING IN ARMS.
1919–1936. 117 pieces. [III 124]

The Royal Commission was appointed in 1935 with Sir John Bankes as chairman.

1–10	1919–1934. Background material including reports to the Minister of Munitions, League of Nations reports, Arms Traffic Conventions of 1919 and 1925, United States Senate Reports.
11–114	Memoranda from Government departments, evidence given by individuals and organisations, legislation in other countries.
115–117	Draft and final report.

T 185   CUNLIFFE COMMITTEE ON CURRENCY AND FOREIGN EXCHANGE.
        1918–1919.   3 pieces.

1–2	Minutes of meeting and final report.
3	Sub-Committee on Silver, report and evidence.

T 186   HARDMAN LEVER PAPERS.
        1919–1922.   74 pieces.

Sir Hardman Lever was appointed Treasury Representative at the Ministry of Transport in 1919, to supervise all financial transactions relating to roads, railways, and canals. (His earlier papers are in T 172.)

1–42	Papers on the establishment of the Ministry of Transport and also on bridges, canals, docks, rivers, London traffic, channel tunnel, unemployment relief, etc.
43–49	Railway Advisory Committee papers.
50–55	Road Improvement Fund papers.
56–64	Motor taxation.
65–73	Irish roads and railways.

T 187   SPECIAL AREAS LOANS ADVISORY COMMITTEE.
        1937–1948.   80 pieces.

The Special Areas (Development and Improvement) Act, 1934, established two Commissioners to initiate and superintend measures designed to improve the Special Areas economically and socially. A Special Areas Fund was voted, and in 1937 the Advisory Committee was formed to advise the Commissioners on loans to be made.

The Special Areas were in North-East England, Cumberland, South Wales, and Scotland.

1–9	General files including minutes of meetings and statements of progress.
10–74	Mainly applications for loans.

See also LAB 23.

OUT-LETTERS.   [II 285–290]

These consist of bound carbon copies of letters sent by the Treasury to government departments, local authorities, the Bank of England, and other banks; and

T 27 General contains correspondence with minor government departments and letters to individuals, firms, and other organisations. In most cases the letters are arranged in chronological order. Out-letters ceased to be filed separately in the early 1920's, after the new registration system came into operation, except for the letters to the India Office which continued until 1925, the D.S.I.R. until 1927, and the Public Trustee until 1934.

Most letters deal with establishment matters and show the control exercised by the Treasury over staffing and all forms of expenditure. Probably other copies of these letters were filed elsewhere, possibly with in-letters and papers in T 1, but most are likely to have been destroyed during the process of weeding.

Some out-letters deal with matters of importance, and they can be used as a means of checking whether a letter on a particular subject was sent by the Treasury at a particular time.

The following classes contain out-letters sent in the inter-war period:

T 5   ADMIRALTY. 1849–1920. 58 pieces.

T 6   AUDITORS. 1810–1921. 42 pieces.

T 7   COLONIAL AFFAIRS. 1849–1921. 44 pieces.

T 9   COUNCIL. 1793–1922. 44 pieces.
           Mainly Orders in Council.

T 11   CUSTOMS. 1667–1922. 137 pieces.

T 12   FOREIGN OFFICE. 1857–1920. 47 pieces.

T 13   HOME OFFICE. 1835–1920. 31 pieces.

T 14   IRELAND. 1669–1921. 112 pieces.

T 18   PARLIAMENTARY. 1875–1922. 18 pieces.
           Letters to Parliamentary Counsel, mainly instructions as to preparation of bills.

T 19   POST OFFICE. 1850–1920. 57 pieces.

T 20   STATIONERY OFFICE. 1849–1922. 20 pieces.

T 21   SUPERANNUATION. 1857–1920. 111 pieces.
           Volumes are indexed.

T 22   TAXES. 1704–1921. 62 pieces.
           Letters to Board of Inland Revenue, and a few to National Debt Commission.

T 24   WAR OFFICE. 1855–1920. 63 pieces.

T 25   WOODS AND FORESTS. 1773–1920. 47 pieces.

T 26   WORKS AND PUBLIC BUILDINGS. 1852–1920. 34 pieces.

T 27   GENERAL. 1668–1920. 260 pieces.
           Letters to organisations and individuals, including civil servants, members of committees, High Commissioners of the Dominions, and foreign representatives.

T 101   SCOTLAND. 1886–1920. 21 pieces.

T 109   AGRICULTURE AND FISHERIES. 1914–1920. 4 pieces.

T 110   AIR MINISTRY. 1918–1921. 3 pieces.

T 111   BANK OF ENGLAND. 1917–1921. 4 pieces.

T 112   CENTRAL CONTROL BOARD (Liquor Traffic). 1915–1919. 1 piece.
Letters up to 10.1.1919, later letters in T 147.

T 113   CIVIL SERVICE COMMISSION. 1914–1920. 2 pieces.

T 114   COMMISSIONS (TEMPORARY). 1914–1920. 7 pieces.
Letters to commissions, committees, councils, departments or offices
set up during the war *e.g.* Department of Overseas Trade, Royal
Commissions on the Sugar Supply, and on Wheat Supplies, and the
London Exchange Committee, and some set up after the war, *e.g.*
Coal Industry Commission, Reparation Commission, Official Com-
mittees for Relief in Europe.

T 115   DEVELOPMENT COMMISSION. 1914–1922. 2 pieces.

T 116   EDUCATION, BOARD OF. 1914–1921. 2 pieces.

T 117   FOOD, MINISTRY OF. 1917–1921. 2 pieces.

T 118   FRIENDLY SOCIETIES. 1914–1919. 1 piece.
Letters to January, 1919, later letters in T 147.

T 119   HOUSEHOLD (ROYAL). 1895–1922. 3 pieces.

T 120   INDIA OFFICE. 1914–1925. 2 pieces.

T 121   INFORMATION, MINISTRY OF. 1918–1920. 1 piece.

T 123   INSURANCE COMMISSION (ENGLAND). 1914–1919. 1 piece.

T 124   INSURANCE COMMISSION (WALES). 1914–1919. 1 piece.

T 125   SCIENTIFIC AND INDUSTRIAL RESEARCH. 1919–1927. 1 piece.

T 126   LABOUR, MINISTRY OF. 1917–1921. 4 pieces.

T 127   LOCAL AUTHORITIES. 1914–1922. 2 pieces.
Letters to various officials of local authorities, also to judges, registrars
of county courts, governors of prisons, harbour authorities, river
conservancy and drainage boards, and local pension committees.

T 128   LOCAL GOVERNMENT BOARD. 1914–1919. 2 pieces.

T 129   LORD CHANCELLOR. 1914–1921. 3 pieces.

T 130   MINT. 1914–1924. 2 pieces.

T 131   TRANSPORT, MINISTRY OF. 1919–1922. 1 piece.

T 132   MUNITIONS, MINISTRY OF. 1915–1921. 10 pieces.

T 133   NATIONAL DEBT COMMISSION (*see also* T 22). 1914–1923. 2 pieces.

T 134   NATIONAL SERVICE AND RECONSTRUCTION. 1917–1920. 2 pieces.

T 135   PAYMASTER GENERAL. 1914–1921. 2 pieces.

T 136   PENSIONS, MINISTRY OF. 1917–1921. 4 pieces.

T 138   PUBLIC TRUSTEE. 1914–1934. 2 pieces.

T 139   ROAD BOARD. 1914–1919. 2 pieces.

T 140   SHIPPING, MINISTRY OF. 1917–1921. 4 pieces.

T 141   SOLICITOR (TREASURY). 1914–1921. 3 pieces.

T 142   TRADE, BOARD OF. 1914–1920. 9 pieces.

T 144   BRITISH MUSEUM. 1914–1922. 1 piece.

T 145   LONDON MUSEUM AND WALLACE COLLECTION. 1914–1922. 1 piece.

T 146   NATIONAL GALLERY. 1914–1922. 1 piece.

T 147   MISCELLANEOUS DEPARTMENTS. 1914–1923. 1 piece.
         Letters to small departments: Registrar of Friendly Societies from
         Jan. 1919; Central Control Board (Liquor Traffic), Jan. 1919–Oct.
         1921, then to State Management Districts Central Office; Land
         Registry; and after July, 1922, several others listed in P.R.O. *Guide* II,
         p. 287.

T 148   NATIONAL INSURANCE AUDIT DEPARTMENT. 1914–1922. 1 piece.

T 149   PARLIAMENTARY OFFICES. 1914–1922. 1 piece.
         Apart from staffing, letters deal with cost of Parliamentary committees,
         of recording debates, etc.

T 150   PUBLIC RECORD OFFICE AND REGISTRAR GENERAL. 1914–1922.
         1 piece.

T 151   PUBLIC WORKS LOAN COMMISSIONERS. 1914–1922. 1 piece.

T 152   BANKS, MISCELLANEOUS. 1919–1921. 1 piece.

T 153   CIVIL SERVICE ARBITRATION. 1919–1923. 1 piece.

T 154   HEALTH, MINISTRY OF. 1919–1920. 1 piece.

T 155   OVERSEAS TRADE. 1919–1922. 1 piece.
         Letters from 3.9.1919, earlier letters in T 114.

T 157   CHARITY COMMISSION. 1914–1920. 1 piece.

T 158   TREASURY (IRELAND). 1920–1922. 9 pieces.

BOARD OF CUSTOMS AND EXCISE

A single Board of Customs for the United Kingdom was appointed in 1823, and
in 1909 administration of the excise was transferred to the Board from the Commissioners of Inland Revenue. Most records are retained by the Board of Customs
and Excise for 100 years; the only inter-war material transferred to the P.R.O. is as
follows:

CUST 44   BOARD AND SECRETARIAT: ANNUAL REPORTS.
                 1856–1960.   49 pieces.   [III 33]
    21–28   1910–1938. Annual Reports.

EXCHEQUER AND AUDIT DEPARTMENT

This department was set up under the Exchequer and Audit Departments Act, 1866, which combined the two separate offices of the Comptroller General of the Exchequer and the Commissioners of Audit. Its function is to ensure that all money paid out of the Exchequer has been authorised by Parliament, and to audit the accounts of departments after the money has been spent. The Comptroller and Auditor General is responsible to Parliament for auditing, certifying, and reporting upon departmental accounts.

AO 15   ENROLMENT BOOKS
           1563–1927.   184 pieces.   [II 121]

  184   1879–1927. Warrants, Commissions, Appointments, etc.

AO 24   AUDIT INSTRUCTIONS
           1849–1967.   37 pieces.   [III 50]

  9   1927. Manual: General Guide to the Control and Audit of Receipts and Expenditure.

  11   1918–1938. Old Conspectus; a summary of important or instructive audit decisions and reports.

BOARD OF INLAND REVENUE

The Board of Commissioners of Inland Revenue was formed in 1849 when the Boards of Excise and of Stamps and Taxes were amalgamated. Responsibility for excise duties was transferred to the Board of Customs in 1909.

The Board of Inland Revenue is now responsible for the management and collection of direct taxes, and also for valuations of freehold and leasehold property for its own purposes and on behalf of other government departments and public authorities; and in England and Wales for local authority rating. It is also responsible for the collection and redemption of tithe redemption annuities, inherited from the former Tithe Redemption Commission in 1960.

IR 2   PAROCHIAL TAX LEDGERS, INSPECTORS' LEDGERS, AND LAND TAX LEDGERS.
       1857–1937.   1,791 pieces.   [II 197]

Parochial Tax Ledgers show the amount of income tax, inhabited house duty, and land tax, paid in each parish. They were discontinued after the year 1916–1917. Their place was taken by inspectors' ledgers kept in the office of the Chief Inspector of Taxes, and charge duplicates, balancing statements, discharge schedules, and default schedules, belonging to the Accountant and Comptroller General's office. These latter are now in IR 11 and this class is not open to public inspection.

INSPECTORS' LEDGERS

These show the amount of income tax, inhabited house duty (ended in 1929–1930), and land tax, in each parish. Ledgers for the years 1924–1925, and every tenth year thereafter are preserved.

  559–1433   1924–1925. Inspectors' ledgers, arranged alphabetically by districts.

1490–1503   1924–1925. Additional districts.

1559–1789   1934–1935. Inspectors' ledgers, arranged alphabetically by district.

LAND TAX LEDGERS

These continue a section of the parochial registers; the following have been preserved:

1434–1489   1921–1925. Ledgers arranged alphabetically by county or group of counties.

1504–1558   1933–1937. Ledgers arranged as above.

IR 9   INLAND REVENUE OFFICE: SPECIMEN FORMS, VARIOUS.
        1798–1944.   154 pieces.   [II 198]

Specimen forms of all kinds used by the Inland Revenue Office.

IR 15   COMMISSIONERS OF INLAND REVENUE: ANNUAL REPORTS.
         1856–1962.   105 pieces.   [III 91].   Open without restriction.
62–82   1919–1939. Annual Reports.

IR 22   LAND TAX REDEMPTION OFFICE: PARISH BOOKS OF REDEMPTION.
         1799–1958.   247 pieces.   [III 92]

These volumes contain particulars of redemption of land tax, which are arranged by county and within each county by hundred and by land tax 'parish'. This is not necessarily the same as the ecclesiastical parish of the nineteenth century, or the civil parish of this century.
Parish Book Index, IND 27763 and 27764, shows the county volume and folio therein for each parish. The details given are the name of the redemptioner, name of occupier, amount of tax redeemed, and the registered number of the redemption contract. The complete contract is in IR 24.

IR 24   LAND TAX REDEMPTION OFFICE: REGISTERS OF REDEMPTION CERTIFICATES.
         1799–1963.   599 pieces.   [III 92]

The redemption certificates contain the complete contract of redemption of land tax; from 1905–1950, these include plans of the property concerned. The certificates are in numerical order of the registered numbers. The Finance Act of 1949 made redemption compulsory and the procedure was altered.

IR 32   RAILWAY ASSESSMENT AUTHORITY.
         1930–1948.   87 pieces.

The Railways (Valuation for Rating) Act, 1930, changed the way in which railway companies were valued for rating purposes. The Railway Assessment Authority was set up to assess railway properties and apportion the rateable value between local authorities.

1–28   Valuation Rolls of the Southern Railway, Great Western Railway, London, Midland, and Scottish Railway, and London and North-Eastern Railway.

29–87   Minutes of meetings and papers submitted to the Railway Assessment Authority, the Panel of Railway Valuers and Accountants, and the Joint Authority of the Anglo-Scottish Railway Assessment Authority.

MINT

In 1553 the Mint lodged in the Tower of London became the sole mint for England and Wales. It was an independent department under the king until 1688 when it was made responsible to the Chancellor of the Exchequer. The Mint moved into a new building on Tower Hill in 1811–1812. There have been six branch mints at Sydney, Melbourne, Perth, Ottawa, Bombay, and Pretoria.

The Mint's main function is the production of coins for the United Kingdom, the mint at Edinburgh having been abolished in 1817. It also produces medals and is responsible for the standard of hall-marking of all articles of bullion made by bodies other than the London Company of Goldsmiths.

The Mint produces plates for printing postage and revenue stamps, dies for stamps on legal documents, plates for National Insurance stamps, and plates for printing parts of passports.

Foreign coins were first produced by the Mint in the reign of Mary I, when Spanish coin was made. During the nineteenth century, coins were made for France and for the new countries of Central and South America as well as for the colonies. After reorganisation in 1870, foreign orders were discouraged until 1923 when depression led to a search for foreign orders. Sixteen foreign countries were supplied with coin during the inter-war period, and the Mint also produced the Maria Theresa thaler which although not legal tender was accepted as currency in parts of Africa and the Middle East.

Regular minting of gold sovereigns ceased in 1917. The fineness of silver coin was reduced from 925 to 500 in 1920, and these continued to be minted until superseded by cupro-nickel in 1946.

The Pyx is a box at the Mint in which sample coins are kept for testing. Each spring a Trial of the Pyx is held to test any gold or silver coins minted the previous year. The trials, held since the thirteenth century, were in Westminster Hall and then at the Goldsmiths' Hall; the Standards Department of the Board of Trade now provides the weights (*see* BT 101, sections 11 *and* 15).

MINT 3   ESTABLISHMENT AND ORGANISATION.
              1657–1935.   169 pieces.

There is very little inter-war material in this class; the following are of interest:

67   1925. Area of control of the Operative Department and plan of the Department.

68   1922. Report of the Pyx Office Special Committee.

134   1912–1923. Workmen's wages book.

135   1932–1935. Quarterly accounts of staff salaries.

MINT 4   ADMINISTRATION AND MANAGEMENT.
              1601–1920.   92 pieces.

15–16	1920. Coinage Acts.
70	1912–1920. Order Book of the Master, Deputy Master, and Comptroller.

MINT 5   BUILDING AND MACHINERY.
1653–1935.   140 pieces.

There is little inter-war material.

MINT 6   ACCOUNTS
1677–1951.   87 pieces.

4	1924–1928. General cash book.
18–20	1912–1938. Register of receipts into the cash and bullion accounts at the Bank of England.
29–31	1916–1940. Master and Worker's General Accounts: accounts include bullion suspense, currency note reserve, alloys, imperial gold bullion, bronze and silver, colonial and foreign coinages.
62–63	1927–1938. Mint office ledgers.
87	1926. Instructions concerning cost accounts.

MINT 7   COINAGE: IMPERIAL (GENERAL).
1603–1947.   154 pieces

29	1919. Notes by Sir J. Cawston on the Mint with regard to Decimal Bills.
30	1920. Report of the Royal Commission on Decimal Coinage, with appendices.
42	1925–1932. Illustrations of designs of new coins.

MINT 8   COINAGE: IMPERIAL (COPPER, BRONZE, AND BASE METAL).
1672–1943.   37 pieces

13	1925–1940. Imperial bronze coinage costs.
22	1933–1937. Bronze ledger.

MINT 9   COINAGE: IMPERIAL (GOLD AND SILVER).
1625–1945.   242 pieces

25	1925–1940. Imperial silver coinage costs.
96–101	1913–1939. Gold and silver account books and ledgers.
116	1926–1928. Maundy money coinage costs.
129	1925. Imperial sovereign coinage costs.

MINT 12   COINAGE: CHANNEL ISLANDS, IRELAND, ISLE OF MAN, AND SCOTLAND.
1661–1940.   26 pieces

5	1926–1937. Jersey coinage costs.
22	1928–1940. Irish Free State coinage costs.

MINT 13   COINAGE: COLONIAL AND FOREIGN.
1684–1943.   247 pieces

The following sections contain some inter-war material:

1–21   General.

22–191   Colonial and foreign currencies, papers arranged by states grouped
             as follows:

             Africa: British East Africa, British West Africa, Egypt, South
                 Africa.
             America: Central, including the West Indies; North, including
                 Mexico; South.
             Asia: including Cyprus.
             Australia.
             Europe.
             Fiji.
             New Zealand.

192–235   Colonial and foreign mints and refineries, some inter-war material
             on European mints.

MINT 14   DIES, MATRICES, AND PUNCHEONS.
1685–1943.   54 pieces.

Accounts of dies, matrices, and puncheons, left good and sunk or defaced, and
correspondence and papers concerning preparation of dies and plates for postage,
revenue, and other stamps.

MINT 16   MEDALS.
1805–1948.   122 pieces.

This class contains medal books of orders received, medal sales day books, and
one folder each on medals and plaquettes for the British Empire Exhibition, 1924,
and Royal Prize Medals, 1931.

MINT 17   BRANCH MINTS.
1853–1937.   203 pieces.

1–186   Australia; inter-war material in pieces 3, 77, 151, 184, and 185.

187–198   Canada; inter-war material in pieces 195, 196, and 198.

199–200   India.

201–203   South Africa; Pretoria Branch Mint.

MINT 20   REGISTERED FILES.

Many files for the inter-war period are expected to be transferred in this class,
probably during 1971. They will include correspondence on decimalisation and
on the effect of the General Strike on the Mint.

NATIONAL DEBT OFFICE

This office was set up to administer the sinking fund started by William Pitt in 1786. In 1808, it became responsible for granting life annuities and for the administration of annuities and tontines granted under eighteenth century acts. It became responsible for the investment and management of many public funds. Its main function now is to control Trustee Savings Banks, and it also deals with applications to commute service pensions and civil compensation allowances.

NDO 6 ESTABLISHMENT PAPERS.
     1822–1927.   17 pieces.   [II 221]

11–17   1919–1927. Books containing bound staff files, list of contents at beginning of each volume.

NDO 7 CORRESPONDENCE.
     1873–1924.   45 pieces.   [II 221]

39–44   1919–1924. Correspondence files bound, one volume per year, and a list of contents at the beginning of each volume.

45   Index to the whole class.

NDO 9 MINUTES OF THE NATIONAL DEBT COMMISSIONERS.
     1786–1946.   26 pieces.   [III 97]

21–24   1919–1938. The Commissioners have not held formal meetings since 1860. The papers are reports by the Comptroller General of financial transactions, and statements of action taken. Many papers set out advances made to the Exchequer.

NATIONAL INSURANCE AUDIT DEPARTMENT

This department was appointed by the Treasury in 1912 to audit the accounts of approved societies and their branches and of the insurance committees, as laid down by the National Insurance Act, 1911. Under this Act the approved societies were the friendly societies and other organisations which were approved to administer the sickness benefits to insured persons; and the insurance committees in England, Wales, and Scotland, were responsible for administering the medical services. Following the National Health Service Act, 1946, the approved societies were dissolved and the property and liabilities of the insurance committees were transferred to the newly appointed executive councils. Most of the records of the department have been destroyed.

NIA 2 ANNUAL REPORTS.
     1912–1946.   1 piece.   [III 98]

A set of the printed annual reports, with appendices.

NIA 3 SPECIMENS OF DESTROYED DOCUMENTS.
     1913–1943.   3 pieces.   [II 222]

These are selected records to show the work of the department and consist of copies of auditors' reports on the certified accounts of approved societies, branches of approved societies, and insurance committees.

NATIONAL SAVINGS COMMITTEE

The National Savings Movement was formed in 1915. The following year the two committees that had been set up combined as the National War Savings Committee. This was changed to the present name in 1919.

NSC 1   MINUTE BOOKS.
        1916–1937.   11 pieces.   [III 99]

6–11   1919–1937. Each volume is indexed.

NSC 2   ANNUAL REPORTS.
        1916–1969.   47 pieces.   [III 99]

4–23   1919–1939. Reports made to the Treasury.

NSC 3   JOURNALS.
        1916–1963.   17 pieces.   [III 99]

3–7   1919–1939. Copies of the official printed bulletin circulated to savings groups.

NSC 5   POSTERS.
        1917–1968.   528 pieces.   [III 100]

9–31   1920–1939.

NSC 6   LEAFLETS.
        1916–1962.   5 pieces.   [III 100]

NSC 7   ORGANISATION AND DEVELOPMENT FILES.
        1915–1958.   88 pieces.   [III 100]

2–63; 82   1919–1939.

PAYMASTER GENERAL

The office of Paymaster General was created in 1835 by the consolidation of the four separate pay departments then existing, that is Paymaster General of the Forces, the Paymaster and Treasurer of Chelsea Hospital, the Treasurer of the Navy, and the Treasurer of Ordnance. In 1848 the offices of the Paymaster of Exchequer Bills, and the Paymaster of the Civil Service were also incorporated.

The Paymaster General is today the principal paying agent of the Government and for most purposes he is the banker for all government departments except the revenue departments and the National Debt Commissioners. The payments made on behalf of departments are in respect of such items as salaries, contractors' accounts, grants for subsidies, compensation payments, and payments relating to social and other services. The Paymaster General is also responsible for the payment of retired pay and pensions to staff of the defence and civil services and their widows and dependents and members of the Royal Irish Constabulary. He is also responsible for the payment of Health Service pensions and pensions borne upon the Consolidated Fund. In 1916 the administration of pensions for wounds was transferred to the Ministry of Pensions. In 1919, the payment of teachers' pensions was transferred from the Paymaster General to the Board of Education but in 1926 it was returned. In 1925, functions of the pay officer under Court of Chancery Funds Act, 1872, were transferred from the Paymaster General to the Lord Chancellor's Department.

There is a separation of functions between the Paymaster General and his Office. The Paymaster General is usually a non-departmental minister, or minister without portfolio, or the post is combined with another office. The Paymaster General's Office is under the supervision of a permanent Assistant Paymaster General who would regard the Chancellor of the Exchequer as his chief.

The records in this group consist mainly of registers of names of those awarded pensions, etc. They relate to the work of the Office not that of the Paymaster General. Many of the records of the Office have not been transferred because they are in current use, so at present many classes end at 1920 for the Services, and a little later for civil pensions. For nearly all the classes the volumes are listed chronologically and the names are in alphabetical order within each volume.

The main account ledgers of the Paymaster General's Office are in PMG 49, and registers and ledgers relating to the Civil Establishment are in PMG 27 and 28. They include payments made out of the Consolidated Fund as follows:

(a) Civil List Classes 1–6: payments relating to salaries, retired allowances, and expenses of the royal household, royal bounty alms, special services, and Commissioners of Works.

(b) Salaries and allowances: salaries of the Speaker of the House of Commons, the Comptroller and Auditor-General, the inspectors of anatomy, and compensation payable under the Copyright Act to various universities for loss of the right to copies of all works published in the United Kingdom.

(c) Courts of Justices: salaries of the superior judicial body, the county court judges, magistrates attached to the metropolitan police courts, and the Sheerness and Chatham police magistrates.

(d) Miscellaneous services: e.g. compensation for loss of duties on coinage of tin, payments to Greenwich Hospital.

(e) Advances: payments specially sanctioned by the Treasury to meet expenditure incurred for public purposes under the authority of special acts, e.g. The Barracks Act, 1890.

(f) Annuities and pensions: annuities to the Royal Family and pensions for naval, military, civil, and political services.
    Each volume is indexed.

Registers and records relating to the Army Establishment are in PMG 3, 4, 9–11, 33–36, 57 [II 226–227].

Registers and records relating to the Naval Establishment are in PMG 15, 16, 18–20, 23–25, 56, 69–72 [II 228–230].

Registers of the Royal Irish Constabulary are in PMG 48 [II 230].

Registers of teachers' pensions are in PMG 55 and 68 [II 231].

Records concerning pensions for wounds are in PMG 9 [II 226].

Records concerning payments arising out of the War of 1914–18 are in PMG 9 and PMG 42–47 [II 231]. These cover: disability retired pay, supplementary allowances, pensions to relatives of deceased officers, widows' pensions, and children's allowances.

To date, no R.A.F. records have been transferred.

PUBLIC WORKS LOAN BOARD

The Board was set up in 1817 to advance money 'for the carrying on of Public Works and Fisheries in the United Kingdom and Employment of the Poor'. It makes loans to local authorities and other public bodies for public works. It can also lend money to harbour authorities and to associations, companies, and private persons for the provision of housing. Special legislation allows loans for other purposes, the most important being long term credits to farmers.

PWLB 1   SOLICITOR'S REPORTS: ADVANCES FROM THE LOCAL LOANS FUND.
        1866–1961.   737 pieces.   [II 256].   Records open after 5 years.

170–345   1919–1939. Reports sent by the Public Works Loan Board's Solicitor to the Accounts Branch giving notification of loans and the information necessary for the opening of loan accounts. Indexed to March 1919.

PWLB 2   MINUTE BOOK.
        1817–1945.   229 pieces.   [II 256]

167–225   Minutes for the years 1919 to 1939.

PWLB 3   SOLICITOR'S REPORTS: ADVANCES UNDER THE LAND SETTLEMENT ACTS.
        1919–1926.   5 pieces.   [III 111].   Records open after 5 years.

Reports to the Accounts Branch, similar to PWLB 1.

PWLB 4   SOLICITOR'S REPORTS: MISCELLANEOUS AMALGAMATIONS AND RE-ARRANGEMENTS.
        1875–1954.   13 pieces.   [III 111].   Records open after 5 years.

7–13   1911–1954. Reports to the Accounts Branch giving details of variations in the terms of mortgages securing loans.

PWLB 5   ACCOUNT LEDGERS.
        1894–1938.   5 pieces

4–5   1916–1938. Volumes dated. Ledgers contain completed accounts giving debtor's name, amount paid, and property concerned.

PWLB 6   REGISTERS OF APPLICATIONS FOR LOANS.
        1811–1938.   61 pieces.

Registers of applications from local authorities and other public bodies.

31–60   1915–1938. Applications for loans from the Local Loans Fund.

61   1919–1926. Applications for loans under the Land Settlement Act.

PWLB 7   APPLICATIONS FOR LOANS: FILES.
　　　　　1894–1968.　　18 pieces.

1–10　　　　1921–1968. Applications from individuals under Agricultural
　　　　　　Credits Act, 1923. Some files extend beyond 1940.

11–18　　　1900–1964. Applications from harbour authorities. All files extend
　　　　　　beyond 1940.

TITHE REDEMPTION COMMISSION

Tithes, originally a tenth of annual produce payable to the church, were changed into
rentcharges following the Tithe Commutation Act, 1836. This Act set up three
Tithe Commissioners and under their supervision all parishes where tithes were
still paid were surveyed, the amount of tithe established, and usually the tithe
rentcharge was apportioned among the various properties.

The Tithe Commissioners were later given the work of supervising inclosures
and enfranchisement of copyholds. This work was amalgamated in 1882 and carried
on by Land Commissioners operating as part of the Home Office. Their functions
were transferred to the Board of Agriculture in 1889.

In 1936, following the report of a Royal Commission, a new Tithe Act was passed
providing that all tithe rentcharges should be redeemed by annual payments, the
process to be completed by the end of the century. The Tithe Redemption Commission was appointed to administer this work, and to it were transferred the remaining
duties of the Ministry of Agriculture concerning tithes, and custody of the tithe
maps and apportionments. In 1960, the Tithe Redemption Commission was
dissolved and the remaining work and records were transferred to the Board of
Inland Revenue.

Three classes were transferred to the P.R.O. in this group. Papers and correspondence relating to the commutation process in the various parishes are in IR 18,
apportionments in IR 29, and maps in IR 30. Files concerning tithes in the City of
London are in MAF 8, papers on payment of tithe by local authorities are in HLG 35,
and 1936 Bill Papers are in HLG 29.

A P.R.O. leaflet *Tithe Records 1836–1936 preserved in the P.R.O.* is available in the
search rooms.

TITHE 3   DECLARATIONS OF MERGER.
　　　　　1837–1937.　　277 pieces.　　[II 266].　　No restriction on access.

In some districts when tithes were commuted there was no apportionment
because the landowner was also the owner of the tithe. In such cases the tithe rentcharge could be extinguished by a deed of merger; as a result the rentcharge was
absolutely merged in the freehold and inheritance of the land on which it had been
charged. Mergers were confirmed under the seal of the Tithe Commissioners and
their successors, and continued to be made up to 1936.

Mergers are arranged numerically and the number of a merger can be found on
the appropriate apportionment in IR 29.

209–276　　1919–1937. Mergers numbered 17,851–26,354.

FOREIGN AFFAIRS

FOREIGN OFFICE

A single department of state to deal with foreign affairs came into existence in 1782. During the inter-war period, 1919–1939, the Foreign Office was responsible for conducting relations with all fully independent foreign countries, except states near India which had special treaty relations with Britain. These countries were dealt with by the Government of India acting under the control of the India Office in consultation with the Foreign Office.

The Foreign Office was also responsible for Egypt, and for the Anglo-Egyptian Sudan, although this country did not become independent until 1955. Relations with other dependent countries were transferred to the Foreign Office when they became independent, for example, Iraq in 1932, Burma, Israel, Jordan, etc., since the last war.

The conferences following the First World War and the formation of the League of Nations were the responsibility of the Cabinet, the Foreign Office taking over control in 1922 after the ending of the Coalition Government. Since the Second World War the Foreign Office has been responsible for relations with the United Nations, North Atlantic Treaty Organisation, and similar bodies.

The Foreign Office is responsible for the correlation of commercial policy with political relations, and it controlled the Commercial Diplomatic Service and the Consular Service before they became combined with the Foreign Office and Diplomatic Service to form a single Foreign Service after 1943. Negotiations of commercial treaties and representations to foreign governments to protect British interests are carried on by the Foreign Office, acting on the advice of the Commercial Department of the Board of Trade. The Department of Overseas Trade which existed from 1917 until 1946 was responsible jointly to the Foreign Office and the Board of Trade. Its function was to assist British traders in their relations with foreign traders. When it was dissolved, most of its functions were transferred to the Board of Trade, and its records are in the BT group.

In 1968 the Foreign Office combined with the Commonwealth Office to form the Foreign and Commonwealth Office.

In 1961 the Department of Technical Co-operation was formed to organise aid to underdeveloped countries, taking over functions from the Foreign Office, Colonial Office, Commonwealth Relations Office, and the Ministry of Labour. In 1964 this department was absorbed by the new Ministry of Overseas Development which became responsible for the overseas aid programme. Functions exercised by the Board of Trade, the Department of Education and Science, and the Ministry of Agriculture and Fisheries in connection with the United Nations and its specialised agencies, were transferred to the new ministry which was also responsible for the Commonwealth Development Corporation and the Technical Products Institute. In 1970 this ministry was merged with the Foreign and Commonwealth Office.

The Foreign Office is a very large group, having over 900 classes. In this case it has been thought better to arrange according to subject the classes with inter-war material which may possibly be of interest to social scientists. In most cases the classes are merely listed as there is a detailed P.R.O. Handbook called *The Records of the Foreign Office, 1782–1939*, which should be consulted. No reference is made in this guide to the numerous classes of embassy and consular archives which may contain material concerning British companies and persons overseas, or to the classes of Confidential Print, which consist of printed correspondence and reports circulated within the Foreign Office, to the Cabinet, to other government departments, and to missions abroad, and which are duplicates of material found elsewhere.

The classes listed here are arranged as follows:

General Correspondence.
Archives of Commissions.
Treaties.
War of 1914–18 and Subsequent Conferences.
Private Office.
Private Collections.
Miscellaneous.

The Foreign Office at times collected information concerning social conditions in this country in response to enquiries from abroad. Such material was usually obtained from other departments and may be found in the Foreign Office records in general correspondence by looking in the index under headings such as Labour, Legislation, etc.

GENERAL CORRESPONDENCE

FO 366 CHIEF CLERK'S DEPARTMENT.
1719–1940. 1,316 pieces. [II 158]. Various files are closed for 50 or 75 years.

FO 368 COMMERCIAL.
1906–1920. 2,269 pieces. [II 128]

FO 369 CONSULAR.
1906–1944. 3,039 pieces. [II 128]. Various files are closed for 50 or 75 years.

FO 370 LIBRARY.
1906–1944. 1,086 pieces. [II 128]. Various files are closed for 50 or 75 years.

FO 371 POLITICAL.
1906–1943. 37,665 pieces. [II 128]. Various files are closed for 50 or 75 years.

FO 372 TREATY.
1906–1944. 4,066 pieces. [II 128]. Various files are closed for 50 or 75 years.

This includes Prize Court Department correspondence, and that of Dominions Information Department before 1928 and after 1933. This department also dealt with international conventions concerning social conditions, Red Cross, etc.

FO 382 CONTRABAND.
1915–1920. 2,523 pieces. [II 128]

FO 383 PRISONERS OF WAR AND ALIENS.
1915–1919. 547 pieces. [II 128]

FO 395   NEWS.

   1916–1939. 666 pieces. [II 128]. Various files are closed for 50 or 75 years.

  The functions of this department were carried on by the Ministry of Information during the war 1939–45. *See* INF group.

FO 627   DOMINIONS INFORMATION.

   1929–1933. 58 pieces. [II 128]

FO 850   COMMUNICATIONS.

   1936–1944. 158 pieces. [III 52]

In 1906 a new registry procedure based on subject files was introduced for general correspondence; this did not prove satisfactory and a revised system began in 1920. A card index was prepared for the correspondence up to 1919 and can be consulted in the Enquiries Room at the Land Registry. This index covers the 1920 correspondence of the Commercial and Contraband classes as these departments were wound up during 1920 and were not included in the new registry scheme. The index also includes some 1920 correspondence of other departments for the period before they adopted the new system.

For general correspondence from 1920 onwards, a very detailed index was made each year by the Foreign Office. This has been published by the Kraus-Thomson Organisation, four volumes per year, and is the only detailed means of reference to most files in these classes. In some cases the files are named in the class list, for example in FO 371 for the years 1938 and 1939, but the names do not always indicate all the material contained in the files.

The index was compiled at the time when the documents came into existence and the papers have since been weeded, so some of the documents listed in the index no longer exist. When correspondence of the Chief Clerk's Department, which deals mainly with establishment matters, was included after 1930, only selected papers were preserved and indexed.

Secret correspondence was placed in green docket sheets and these were not included in the index. Separate indexes on the same lines as the main index have been made for the 'green papers' which are now open.

The index was compiled by the Foreign Office for its own use, and the references given have to be turned into P.R.O. class and piece numbers. Each volume of the index has a page at the front giving index numbers and departmental designations. These vary in detail from year to year so should always be checked. The following particulars apply from 1920–1939:

Numbers between 0 and 100 indicate countries, regions or subjects, and these are to be found in the class FO 371, POLITICAL.

The same numbers for countries, prefixed by 2, indicate FO 369, CONSULAR.

The 100's denote the class FO 395, NEWS.

The 300's denote the class FO 372, TREATY.

The 400's denote the class FO 370, LIBRARY.

The 500's from 1931 onwards denote the class FO 366, the CHIEF CLERK'S DEPARTMENT.

The 600's denote the class FO 850, COMMUNICATIONS.

The 700's denote the class FO 627, DOMINIONS INFORMATION, between 1929 and 1933.

A typical FO reference consists of a letter and three sets of figures. The letter and the final number indicate the department of the Foreign Office which dealt with the papers. The penultimate number gives the file number (which is the registry number of the first paper on that subject for the year), and the first number indicates the paper number (that is the registry number given to an in-coming paper and the related minutes and drafts).

For example, take the following entry in the index for 1930:

Banks: Bank for International Settlements; Agreement reached at the Hague: Text. Reference C738/80/62.

'C' here stands for the Central Department; 62 being a figure below 100 also indicates that a Political Department is concerned, and 62 stands for Central General. Correspondence of Political Departments is in class FO 371, so it is necessary to get out the class list for FO 371 covering the year 1930; turn to Political (Central) and under General find file 80. This is a very large file covering several piece numbers, but using the first number in the reference, the piece number 14340 is found. The FO reference C738/80/62 therefore corresponds to the P.R.O. reference FO 371/14340.

ARCHIVES OF COMMISSIONS

The following Commissions have material for the inter-war period. *See also* WO 155.

FO 175   ARCHANGEL: ALLIED HIGH COMMISSION: CORRESPONDENCE.
  1918–1919.   29 pieces.

Registers of correspondence are in FO 176.

MIXED ARBITRAL TRIBUNALS, WAR OF 1914–1918.   [II 153]

FO 324   ANGLO-AUSTRIAN. 1921–1930. 1 piece.

FO 325   ANGLO-BULGARIAN. 1921–1927. 4 pieces.

FO 326   ANGLO-GERMAN. 1921–1931. 19 pieces.

FO 327   ANGLO-HUNGARIAN. 1921–1931. 1 piece.

FO 328   CLAUSE 4 ARBITRATIONS. 1922–1930. 1 piece.

FO 538   VLADIVOSTOK: ALLIED HIGH COMMISSION.
  1918–1921.   4 pieces.   [II 154]

FO 852   INTERNATIONAL PLEBISCITE COMMISSION IN SLESVIG.
  1919–1921.   26 pieces.   [III 67]

FO 890   UPPER SILESIA (BRITISH SECTION): INTER-ALLIED ADMINISTRATIVE AND PLEBISCITE COMMISSION.
  1920–1922.   16 pieces.   [III 67]

FO 894 GERMANY: INTER-ALLIED RHINELAND HIGH COMMISSION.
1920–1930. 33 pieces. [III 68]

FO 895 AUSTRIA: KLAGENFURT PLEBISCITE COMMISSION (BRITISH SECTION).
1920. 3 pieces. [III 68]

FO 896 AUSTRIA: INTER-ALLIED COMMISSION OF CONTROL.
1926–1928. 3 pieces. [III 68]

FO 897 MIXED ARBITRAL TRIBUNALS: ANGLO-AMERICAN PECUNIARY CLAIMS.
1896–1923. 24 pieces. [III 68]

FO 919 INTERNATIONAL COMMITTEE ON REFUGEES, 1938.
1937–1938. 9 pieces.

TREATIES

FO 93 PROTOCOLS OF TREATIES.
1778–1966. 152 pieces. [II 129]

FO 94 RATIFICATION OF TREATIES.
1782–1966. 2,307 pieces. [II 129]

WAR OF 1914–1918 AND SUBSEQUENT CONFERENCES

PEACE CONFERENCE OF 1919–1920.

FO 373 HANDBOOKS OF THE CONFERENCE.
1918–1919. 7 pieces. [II 159]

FO 374 ACTS OF THE CONFERENCE.
1919 and 1922–1935. 34 pieces. [II 159]

FO 608 CORRESPONDENCE.
1919–1920. 281 pieces. [II 159]

See also FO 893.

FO 686 JEDDA AGENCY: PAPERS.
1913–1925. 148 pieces. [III 70]

FO 801 REPARATION COMMISSION, 1919.
1919–1931. 126 pieces. [III 68]

FO 833 FOREIGN TRADE DEPARTMENT.
1916–1919. 18 pieces. [III 52]

FO 839 EASTERN CONFERENCE: LAUSANNE.
1922–1923. 53 pieces. [III 69]

FO 840 INTERNATIONAL CONFERENCES: VARIOUS.
1920–1929. 8 pieces. [III 69]

FO 845 RESTRICTION OF ENEMY SUPPLIES DEPARTMENT.
1916–1919. 11 pieces. [III 70]

FO 882 ARAB BUREAU: PAPERS.
   1911–1920. 28 pieces. [III 69]

FO 893 CONFERENCE OF AMBASSADORS: PARIS.
   1920–1930. 33 pieces. [III 69]

FO 902 RECORDS OF TEMPORARY DEPARTMENTS.
   1915–1919. 41 pieces. [III 70]

This class contains records of the War Trade Intelligence Department and of the Ministry of Blockade. *See also* TS 14.

PRIVATE OFFICE

FO 794 INDIVIDUAL FILES.
   1904–1942. 20 pieces. [III 71]

Correspondence between the Foreign Secretary or senior officials and ambassadors, etc.

PRIVATE COLLECTIONS

FO 350 JORDAN PAPERS.
   1901–1919. 16 pieces. [II 162]

Sir John Jordan was envoy to China, 1906–1920.

FO 800 MINISTERS AND OFFICIALS: VARIOUS.
   1824–1949. 400 pieces. [III 71]. Various files are closed for
                       for 50 or 75 years.

Collections of papers belonging to Foreign Secretaries, junior ministers, and Foreign Office, diplomatic, and consular officials.

MISCELLANEOUS

PASSPORT OFFICE. [II 158; III 69]

 FO 610 PASSPORT REGISTERS. 1795–1939. 385 pieces.

 FO 612 CORRESPONDENCE. 1815–1905; 1920–1940. 200 pieces.

 FO 655 EXAMPLES OF PASSPORTS ISSUED. 1802–1961. 1,895 pieces.

 FO 737 REPRESENTATIVE CASE PAPERS. 1920–1954. 24 pieces.

FO 837 MINISTRY OF ECONOMIC WARFARE.
   1931–1951. 1,309 pieces. [III 70]

FO 849 INTERNATIONAL COMMITTEE FOR THE APPLICATION OF THE AGREEMENT
   REGARDING NON-INTERVENTION IN SPAIN.
   1936–1939. 41 pieces. [III 68]

See also CAB 62.

FO 899   CABINET PAPERS.
          1900–1921.   20 pieces.

MISCELLANEA.   [II 160]

  FO 95   SERIES I.   1639–1942.   805 pieces.

  FO 96   SERIES II.   1816–1929; 1937.   218 pieces.

COLONIAL OFFICE

The distinct post of Secretary of State for the Colonies was established in 1854.
In 1925 business relating to 'autonomous communities within the Empire', for
many years dealt with by a separate department within the Colonial Office, was
transferred to a new Secretaryship of State for Dominion Affairs. One Minister
combined the duties of Secretary of State for Dominion Affairs and Secretary of
State for the Colonies until 1930. In 1966 the Commonwealth Office was formed
from the merger of the Commonwealth Relations Office, which the Dominions
Office had become, and the Colonial Office. Transfers of functions include:

  1922.   From Admiralty, responsibility for Island of Ascension.
           From Lord Lieutenant of Ireland, responsibility for Irish Free State.
           To Home Office, the Royal Irish Constabulary.
  1925.   To Board of Trade, Imperial Institute.
  1926.   To Dominions Office, relations with Irish Free State.
  1927.   From India Office, certain responsibilities in relation to Aden.
  1932.   To Foreign Office, relations with Iraq.
  1937.   From India Office, total responsibility for Aden.
  1946.   To Foreign Office, relations with Jordan.
  1948.   To Commonwealth Relations Office, relations with Ceylon.
           To Foreign Office, relations with Israel.
  1949.   From Board of Trade, scientific and technical work of the Imperial
           Institute.
  1951.   From Ministry of Food, Overseas Food Corporation.
  1957.   To Commonwealth Relations Office, relations with Ghana and Malayan
           Federation.
  1958.   To Australian Government, Christmas Island.
  1959.   To Department of Scientific and Industrial Research, Tropical Products
           Research Institute.
  1960.   To Foreign Office, relations with Somalia.
           To Commonwealth Relations Office, relations with Cyprus, Nigeria.
  1961.   To Foreign Office, relations with Southern Cameroons.
           To Commonwealth Relations Office, relations with Northern Came-
           roons, Sierra Leone, and Tanganyika.
           From Commonwealth Relations Office, responsibility for Basutoland,
           Bechuanaland, and Swaziland.
  1962.   To Department of Technical Co-operation, functions re development.
           To Commonwealth Relations Office, relations with Jamaica, Trinidad,
           Tobago, Uganda.
  1963.   To Commonwealth Relations Office, relations with Singapore,
           Sarawak, North Borneo, Zanzibar, Kenya, Brunei.
  1964.   To Commonwealth Relations Office, relations with Malta.

The CO classes fall into two main groups, corresponding to the division of work in the Colonial Office: those that deal with geographical areas, for example Ireland, Malay States, Middle East, and those that are general in character, for example Economic, Appointments, Empire Marketing Board. The class lists are correspondingly divided into these two groups. For the most part the pieces in the class lists are not given full descriptive titles. Each class of correspondence or papers has a companion register, which is not always transferred at the same time as the documents. For example, the class list of CO 232 containing original correspondence gives for each year several piece numbers and the file numbers of the papers each contains. The registers list the papers in numerical order of their file numbers and give a precis of the contents of each file. Some registers contain indexes for a year, and some have lists of topics at the beginning of each volume. Registers may cover part of a year, a whole year, or more rarely a group of years. The registers do not give the P.R.O. reference number, so it is only by comparing dates and file numbers that the relevant file can be found.

The geographical classes contain much inter-war material but it is an enormous research task to sift out that dealing specifically with social or economic policy. In general for each colony the records include correspondence, registers of correspondence, sessional papers, government gazettes, and miscellanea consisting mainly of Blue Books of statistics. The registers should be consulted for topics of interest. The general classes which contain inter-war material are listed below.

The P.R.O. handbook *The Records of the Colonial and Dominions Offices,* published in 1964, should be consulted.

CO 323   COLONIES (GENERAL): ORIGINAL CORRESPONDENCE.
1689–1952.   1,924 pieces.   [II 87]

Broadly speaking these are documents that concern more colonies than one or no colony in particular. They consist of the records of the General Department of the Colonial Office. This was set up in 1870 and eventually was responsible for defence, copying departments, library and registry, governors' pensions, naval cadetships, uniforms, the drafting of formal instruments, what was called 'establishment proper', the scrutiny of Parliamentary notices, and circular dispatches. In 1894, the General and Emigration Departments were fused and in 1896 the General and Financial Departments were merged and the Chief Clerk put in charge of them. In 1901, the General and Financial Department was renamed the General Department. In 1928, the General Department was split in two. One of these branches dealt mainly with personnel questions, the other mainly with the rest of the subjects which had customarily belonged to the General Department. In 1930, a Personnel Division was created and all personnel work taken away from the General Department. In 1934 the Department was renamed the General Division and split into two departments. Early in 1938, the first of these was handling defence, international relations, mandates, labour education, public health, communications, and currency. The second called the Economic Department dealt with the marketing and development of colonial products, and with trade relations. In the same year a third department, called the Social Service Department, was added to the General Division.

The content of CO 323 reflects the work of the department described in the above historical note.

The registers are CO 378 for registered correspondence, CO 652 for unregistered correspondence, and CO 379 for out-letters.

For other aspects of the work of the General Department, see CO 380, 449, 523, 537, 854, 866, and 877.

CO 380   COLONIES, GENERAL: DRAFT LETTERS PATENT, COMMISSIONS, ROYAL
          INSTRUCTIONS, WARRANTS, ETC.
          1764–1925.   215 pieces.   [II 88]

The pieces are dated and listed by the name of the relevant colony. There is no index.

CO 382   REGISTERS: DAILY CORRESPONDENCE.
          1849–1929.   82 pieces.   [II 91]

A daily register of letters received at the Colonial Office with brief account of their content.

CO 429   PATRONAGE: ORIGINAL CORRESPONDENCE.
          1867–1919.   131 pieces.   [II 90]

The Colonial Secretary exercised a wide patronage: in 1910 a special assistant private secretary was appointed to deal with it. Later correspondence is in CO 877.

CO 431   ACCOUNTS BRANCH: ORIGINAL CORRESPONDENCE.
          1868–1925.   152 pieces.   [II 87]

The Accounts Branch was formed at the end of the nineteenth century and dealt with lesser financial questions, not major policy decisions. The class consists of correspondence on financial matters with colonial governors, the Treasury and other departments, and with individuals.
The register for this class is CO 622.

CO 447   ORDER OF ST. MICHAEL AND ST. GEORGE.
          1836–1932.   129 pieces.   [II 92]

Original correspondence. Entry books and registers of out-letters are in CO 734, miscellanea in CO 745, and register of correspondence in CO 845.

CO 448   HONOURS: ORIGINAL CORRESPONDENCE.
          1858–1943.   71 pieces.   [II 90]

The register is CO 728 and CO 729 contains a register of out-letters up to 1934.

CO 449   GOVERNORS' PENSIONS: ORIGINAL CORRESPONDENCE.
          1863–1925.   10 pieces.   [II 89]

This class owes its origin to the Governors' Pension Act of 1865. From 1925 to 1931, it was absorbed into CO 323, and after that into CO 850.

CO 523   CHIEF CLERK: ORIGINAL CORRESPONDENCE.
          1843–1931.   92 pieces.   [II 87]

3

This includes the correspondence of the General Department on such formal matters as precedence, seals, the consecration of colonial bishops, medals, titles, and the drafting of governors' instructions. For later correspondence see CO 323.

The register for this class is CO 863, and CO 864 is a register of out-letters.

CO 524   IMPERIAL SERVICE ORDER: ORIGINAL CORRESPONDENCE.
          1902–1932.   14 pieces.   [II 90]

This Order was instituted in 1902 as a means of rewarding long and meritorious service performed by civil servants within the Empire. The pieces consist of bound volumes listed chronologically.

The register is CO 834 and CO 835 is a register of out-letters.

CO 532   DOMINIONS: ORIGINAL CORRESPONDENCE.
          1907–1925.   335 pieces.   [II 88]

Correspondence relates to Australia, Canada, the Irish Free State, Newfoundland, New Zealand, and the Union of South Africa. The register for this class is CO 708 and the register of out-letters CO 709. For a continuation of this series see the DO group.

CO 537   SUPPLEMENTARY CORRESPONDENCE.
          1759–1929.   1,208 pieces.   [II 86]

These papers relate to various colonies. The class contains secret despatches, telegrams, correspondence on the Civil Service Commission, defence, emoluments of governors and their staff, personal cases, reports on unrest, and sundry unregistered correspondence.

The pieces from 601 to 1,208 cover the period 1915–1929 and are arranged in the following way: general, colonies by name, not in strict alphabetical order, dominions general, and dominions by name. Within each section the files are in chronological order and each is fully described.

CO 694 is the register for this class and also provides a key to the secret despatches and telegrams.

CO 571   IMMIGRATION: ORIGINAL CORRESPONDENCE.
          1913–1920.   7 pieces.   [II 90]

These concern the entry of Indian indentured labour into the West Indies and Mauritius. The register is CO 780.

CO 616   DOMINIONS: WAR OF 1914–1918: ORIGINAL CORRESPONDENCE.
          1914–1919.   82 pieces.   [II 89]

The volumes are listed chronologically. The class list indicates the government departments concerned and some volumes are of correspondence with individuals.

The registers are CO 752 for correspondence and CO 753 for out-letters.

CO 687   DOMINIONS: WAR OF 1914–1918: TRADE.
          1916–1919.   68 pieces.   [II 89]

Listed as for CO 616. The registers are CO 756 for correspondence and CO 757 for out-letters.

CO 693 DOMINIONS: WAR OF 1914–1918: PRISONERS: ORIGINAL CORRESPON-
DENCE.
1917–1919. 10 pieces. [II 89]

Listed as for CO 616. The registers are CO 754 for correspondence and CO 755 for out-letters.

CO 721 OVERSEAS SETTLEMENT: ORIGINAL CORRESPONDENCE.
1918–1925. 118 pieces. [II 90]

A Government Emigration Committee, later renamed the Oversea Settlement Committee, was appointed in 1919 as the Government found it necessary to take closer responsibility for the movements of British subjects wishing to settle overseas within the Empire, or to emigrate to foreign countries. It was served by the Oversea Settlement Office. The Committee advised the Government on settlement within the Empire and the administration of the Empire Settlement Act of 1922. The Oversea Settlement Department was a branch of the Dominions Division and later of the Dominions Office.
The registers are CO 791 and CO 792. *See also* DO 57.

CO 758 EMPIRE MARKETING BOARD: ORIGINAL CORRESPONDENCE.
1922–1934. 107 pieces. [II 89]

From 1926 to 1933 this Board, with the Dominions Secretary as chairman, promoted the marketing of Empire produce in the United Kingdom, and fostered trade between different parts of the Empire. CO 759 is a card index to the correspondence, both nominal and subject.

CO 760 EMPIRE MARKETING BOARD: MINUTES AND PAPERS.
1926–1933. 39 pieces. [II 89]

This class contains the minutes and papers of the Board and papers of its various committees and sub-committees.

CO 766 PRIVATE ENTERPRISE COMMITTEE.
1923. 1 piece. [II 91]

The Committee was set up to consider measures to encourage private enterprise in the development of the British colonies in East and West Tropical Africa. Its papers consist of in-letters and out-letters, records of oral and written evidence, and the draft report.

CO 820 MILITARY: ORIGINAL CORRESPONDENCE.
1927–1946. 60 pieces. [II 90]. Various files are closed for 50 years.

The files are numbered and dated; the register is CO 871.

CO 836–839 PRIZE COURT. [II 91]

These are bound volumes covering the period 1914–1921. The subjects covered are: naval appeals, overseas appeals, United Kingdom appeals, and the Naval Prize Tribunal. All the classes consist of extracts from Lloyds List and occasionally from other printed works. A few not very significant minutes have been written on the pages. The volumes are indexed.

CO 848 CLAIMS, 1914–1918 WAR: ORIGINAL CORRESPONDENCE.
1920–1938. 7 pieces. [II 87]

The list consists of dated file numbers.

CO 850 PERSONNEL: ORIGINAL CORRESPONDENCE.
1932–1949. 238 pieces. [II 90]

This class contains correspondence of the Personnel Division, formed in 1930, later called the Colonial Service Division. It deals with organisation and discipline of the service, promotion and transfer within it, conditions of employment, etc., and training until 1937. There is also correspondence concerning appointment of colonial governors. Other correspondence on appointments, and after 1937 on training will be found in CO 877. The files are bound in dated volumes, the register is CO 919.

CO 852 ECONOMIC: ORIGINAL CORRESPONDENCE.
1935–1949. 1,054 pieces. [II 89]

The records of the Economic Department. The register is CO 920.

CO 854 COLONIES, GENERAL: CIRCULAR DESPATCHES.
1808–1956. 181 pieces. [II 88]

These are listed in dated volumes. The index is CO 949; CO 862 contains a register of replies to circular despatches.

CO 859 SOCIAL SERVICE: ORIGINAL CORRESPONDENCE.
1939–1949. 164 pieces. [II 92]

The Social Service Department was set up in 1939 as part of the General Division. The files in this class are continuations of those previously registered under Colonies, General, CO 323. Nineteen boxes cover 1939:

1–5   Education: Education Advisory Committee and sub-committees; examinations; welfare of colonial students in Great Britain; work of British Council; survey of vocational and technical education in colonies; teaching about the Empire in British schools; higher education and political development. See also BT 59.

6   Education: general policy; Rhodes Scholarships; International Conference on the Educational Implications of the Changing Attitude of Europe to the Colonies.
Films: use of for education in colonies.

7	Films: continued.

7   Films: continued.
Labour: Forced Labour Convention, 1930, annual reports, 1938–39; colonial legislation.

8–11   Labour: International Labour Convention, annual reports; trade union legislation; League of Nations Committee on Slavery.

12–14   Medical: infectious diseases, Sanitary Control of Aircraft Convention; nutrition.

15   Opium; dangerous drugs; native welfare; penal reform; juvenile offenders.

16–19   Penal reform; native courts; welfare of coloured students in Great Britain; preparation for census, 1941; sociological research and anthropology; the churches and social welfare.

CO 866   ESTABLISHMENT: ORIGINAL CORRESPONDENCE.
1922–1946.   40 pieces.   [III 28]

The pieces are dated volumes. After 1933 the files are bound in pieces continuing to 1946. The register is CO 867.

CO 868   COLONIAL EMPIRE MARKETING BOARD.
1938–1939.   7 pieces.   [III 27]

The Board was set up in 1937. Its object was to help the colonies to 'develop their own sources of wealth, to sell more goods, and to sell those goods to better advantage'. It started work in 1938, presented its first report in 1939, but did not survive the Second World War. For its predecessor, the Empire Marketing Board, see CO 758–760. The last piece, 7, in this class contains a list of the Board's papers.

CO 877   APPOINTMENTS: ORIGINAL CORRESPONDENCE.
1920–1949.   31 pieces.   [III 27]

This is a continuation of CO 429. After 1937 the class contains correspondence about training of Colonial Service officers. The register for the class is CO 918. *See also* CO 850.

CO 878   ESTABLISHMENT: MISCELLANEA.
1794–1965.   34 pieces.   [III 28]

This class consists of a series of office minutes (1836–1929), a set of Colonial Office Bulletins (1920–1932), and a series of Establishment notices (1935–1965). The volumes contain details of instructions to staff, regulations, appointments, and other allied matters affecting the internal administration of the office.

CO 888   COLONIAL LABOUR ADVISORY COMMITTEE: PAPERS AND MINUTES.
1931–1961.   11 pieces.   [III 28]

The only inter-war material is in piece 1, the Colonial Labour Committee, 1931–1941. This was an interdepartmental committee appointed to review the general principles on which colonial labour legislation should be based. *See also* CO 885.

CO 912 TREATMENT OF OFFENDERS IN THE COLONIES: ADVISORY COMMITTEE: PAPERS.
1937–1961.   10 pieces.   [III 31]

Minutes and papers of the Committee originally set up in 1937 as the Colonial Penal Administration Committee.

CO 916 COMMITTEE ON THE DEPORTATION OF BRITISH SUBJECTS FROM THE COLONIES: PAPERS.
1932–1933.   1 piece.   [III 31]

Minutes and papers of a committee appointed to consider the conditions which should govern the deportation of British subjects from colonies not possessing responsible governments, protectorates, and mandated colonies.

CO 959 PRIVATE COLLECTIONS: VARIOUS.
1869–1922.   4 pieces.

2–3   1909–1922. Papers and correspondence of Captain H. L. Norton Traill, Resident in Northern Nigeria.

CONFIDENTIAL PRINT

The following classes of confidential print consist of collections of the main correspondence and reports on a particular subject, duplicating material found elsewhere. They cover social, economic, and political policies and relations with the respective colonies. Up to 1934 there exist indexed catalogues for these classes (CO 601), thereafter the pieces are fully described.

CO 879 AFRICA.
1642–1961.   190 pieces.   [III 27]

CO 881 AUSTRALIA.
1833–1923.   15 pieces.   [III 27]

CO 882 EASTERN.
1847–1939.   23 pieces.   [III 27]

CO 883 MEDITERRANEAN.
1844–1936.   10 pieces.   [III 27]

CO 884 WEST INDIES.
1787–1961.   13 pieces.   [III 27]

CO 885 MISCELLANEOUS.
1839–1918; 1922–1966.   140 pieces.   [II 88]

Material in this class covers more than one colony and concerns topics of very general interest. Subjects covered include: workmen's compensation, industrial development of the Empire, recruitment of native labour, and the report of the Colonial Labour Committee (1935).

CO 886   Dominions.
        1907–1925.   11 pieces.   [III 27]

Continued in DO 114.

CO 934   Pacific, Western.
        1921–1960.   8 pieces.

CO 935   Middle East.
        1920–1956.   25 pieces.

COMMONWEALTH RELATIONS OFFICE

In 1925 a new Secretaryship of State for Dominion Affairs was created, to take over from the Colonial Office relations with the self-governing Dominions, Southern Rhodesia, and the High Commission Territories.

In 1947 the Secretaryship of State for Commonwealth Relations replaced that for Dominion Affairs and responsibility for India and Pakistan was transferred from the Secretary of State for India. The Office remained responsible for relations with Eire after 1949.

1961.   To Department of Technical Co-operation, some functions concerning development and aid.
        To Foreign Office, relations with Republic of South Africa.
1962.   Relations with the Federation of Rhodesia and Nyasaland transferred to the newly created Central African Office, responsible to the Home Secretary.
1963.   Zambia (Northern Rhodesia) and Malawi (Nyasaland) became independent. Central African Office made responsible to the Commonwealth Relations Office, and merged with the office in 1964.
1966.   Commonwealth Relations Office merged with the Colonial Office to form Commonwealth Office.
1967.   From Department of Education and Science, the Commonwealth Institute.
1968.   Commonwealth Office combined with Foreign Office to form Foreign and Commonwealth Office.

See Colonial Office for other transfers.

The records of the DO group are arranged, for the most part, like those of the Colonial Office, geographically under countries with separate classes for each territory covering acts, government gazettes, sessional papers, etc. These classes are supplemented by a few general or special subject classes. All original correspondence relating to particular territories is preserved in Dominions Original Correspondence DO 35 and 117, with the exception of two classes of Original Correspondence relating to Southern Rhodesia and the South African High Commission Territories for the period 1926–1929.

DO 9   South Africa: Original Correspondence.
        1926–1929.   15 pieces.   [II 93]

The register of correspondence is DO 1 and the register of out-letters is DO 2.

DO 35   DOMINIONS: ORIGINAL CORRESPONDENCE.
       1926–1953.   1,231 pieces.   [II 95]

This class which is a continuation of CO 532 contains only numbered files. DO 117 which covers the period 1926–1929 is supplementary to DO 35. It contains named files originally retained by the Commonwealth Office owing to their security classification. The registers to both classes are in DO 3. DO 4 is a register of out-letters for the period 1927–1929.

DO 36   HONOURS (DOMINIONS): ORIGINAL CORRESPONDENCE.
       1927–1929.   2 pieces.   [II 95]

DO 57   OVERSEAS SETTLEMENT: ORIGINAL CORRESPONDENCE.
       1926–1936.   189 pieces.   [II 96]

Continues CO 721. The registers are DO 5, and DO 6 (1928–1929 only).

DO 63   RHODESIA, SOUTHERN: ORIGINAL CORRESPONDENCE.
       1926–1929.   6 pieces.   [II 97]

The register of correspondence is DO 7 and the register of out-letters is DO 8.

DO 81   IMPERIAL SERVICE ORDER (DOMINIONS): ORIGINAL CORRESPONDENCE.
       1927–1929.   1 piece.   [II 95]
  See CO 524.

DO 89   ORDER OF ST. MICHAEL AND ST. GEORGE.
       1927–1928.   1 piece.   [II 97]
  See also CO 447.

CONFIDENTIAL PRINT

All the pieces in these classes are fully described in the class-lists.

DO 114   DOMINIONS.
       1924–1951.   119 pieces.

Continues CO 886. The files contain papers on social and economic questions, for example:

10	1926. Dominion legislation for the prevention of strikes and lock-outs.
16	1927–1931. Treatment of Asiatics in the Dominions.
74	1936–1938. Migration.
93	1937–1939. Trade negotiations with the United States.

DO 115   AUSTRALIA.
       1928–1936.   3 pieces.

Continues CO 881. All the papers so far transferred relate to Australian constitutional questions.

DO 116   SOUTH AFRICA.
         1913–1944.   8 pieces.

Continues CO 879. The papers cover the territories administered by the High Commissioner for South Africa including their possible transfer to the Union of South Africa and the question of mineral concessions in the Bechuanaland Protectorate.

DO 117   ORIGINAL CORRESPONDENCE: SUPPLEMENTARY.
         1926–1929.   189 pieces.
   See DO 35.

The records of the India Office are kept at the India Office Library and Records, Orbit House, 179 Blackfriars Road, London, SE1 89G.

CROWN AGENTS FOR OVERSEAS GOVERNMENTS

Crown Agents were set up in 1833 to act as business and financial agents for the Crown Colonies. Subsequently they have come to act for many dependent territories, for some Commonwealth and other independent countries, for the United Nations, and municipalities and public utilities.

Many of the papers of the Crown Agents are not public records, but representative papers have been deposited at the P.R.O. together with printed bulletins.

CAOG 1   ACCOUNTS AND FINANCE DEPARTMENT: REPRESENTATIVE PAPERS.
         1930–1959.   10 pieces.   [II 98]

Reports of the Joint Colonial Fund, and Joint Miscellaneous Funds, and accounts of Colonial Funds; all files extend beyond 1945.

CAOG 2   APPOINTMENTS AND PASSAGES DEPARTMENT: REPRESENTATIVE PAPERS.
         1933–1953.   10 pieces.   [II 98]

1   1933. Appointment and passage agreements.

2   1939. Colonial appointments.

CAOG 5   STORES PUCHASING DEPARTMENT: REPRESENTATIVE PAPERS.
         1925–1956.   6 pieces.   [II 98]

1   1925–1929. Civil and Mechanical Engineering Advisory Service
               Papers.

CAOG 6   BULLETINS.
         1928–1932.   8 pieces.

The bulletins were printed and circulated to the governments for whom the Crown Agents act, to give them the benefit of the information the Crown Agents collected in the course of their work. The bulletins deal very largely with aspects of the engineering industry, particularly railways, road bridges, ships, and motor vehicles. There are also articles on refrigeration in the tropics, travelling entomological laboratory, standardisation of textiles and other materials. The preface to Bulletin 8 gives a list of the subjects covered.

INDUSTRY AND TRADE

BOARD OF TRADE

The Board of Trade began in the seventeenth century as a committee of the Privy Council dealing with trade, particularly trade with the colonies. During the nineteenth century it was given various powers to regulate industry and commerce. During the present century some of its functions have been transferred to new ministries, for example, the functions and relevant records of the Harbour, Marine, and Railway Departments, to the Ministry of Transport. The department also contains some records of defunct ministries, such as branches of the Ministry of Munitions, and six files from the Ministry of Reconstruction.

The main changes in the Board of Trade since 1918 are set out below because there have been so many and because the location of records in the P.R.O. depended on which department held the records at the time of transfer to the P.R.O.

CHANGES IN FUNCTIONS OF THE BOARD OF TRADE

1918–1939.

1918. Department of Overseas Trade established, responsible jointly to Board of Trade and Foreign Office.

1919. Export Credits Department established as part of the Board of Trade, became a separate department in 1930. (*See* ECG)

War Trade Department, established in 1915, transferred to Board of Trade and became the Export Licensing Department (BT 73)

From Ministry of Munitions, sections dealing with electrical power, optical glass, and potash.

To Department of Scientific and Industrial Research, custody and maintenance of electrical standards.

To Home Office, power to appoint to Railway and Canal Commission.

To Ministry of Transport, most powers relating to inland transport, harbours, docks, and piers.

1920. Mines Department established, headed by a Parliamentary Secretary to the Board of Trade, taking over from the Home Office powers relating to mines and quarries.

From Ministry of Health, powers relating to gas undertakings belonging to local authorities.

To Ministry of Health, powers relating to private water undertakings in England and Wales.

To Ministry of Transport, powers relating to electricity, property in Ramsgate and Holyhead harbours, and two colliery railways.

1921. Marine Department of the Board renamed Mercantile Marine Department, taking over residual functions of the dissolved Ministry of Shipping, including Transport Services which before 1917 had been part of Admiralty.

From the dissolved Ministry of Food, residual functions dealing with civil emergency food organisation.

From the dissolved Ministry of Munitions, powers under the Petroleum Act, to be exercised by the Mines Department.

1922.   Petroleum Department merged with Board of Trade.

From Registrar General, then at Ministry of Health (from Local Government Board), registration of business names. Following year transferred to Inland Revenue, returned to Board of Trade in 1948.

To Ministry of Transport, some powers over railway and canal traffic, and the Port of London.

1923.   From Admiralty, responsibility for the coastguard service.

1925.   From Colonial Office, responsibility for the Imperial Institute, to be exercised by the Department of Overseas Trade. Returned to Colonial Office and Ministry of Education in 1949; now called Commonwealth Institute.

From Public Trustee, custodianship of enemy property. Delegated to Public Trustee in 1939, and returned to Board of Trade in 1948.

1936.   Food (Defence Plans) Department established, transferred to new Ministry of Food in 1939.

1937.   To Scottish Office, functions relating to provisional orders for harbour, pier, and ferry works.

1939.   To the new Ministry of Supply, functions relating to raw materials.

WAR 1939–1945.

1939.   To Ministry of Food, the Food (Defence Plans) Department.

To Ministry of Shipping, everything to do with ships and the coastguard service.

To Ministry of Supply, some powers over petroleum.

1940.   Petroleum Department established, controlled by Secretary for Petroleum.

1941.   Board of Trade responsible for war damage claims for chattels and for clothes rationing scheme.

From Ministry of War Transport, powers relating to electricity.

1942.   Trading with Enemy Department set up jointly by Treasury and Board of Trade.

To Ministry of Fuel and Power, powers relating to mines, petroleum, gas, hydraulic power, and electricity. Mines Department and Petroleum Department abolished.

To Ministry of Works and Buildings, responsibility for the building industry.

1943.   Board of Trade responsible for utility furniture scheme.

1945–1970.

After the war, the Board of Trade merged with the Ministry of Production. Responsibility for the engineering industry was transferred to the Ministry of Supply. Control of raw materials was divided between the Board and the Ministry of Supply until 1951 when a Ministry of Materials was set up, taking over from both departments. The Ministry of Supply, however, kept control over iron and steel and non-ferrous metals. The Ministry of Materials was dissolved in 1954, all its functions being transferred to the Board of Trade. In 1955, control of metals, retained by the Ministry of Supply, transferred to the Board of Trade, but in 1957 went to the newly named Ministry of Power (former Fuel and Power), later to the Ministry of Technology, and in 1970 to the Department of Trade and Industry.

Responsibility for the distribution of industry and policy for Development Areas (Special Areas renamed) passed from the Ministry of Labour and National Service to the Board of Trade in 1945. Regional Boards for Industry were set up under the Board and in 1947 transferred to the newly formed Ministry of Economic Affairs which later that year was absorbed by the Treasury. They returned to the Board of Trade in 1952.

The Department of Economic Affairs was formed in 1964 to be responsible for long term economic planning. In 1967 some of its work, particularly in the field of overseas economic policy and relations with industry in preparation for entry into the European Economic Community, was transferred to the Board of Trade.

The Board of Trade took over from the Treasury the co-ordination of work of government departments on industrial productivity, from the Ministry of Food supervision of labelling of food, and from the Home Office functions under the Fabric (Misdescription) Act, 1913.

The Board lost the following:

To Ministry of Agriculture, functions relating to home grown wool. (Transferred from Ministry of Supply in 1946.)
To the Forestry Commission, licensing of felling of growing trees.
To the Treasury Solicitor, legal work for the Ministry of Power.

Other functions left the Board but returned when in 1970 it merged with the Ministry of Technology to form the Department of Trade and Industry.

BT 7   TEMPORARY DEPARTMENT: COTTON CONTROL BOARD.
        1917–1919.   46 pieces.   [II 276]

Summaries of census returns, minutes, ledgers, miscellaneous papers.

BT 8   TEMPORARY DEPARTMENT: ENEMY DEBTS COMMITTEE.
        1916–1919.   26 pieces.   [II 276]

Correspondence, minutes, evidence, reports, returns from Public Trustee, miscellaneous papers.

BT 10   TEMPORARY DEPARTMENTS: IMPORT DUTIES ADVISORY COUNCIL.
        1932–1939.   56 pieces.   [II 276].   Closed for 50 years.

BT 11   COMMERCIAL DEPARTMENT: CORRESPONDENCE AND PAPERS.
        1866–1953.   2,834 pieces.   [II 269, III 162].   Various files are
                                                             closed for 50 years.

The department's original function was the revision of the tariff and negotiation of tariff agreements with foreign countries. This was transferred to the Foreign Office in 1872, and the department became adviser to the Foreign Office on commercial policy. In 1917 the Department of Overseas Trade was formed to administer the overseas commercial services; the Commercial Department continued to advise the Foreign Office on commercial agreements, protection of the interests of British traders abroad, and control of imports and exports.

In 1908, work connected with Merchandise Marks, Patents, Designs and Trade Marks, was transferred from the Finance Department to the Commercial Department until it moved to the General Department (BT 63) in 1928, and to the Industries and Manufactures Department (BT 64) in 1934.

13–42   1919–1930. Files are listed chronologically. The papers deal with the subjects indicated by the sections into which records after 1930 were divided, see below. In addition this section of the class contains papers dealing with the Reparation Commission, the economic clauses of peace treaties, various international economic conferences and commissions dealing with the Danube and the Elbe. Subject index is available in search rooms.

43–1,401   1931–1939. Files named and arranged in sections and under countries:

Codes:
1. Arms trade control
2. Certificates of origin
3. Commodities:
   A. Apparel and textiles
   B. Chemicals
   C. Consumer goods
   D. Food and drink
   E. Fuel
   F. Metals
   G. Raw materials
   H. Vehicles and parts
   J. Miscellaneous
4. Commonwealth trade
5. Customs
6. Denunciation of treaties
7. Discriminations and sanctions
8. Dumping
9. Exchange control (including currency, stabilisations, safeguards, and monetary restrictions)
10. Foreign taxation (including double taxation)
11. Insurance
12. League of Nations
13. Legislation
14. Merchandise and trade marks
15. Most Favoured Nations
16. Payments and debts (including credits, clearings, loans, banking and other kinds of money transactions, also claims, compensations, and activities of the Export Credits Guarantee Dept.)
17. Quotas
18. Shipping
19. Tariffs
20. United Kingdom (departmental and general)

Where appropriate, files are also listed under countries.

70

BT 12   COMMERCIAL DEPARTMENT: OUT-LETTERS.
          1864–1921.   160 pieces.   [II 269]

142–160   1919–1921. Each year letters to firms and to government
            departments are filed alphabetically; except that letters to
            Foreign Office take precedence.

BT 13   ESTABLISHMENT DIVISION: CORRESPONDENCE AND PAPERS.
          1865–1964.   233 pieces.   [II 270].   Various files are closed
                                                      for 50 years.

92–174   1919–1939. Apart from establishment matters, the class con-
            tains minutes of the Advisory Council of the Board of Trade,
            reports of other committees, transfers of functions between
            departments, etc.

BT 15   FINANCE DEPARTMENT: CORRESPONDENCE AND PAPERS.
          1865–1954.   215 pieces.   [III 163]

The department supervises the financial policy, revenue, and expenditure
of the Board of Trade, and in addition has administrative functions concerned
with merchant seamen, lighthouses, wrecks, and other marine matters.

71–88   1919–1930. Files are listed chronologically. The papers deal
            with the subjects indicated by the sections into which the
            records were grouped after 1930, see below. Most papers
            relate to the marine work of the department, and there are also
            reports on the coal industry, 1920, and papers on the transfer
            of the Food Ministry, 1921, and the Petroleum Department,
            1922, to the Board of Trade. Subject index is available in
            search rooms.

89–215   After 1930 files are arranged in sections. Many files contain
            earlier material, some going back to 1905.

Codes: 1. Accounting
          2. Contracts
          3. Defence and war measures
          4. Establishments
          5. Estimates
          6. Fees (for licences, certificates, etc.)
          7. Industrial assistance and reorganisation
          8. Insurance
          9. Liquidation
          10. Marine
          11. Official enquiries
          12. Pensions and gratuities
          13. War claims

BT 17   FINANCE DEPARTMENT: OUT-LETTERS.
          1864–1919.   226 pieces.   [II 270]

221–6   1919. Letters.

BT 20   ESTABLISHMENT DEPARTMENT: OUT-LETTERS.
         1865–1921.   48 pieces.   [II 270]

BT 26   STATISTICAL DEPARTMENT: PASSENGER LISTS: INWARDS.
         1878–1960.   1,476 pieces.   [II 275].   Records are open after 5
                                                     years.

650–1186   1919–1939. Passenger lists of all ships entering British ports
            coming from ports outside Europe and the Mediterranean Sea;
            giving age and occupation of each traveller. Arranged yearly by
            port of arrival.

BT 27   STATISTICAL DEPARTMENT: PASSENGER LISTS: OUTWARDS.
         1890–1960.   1,922 pieces.   [II 275].   Records are open after 5
                                                     years.

890–1552   1919–1939. Lists similar to BT 26 are arranged yearly by port of
            departure.

BT 31   COMPANIES REGISTRATION OFFICE: FILES OF DISSOLVED COMPANIES.
         1856–1948.   33,943 pieces.   [III 163–4].   Records are open after
                                                         5 years.

This class contains the remaining files of dissolved companies registered after
the passing of the Joint Stock Company Act, 1856. The records are arranged
according to the registered number of the company; this can be found for most
companies incorporated before July, 1937, in the indexes, press reference B 247–250
(Long Room), described below.

    There is one series of numbers up to 370,751, arranged in five sections according
to the date when the company was dissolved. Dissolved companies whose numbers
range from 1–142,657 are in numerical order in the volumes B 186–190, the next
section, from 60–260,957, are in B 191–194, B 195 is a special section described
below. A further section of numbers 384–364,521, is in B 196–197 and a final section
from 270–370,751, is also in B 197. The number of a company may be in any one
of these five sections, depending mainly on when it was dissolved.

    Companies incorporated between 1856 and 1900 and registered in London, and
which were dissolved between 1933 and 1948, have a separate alphabetical index in
B 185. This index gives the number of the company which can then be found in the
special section of numbers in B 195.

    The indexes of companies registered are as follows:

Index of Companies Registered 17.7.1856–30.6.1920
                                                   A–K   B 248
                                                   L–Z   B 249
Index of Companies in the Register 30.6.1930   B 247
Index of Companies on the Register 30.6.1937   B 250

    The registered number of all firms incorporated before July, 1920, can be found
in B 248–9; and the number of all firms which were incorporated between 1920 and
1937 and which survived for more than ten years can be found in B 247 and 250.
Registration numbers of companies not listed in the above indexes can be obtained

from the Companies Registration Office of the Board of Trade, Companies House, 55/71 City Road, London, EC1 1BB.

If a company registered in London has been dissolved its remaining records can be traced either in BT 31, BT 34, or BT 95, except for Truro companies whose records have been retained by the Companies Registration Office.

BT 32   STATISTICAL DEPARTMENT: REGISTERS OF PASSENGER LISTS RECEIVED.
        1906–1951.   15 pieces.   [II 275].   Records open after 5 years.

8–14   1919–1939. The Registers give, under the different ports, the names of the ships and the date of their arrival and departure.

BT 34   COMPANIES REGISTRATION OFFICE: LIQUIDATORS' ACCOUNTS.
        1890–1932.   5,221 pieces.   [II 272].   Records are open after 5 years.

This class contains the accounts of companies which were incorporated between 1856 and 1915 and registered in London, and which were voluntarily dissolved before 1933. Accounts of companies dissolved after 1933 are in BT 31.

There are two sections of numbers arranged in numerical order as the records reached the Board of Trade. Numbers 89–260,139 are in B 198–9, and 24–142,657 in B 200.

The numbers of the companies can be found in indexes B 248–9. *See* BT 31.

BT 37   BANKRUPTCY DEPARTMENT: CORRESPONDENCE AND PAPERS.
        1883–1955.   187 pieces.   [II 271]

27–184   1919–1939. Files are listed chronologically. The department deals with the administration of the law relating to bankruptcy, the appointment of and correspondence with official receivers. The class also contains annual reports produced under the Bankruptcy Act, 1914; consideration of amendments to bankruptcy law; reports of the law in other countries; memoranda on insolvency, 1922; bankruptcy in post-war England and Wales, 1927; observations on legislation dealing with such matters as agricultural credits, hire purchase, and workmen's compensation. There are reports of the Bankruptcy Amendment Committee, 1925, Committee on Law of Arbitration, 1927, Bankruptcy Law and Winding-up of Companies Amendment Committee, 1930, and papers dealing with the Hague Conference on International Private Law, 1926, and the International Congress for the Protection of Creditors' Interests, 1930.

BT 54   BRITISH INDUSTRIES FAIR.
        1936–1939.   4 pieces.   [III 117]

Files are listed chronologically.

BT 55   DEPARTMENTAL COMMITTEES: RECORDS OF.
        1910–1939.   121 pieces.   [III 118]

Committees are arranged alphabetically. There is an index to committees at the beginning of the class list, and there is a separate index of committees set up by the Safeguarding of Industries Committee under 'S'.

BT 56   CHIEF INDUSTRIAL ADVISER.
        1929–1932.   50 pieces.   [III 118]

This class deals mainly with schemes for relief of unemployment in specific places or industries, many proposals being for works to do with coal, drainage, housing, transport (roads, railways, bridges, ferries, tunnels), and water supply. It also contains many files on export credit schemes and particulars of new factories established in depressed areas, and those set up by foreigners. Other subjects dealt with are colonial development and settlement, trade with Russia, rationalisation of industry in Great Britain and various foreign countries. There are reports on various trades, unemployment statistics, and some papers of the Economic Advisory Council and Unemployment Grants Committee. Arrangement haphazard. Subject index is available in search rooms.

BT 57   COUNCIL FOR ART AND INDUSTRY.
        1934–1939.   27 pieces.   [III 118]

The class contains minutes and reports of the Council for Art and Industry, and papers relating to the work of the numerous committees set up by the Council, and enquiries undertaken. The Council dealt with exhibitions in Great Britain, and abroad through the Department of Overseas Trade. There are files dealing with the Conference for the Protection of Literary and Artistic Works, Brussels, 1926, and with the Report of the Working Class Dwelling Committee, 1937. The Council's work ended on the outbreak of the war and was later absorbed by the Council of Industrial Design. Files are arranged by year. *See also* BT 64/49.

BT 58   COMPANIES DEPARTMENT: CORRESPONDENCE AND PAPERS.
        1893–1962.   377 pieces.   [III 115]

This department was formed in 1904 to carry out the duties of the Board of Trade under the Companies Acts, the Assurance Companies Acts, the Registration of Business Names Act, and the Art Union Act.

60–130   1919–1930. Files are named and arranged chronologically, and deal with topics similar to those indicated by the section headings into which records were grouped after 1930, see below. Subject index is available in search rooms.

131–314   1931–1939. Files are arranged in sections under the following headings:
Codes: 1.   Annual Returns.
        2.   Arts Unions.
        3.   Assurance Companies Acts.
        4.   Auditors and accountants.
        5.   Board of Trade's sanction or opinion sought.
        6.   Companies winding-up; liquidation and liquidators.
        7.   Company files questions.
        8.   Company titles applications.

9. Fixed trusts and trusteeship.
10. Insurance and pension matters.
11. Insurance Undertaking Bill.
12. International negotiations (co-ordination of bankruptcy law between countries, third party insurance).
13. Investigations.
14. Liability to show directors' names.
15. Moneylenders Acts.
16. Official Receivers' procedure.
17. Omitting the name 'limited' from title.
18. Prevention of Fraud (Investment) Act, 1939; share pushing.
19. Proposed amendments to company law.
20. Royal charters.
21. Share registration and shareholders interests.
22. War Risks insurance.

BT 59   DEPARTMENT OF OVERSEAS TRADE: OVERSEAS TRADE DEVELOPMENT COUNCIL.
1930–1939.   29 pieces.   [III 117]

The Council was formed in 1930, taking over the work of the Advisory Committee to the Department of Overseas Trade, BT 90. The class contains minutes and memoranda of the Council, records of sub-committees, missions abroad, and investigations into markets for particular trades in various countries.

1–27   Files are listed by year; they include papers of the Committee on Education and Training in United Kingdom of Overseas Students, 1933, see also BT 64 and CO 859.

28   Minutes of meetings 1–41 of the Overseas Trade Development Council, 1930–1936. For minutes of meetings 42, 43, and 44, see pieces 21, 24, and 26, respectively.

29   1930–1939. Memoranda. Handlist is available in search rooms.

BT 60   DEPARTMENT OF OVERSEAS TRADE: CORRESPONDENCE AND PAPERS.
1918–1940.   62 pieces.   [III 117]

The department was formed in 1918 for the collation and dissemination of overseas commercial intelligence, and for the administration of commercial services abroad; it was responsible to the Foreign Office as well as to the Board of Trade. The class contains records of the British Industries Fair, other exhibitions in Great Britain and abroad, trade missions, reports on economic conditions and trade possibilities in various countries, and other miscellaneous files. Subject index is available in search rooms.

BT 61   DEPARTMENT OF OVERSEAS TRADE: ESTABLISHMENT FILES.
1918–1940.   76 pieces.   [III 117].   Some files are closed for 50 years.

Apart from establishment matters, this class contains files on the organisation, and reorganisation, of the department, and reports on its work.

BT 62   FINANCE DEPARTMENT: CONTROLLER OF TRADING ACCOUNTS: CORRESPONDENCE AND PAPERS.

     1918–1930.   26 pieces.   [III 115].   Some files are closed for 50 years.

This department was formed during the war to administer some trading services, and others were transferred to the Board of Trade after the war prior to liquidation. The class includes papers dealing with various food supplies, and flax, forage, lime, matches, meat, nickel, optical and chemical glassware, petroleum, potash, Siberian supplies, timber (*see also* BT 71), and zinc. There are papers concerning Allied debts, and reports on coal and non-ferrous mining industries. Some of these files originated in the Ministry of Munitions.

For out-letters of this department, *see* BT 83.

BT 63   GENERAL DEPARTMENT: CORRESPONDENCE AND PAPERS.

     1928–1940.   26 pieces.   [III 115].   Various files are closed for 50 years.

This department was formed in 1928 to take over the administration of the Merchandise Marks Acts (until 1934) and the Sale of Food Acts.

1–15   1928–1933. All files are concerned with Merchandise Marks Acts except one in piece 10 on the Severn Barrage Scheme.

16–26   1933–1940. Files deal with Merchandise Marks and Sale of Food Acts, and also there are files on the organisation of the Board of Trade and the Department of Overseas Trade, and one on a discussion with Australian ministers on trade policy.

BT 64   INDUSTRIES AND MANUFACTURES DEPARTMENT: CORRESPONDENCE AND PAPERS.

     1919–1947.   93 pieces.   [III 116].   Various files are closed for 50 years.

The department was formed in 1918 to deal with the problems of reconstruction in British industry, and continued to deal with the development of home industry and trade, to administer various Acts such as the Weights and Measures Acts, Gas Regulation Acts, Cinematograph Film Acts, and after 1934, the Merchandise Marks Acts.

1–42   1919–1938. Files are named and listed chronologically. There are files dealing with specific industries, reports of the Import Duties Advisory Council, tariff negotiations with various countries, papers relating to the Safeguarding of Industries Act, 1921, and the operation of s.25 of the Finance Act, 1935, and some records arising from the Imperial Economic (Ottawa) Conference, 1932, and the Imperial Committee on Economic Consultation and Co-operation, 1937. There are some papers on the League of Nations, one on Lloyd George's scheme for industrial reorganisation (piece 10), one on development of trading estates in Special Areas (piece 11), and papers of the Committee on Education and Training of Students from Overseas, 1933. *See also* BT 59.

43–55   1938–1947. These files contain papers dealing with the subjects outlined above for pieces 1–42, and also files of the Shipbuilding Conference, 1939; Royal Commission on Geographical Distribution of the Industrial Population 1939 (*see also* HLG 27); Capital Issues Committee, 1939–1940; Price Control Co-ordination Committee and the Control of Prices and Prices of Goods bills, 1939. It also contains files relating to the film industry.

86–93   1927–1947. Papers relating to the various Cinematograph Film Acts, the British Film Institute, the Cinematograph Film Council, and the Moyne Committee, 1938. *See also* nos. 43–55 above.

BT 65   POWER TRANSPORT AND ECONOMIC DEPARTMENT: CORRESPONDENCE AND PAPERS.
           1906–1929.   13 pieces.   [III 118]

This department was formed in 1919 by merging the General Economic Department with what was left of the Industrial Power and Transport Department when functions to do with electricity were transferred to the Ministry of Transport. Out-letters are in BT 84.

1–12   1918–1922. Files are listed chronologically, and deal with work arising from the Supreme Economic Council, export credits, co-ordination of transport, etc., and reports of committees.

13   1906–1929. Files on proposed Channel Tunnel or Ferry. Also in piece 12 above.

BT 66   MINISTRY OF MUNITIONS.
           1915–1920.   14 pieces.   [III 118]

1–7   1915–1918. Optical Munitions and Glassware Branch.
8–14   1918–1920. Potash Production Board.

BT 67   MINISTRY OF RECONSTRUCTION.
           1917–1919.   1 piece.   [III 119]

1   Files on: proposed conference on conservation of material resources of Allies; excess profits duty; post-war steel trade; mineral exploration in Ireland; revision of contract prices; and proposals for railway nationalisation.

BT 68   PROFITEERING ACT DEPARTMENT.
           1919–1921.   92 pieces.   [III 119]

1–83   Files are listed chronologically, including regulations, orders, and schedules arising from the Act, reports of sub-committees, deputations, etc.

84   Standing Committee on Prices, 1919–1921, minutes of meetings 1–54.

85   Joint meetings of the Standing Committee on Trusts and Standing Committee for the Investigation of Prices, 1920–1921; minutes of meetings 1–4.

| 86–88 | Standing Committee on Trusts, 1919–1920; minutes of meetings 1–71. |
| 89–92 | Complaints Committee, 1919–1921; minutes and evidence. |

BT 69 ROYAL COMMISSION ON COMPENSATION FOR SUFFERING AND DAMAGE BY ENEMY ACTION.
1921–1924.   5 pieces.   [III 119]

Minutes of meetings 1–71, decisions, general papers and parliamentary questions. *See also* BT 102.

BT 70 STATISTICAL DEPARTMENT/STATISTICS DIVISION: CORRESPONDENCE AND PAPERS.
1918–1939.   65 pieces.   [III 117]

Files are listed chronologically. Papers contain statistical returns of all kinds, including those arising from the Census of Production Acts, surveys of factories in 1934 and 1935, and memoranda prepared for the Imperial Economic Conference.

BT 71 TEMPORARY DEPARTMENTS: TIMBER SUPPLIES DEPARTMENT.
1916–1920.   20 pieces.   [III 119]

| 3–4 | 1919–1920. Files are listed chronologically, including pitwood orders, memorandum on world timber production, forestry camps, winding up of department. |
| 5–20 | 1916–1920. Original contracts. |

BT 73 TEMPORARY DEPARTMENTS: WAR TRADE DEPARTMENT.
1916–1927.   1 piece.   [III 119]

Papers are listed chronologically, including records of Export Licensing Department, various restrictions on imports and exports.

BT 82 REGISTERS AND REPRESENTATIONS OF TRADE MARKS.
1876–1938.   1,387 pieces.   [II 274].   Records are open after 5 years.

| 418–486 | 1919–1933. Lodgement of cotton mark representations at Manchester. Cotton marks continued to 1938, but registers for last 5 years are missing. |
| 987–1387 | 1919–1938. Lodgement of non-cotton representations in London. |

BT 83 FINANCE DEPARTMENT: CONTROLLER OF TRADING ACCOUNTS: OUT-LETTERS.
1921–1922.   8 pieces.   [III 115]

Letters arranged chronologically, half-year per volume. For correspondence and papers of this department, *see* BT 62.

BT 84   POWER, TRANSPORT AND ECONOMIC DEPARTMENT: OUT-LETTERS.
         1918–1921.   9 pieces.   [III 118]

Letters for each year arranged alphabetically.

BT 85   INDUSTRIES AND MANUFACTURES DEPARTMENT: OUT-LETTERS.
         1918–1921.   10 pieces.   [III 116]

Letters for each year arranged alphabetically. For correspondence and papers of this department, *see* BT 64.

BT 90   ADVISORY COMMITTEE TO THE DEPARTMENT OF OVERSEAS TRADE
         (DEVELOPMENT AND INTELLIGENCE): MINUTES AND PAPERS.
         1918–1930.   26 pieces.   [III 117]

This committee was formed in 1918 and in 1930 merged with the Overseas Trade Development Council. Records in BT 59.

1–13   Minutes of meetings.
14–26   Papers. 177 papers covering various aspects of the work of the department: collection of information, commercial missions, export credits, help to buyers from abroad, help with overseas development, investigations into specific markets abroad, propaganda, exhibitions and fairs, reports on conditions in foreign countries, tourism. Handlist is available in search rooms.

BT 95   DISSOLVED EXEMPT PRIVATE COMPANIES: CLASSIFIED INDEX.
         1888–1942.   95 pieces.   [III 115].   Records are open after 5 years.

This index contains the particulars of companies dissolved after 1933 which were exempt from furnishing balance sheets and accounts because they had less than 50 shareholders, and their shares were not offered to the public. Only one complete file in every hundred has been kept and they are now in BT 31.

Numbers of most companies registered before July, 1937, can be found in indexes in the Long Room, press numbers B 247–250.

BT 96   TEMPORARY DEPARTMENTS: INDUSTRIAL SUPPLIES DEPARTMENT.
         1937–1942.   22 pieces.   [III 120]

This department formed in 1939 took over from the Industries and Manufactures Department (BT 64) work connected with questions of priority, other than manpower, and of supply of materials for civil requirements at home and for export.

BT 101   STANDARDS DEPARTMENT: CORRESPONDENCE AND PAPERS.
          1829–1966.   1,149 pieces.   [III 116]

Files are listed chronologically within the following sections:

    1. Colonial, commonwealth, and foreign standards.
    2. Committees and commissions; evidence and reports.

3. Comparison of Parliamentary copies of Imperial Standards of Weights and Measures.

4. Fees and payments.

5. Inspectorate of Weights and Measures.

6. Legislation and legal matters.

7. Merchandise marks and hall marks.

8. Metric system.

10. Reputed and ancient and customary weights and measures.

11. Royal Mint and Treasury matters.

12. Specifications of new weighing and measuring appliances.

13. Standard weights and measures.

14. Testing and inspection.

15. Trial of the Pyx.

See also MINT group.

BT 102 REPARATION CLAIMS DEPARTMENT: CORRESPONDENCE AND PAPERS.
1919–1929. 47 pieces.

Department was formed in 1920 to collect and investigate claims in respect of loss and damage suffered by civilians, and later to pay to claimants amounts recommended by the Royal Commission on Compensation (BT 69). The department dealt also with the release of Turkish property in this country, and with payment of claims against German nationals assessed by British Restitution Service at Wiesbaden.

Files are arranged in sections:
Policy.
Claims for Compensation (selected files only).
Reports of damage and casualties caused by air raids or naval bombardment.

BT 103 SOLICITOR'S DEPARTMENT.
1880–1956. 334 pieces.

Files are described and dated, not chronologically arranged; they include:

110–121	Essential Commodities Reserve Act, 1938.
122–186	Export Credits Guarantee Department.
248–253	Committee of Compulsory Insurance, 1936–7.
254–260	Cotton Industry (Reorganisation) Bill, 1939.

BT 104 COMMISSIONERS FOR THE SPECIAL AREAS.
1934–1957. 105 pieces.

Under the Special Areas (Development and Improvement) Act, 1934, two Commissioners were appointed to co-ordinate the work of government departments, local authorities, and other organisations, in developing areas of especially heavy unemployment. The records deal mainly with the establishment and development of trading estates, and are grouped geographically as follows:

1–4	North East Development Board.
5–9	Merthyr Tydfil; clearance of Dowlais Site.
10–16	Jarrow.
17–22	South West Durham Improvement Association.
23–31	North Eastern Trading Estates Ltd.
32–40	South Wales and Monmouthshire Trading Estates Ltd.
41–51	West Cumberland Trading Estate.
52–60	St. Helens, Auckland.
61–80	South Wales and Monmouthshire Trading Estates Ltd.
81–105	Scotland.

See also LAB 23.

BT 110 TRANSCRIPTS AND TRANSACTIONS: SERIES IV: CLOSED REGISTRIES.
　　　　1891–1955.　　1,976 pieces.

Records of the Registrar General of Shipping and Seamen, containing details of each ship registered at United Kingdom and colonial ports.

BT 131 WAR HISTORIES (1939–1945): FILES.
　　　　1916–1952.　　116 pieces.

BT 132 PARLIAMENTARY BRANCH.
　　　　1887–1966.　　36 pieces.

This Branch acts as liaison between the Board of Trade and Parliament, giving advice on parliamentary procedure and watching over the interests of the Board of Trade in respect of all proposals brought before Parliament. The Parliamentary Branch was formed in 1949 from the Intelligence and Parliamentary Branch of the Establishment Division which was set up in 1920. Before 1920 liaison with Parliament was arranged through the Board of Trade Secretariat.

1–7	1908–1940. There are papers on the Safeguarding of Industries Act, 1921, Geneva Convention Act, 1937, Export Guarantees Act, 1939, Companies Act (1929) Amendment Bill, and Prices of Goods Bill, 1939–1940.

DEPARTMENT OF SCIENTIFIC AND INDUSTRIAL RESEARCH

In 1915, a Committee of the Privy Council was set up to promote scientific and industrial research, to be assisted by an Advisory Council composed of eminent scientists. In 1916, £1,000,000 was voted for the purpose of helping industrial firms to form co-operative research organisations. The Imperial Trust for the Encouragement of Scientific and Industrial Research was formed to administer the 'Million Fund'.

In 1916, a separate Department of Scientific and Industrial Research was formed, responsible to the Lord President of the Council. The Department was made responsible for a number of research institutions, including the National Physical Laboratory, and began to give grants for postgraduate research.

By 1932, the 'Million Fund' was exhausted, and financial assistance to research associations was paid from the D.S.I.R. Vote.

The D.S.I.R. was reorganised in 1956, following the report of the Jephcott Committee. The Advisory Council and the Imperial Trust were abolished, and executive powers were vested in a new Council for Scientific and Industrial Research, whose members were at first appointed by the Lord President and from 1959 by the Minister of Science.

In 1965, the Ministry of Technology took over most of the functions of the D.S.I.R., and all its research stations except for Radio Research, the National Institute for Research into Nuclear Science, and Hydrology Research, which were transferred to the Department of Education and Science, and the Road Research Laboratory which was transferred to the Ministry of Transport.

DSIR 1   MINUTE BOOKS.
          1915–1956.   35 pieces.   [III 113]

Minutes of the following:

2–8	1915–1937. Advisory Council.
13–23	1927–1938. Scientific Grants Committee.
24	1923–1927. Million Fund Committee.
25–35	1927–1938. Industrial Grants Committee.

DSIR 2   MEETINGS FILES: ADVISORY COUNCIL AND COMMITTEES.
          1917–1945.   696 pieces.   [III 113]

This class contains complete sets of papers for meetings of the following:

1–167	1925–1939. Advisory Council.
330–360	1918–1927. Applications Committee.
361–446	1927–1939. Scientific Grants Committee.
531–578	1923–1927. Million Fund Committee.
579–667	1927–1939. Industrial Grants Committee.

DSIR 3   RESEARCH BOARDS AND COMMITTEES.
          1915–1940.   344 pieces.   [III 113–114]

This class contains the papers of research boards and committees which were set up by the D.S.I.R. and which had been disbanded before the end of 1939.

1	1917. Abrasions and Polishing Powders Committee; constitution.
2–16	1920–1928. Adhesions Research Committee.
17–25	1919–1938. Advisory Council: research projects: research carried on by Sir William Bragg, Lord Rutherford, Professor Kapitza, and Professor Bone; also research into ventilation of the Houses of Parliament.
26	1917–1919. Brass and Copper Castings Research Committee.

27–46	1922–1929. Bridge Stress Committee.
47–49	1921–1931. British Museum Laboratory.
50–52	1917–1921. Building Materials Research Committee.
53–54	1925–1927. Chemotherapy Committee.
55–56	1920–1929. Co-ordinating Boards, for chemical, engineering, and physics research.
57–62	1917–1920. Copper and Zinc Research Committee.
63–65	1920–1921. Corrosion of Aluminium and its Alloys Research Committee.
66–68	1916–1925. Corrosion of Metals Research.
69–73	1924–1940. Corrosion of Metals Research Committee.
74–94	1921–1937. Dental Investigation Committee.
95–99	1917–1921. Electrical Research Committee.
100–106	1924–1935. Electro-Deposition Committee.
107–118	1920–1929. Engineering Research Board.
119–142	1921–1934. Fabrics Committee and Fabrics Research Committee.
143	1922–1929. Forest Trees Research Committee.
144–166	1919–1931. Gas Cylinders Committee.
167–173	1928–1933. Geophysical Survey Research Committee.
174–176	1925–1936. High Pressures Research Committee.
178–180	1917–1919. Illuminating Engineering: Joint Sub-Committee.
181–182	1917–1921. Industrial Fatigue Research Board.
183–187	1927–1931. Locomotive Experimental Station Enquiry Committee.
188–189	1929–1930. Locomotive Experimental Station.
190–201	1921–1939. Lubrication Committee and Research Committee.
202–211	1925–1939. Materials at High Temperature Committee.
212–232	1920–1939. Metallurgy Committee, and Metallurgical Research Board and Committee.
233–234	1916–1923. Mine Rescue Research Committee.
235–237	1919–1923. Mining Engineering Committee.
238–242	1922–1932. Minor Metals Committee.
243–254	1918–1924. Oxygen Research Committee.
255–261	1919–1921. Interdepartmental Committee on Patents.
262–264	1921–1922. Permitted Explosives Joint Committee.
265–279	1920–1927. Physics Research Board.
280–283	1924–1925. Severn Barrage Committee.
284–306	1920–1931. Springs Research Committee.
307–308	1917–1920. Standardisation of Optical Instruments Committee.
309	1931–1937. Standing Advisory Committee on Testing Work for the Building Industry.

310–311	1915–1921. Engineering, Mining, and Metallurgy Standing Committee.
312–313	1916–1917. Standing Committee on Engineering.
314–318	1916–1918. Standing Committee on Glass and Optical Instruments.
319–320	1916. Standing Committee on Metallurgy.
321–322	1929–1937. Steel Structures Research Committee.
323–324	1917–1920. Timber Research Organisation.
325–329	1915–1921. Tin and Tungsten Research Board.
331–332	1917–1918. Vitreous Compounds and Cements for Lenses and Prisms Research Committee.
333–334	1918–1928. Water Power Committee.
335–343	1926–1939. X-Ray Committee.
344	1918–1920. Zirconium Research Committee.

DSIR 4   BUILDING RESEARCH BOARD.
       1919–1960.   97 pieces.   [III 114]

This class contains papers on the formation of the Board and minutes of its meetings. There is a section on administration and control, and papers of committees on Acoustics, Fire Resistance of Structures, Heating and Ventilation, Re-inforced Concrete, Stone Preservation, Structures Investigation, and of the Standing Chemical and Weathering Committee.

DSIR 5   CHEMICAL RESEARCH BOARD.
       1920–1960.   33 pieces.   [III 114]

This class contains minutes of the Chemistry Co-ordinating Research Board, 1920–1927, and of the Management Committee of the Chemical Research Board, 1927–1939, programmes of research, and papers of the Microbiological Research Conference, 1930.

DSIR 6   FOOD INVESTIGATION RESEARCH BOARD.
       1917–1949.   105 pieces.   [III 114]

This class contains the minutes of the Research Board, 1917–1928, and of the Committee of Management, 1923–1928, and files on the constitution of the Board. There are also papers of the Low Temperature Research Station, Australian Expeditions, 1922–1925, and papers of committees on fish preservation, engineering, fruit and vegetables, meat, oils and fats, canned food, food and cooking, food transport and distribution, and insulation.

DSIR 7   FOREST PRODUCTS RESEARCH BOARD.
       1920–1961.   136 pieces.   [III 114]

The class contains papers on the formation of the Board, agendas and minutes of its meetings. Also there are minutes of the Forest Products Research Laboratory Review Committee, papers of the Forest Products Research Conference, 1924, and of the Standing Conference on Timber Utilisation, and papers on protection of wood.

DSIR 8   FUEL RESEARCH BOARD.
            1915–1948.   80 pieces.   [III 114]

The class contains the agenda and minutes of the Board and papers on its constitution. There are also papers of the Irish Peat Enquiry Committee, and of the Coal Survey committees which were set up for each of the main coal fields. There are papers on carbonisation processes and hydrogenation, and annual reports on safety in mines and fuel utilisation. The Coal Survey was transferred to the National Coal Board in 1947.

DSIR 9   GEOLOGICAL SURVEY BOARD.
            1845–1941.   109 pieces.   [III 114]

The Geological Survey was begun by the Office of Woods and Forests in 1845. The class contains papers of the Geological Survey Board and of the Geological Survey Committee, 1932–1934, also of the Royal Commission on Museums and Galleries, and of the resulting Standing Committee on Museums and Galleries.

DSIR 10   NATIONAL PHYSICAL LABORATORY.
            1906–1960.   277 pieces.   [III 114].   Various files closed for 50
                                                             years.

The files are grouped under the following headings:
    Accommodation.
    Administration and general.
    Establishment.
    Finance.
    Investigations carried out at the N.P.L.
    Standards.
    Patents.
    William Froude National Tank.

DSIR 11   RADIO RESEARCH BOARD.
            1920–1956.   335 pieces.   [III 114]

The class contains minutes of the Radio Research Board, and papers of committees on:

Organisation of radio research work between N.P.L. and R.R.B.
Standards and precision measurement.
Propagation of wireless waves.
Atmospherics.
Directional wireless.
Thermionic valves.
Radio telephony.
Interference of transmitting stations.
Precision measurements and radio standards.
Production and utilisation of short electric waves.

Direction finding.
Propagation of waves through the ionosphere.
Theoretical.
Field strength measurements.

DSIR 12   ROAD RESEARCH BOARD.
          1931–1960.   38 pieces.   [III 114]

The class contains the minutes of the Road Research Board, its constitution, and papers of the Road Tar Research Committee.

DSIR 13   WATER POLLUTION RESEARCH BOARD.
          1923–1960.   91 pieces.   [III 114]

The class contains the minutes of the Board, its constitution, papers of committees on the River Mersey and the River Tees, and investigations into various effluents.

DSIR 14   ATMOSPHERIC POLLUTION RESEARCH COMMITTEE.
          1923–1958.   60 pieces.   [III 114]

The class contains an account of the formation of the Research Committee, its minutes, and papers of the Standing Conference of Co-operating Bodies.

DSIR 15   IMPERIAL TRUST.
          1916–1956.   49 pieces.   [III 113]

The class contains the minutes of the Imperial Trust, its constitution, and accounts of the 'Million Fund'.

DSIR 16   INDUSTRIAL RESEARCH ASSOCIATIONS.
          1916–1960.   223 pieces.   [III 113]

The general section of this class has papers on the scheme for research associations, proposed constitution, and government policy on grants. This is followed by papers including articles of association for the following research associations:

Institute of Automobile Engineers.
British Boot and Shoe Allied Trades.
British Cast Iron.
Coal Utilisation.
Cocoa, Chocolate, Sugar Confectionery, and Jam Trades.
British Colliery Owners.
British Cotton Industry.
British Cutlery.
British Electrical and Allied Industries.
British Flour Millers.
British Food Manufacturers.
Gas Industry.
Glass.
British Iron and Steel.

British Iron Manufacturers.
British Jute.
British Launderers.
British Leather Manufacturers.
British Linen Industry.
British Liquid Fuel.
British Motor and Allied Manufacturers.
British Motor Cycle and Cycle Car.
British Non-Ferrous Metals.
British Paint, Colour, and Varnish Manufacturers.
British Photographic.
British Portland Cement.
British Pottery.
British Printing Industry.
British Refractories.
British Rubber Manufacturers.
British Scientific Instruments.
Scottish Engineering, Shipbuilding, and Metallurgical.
Scottish Shale Oil.
British Silk.
British Sugar.
Woollen and Worsted Industries.

There are papers containing proposals for research associations for British Air-craft, North East Coast Shipbuilding and Marine Engineering, and X-Ray Apparatus.

Most files up to piece 160 are open and cover the inter-war period.

DSIR 17   REGISTERED FILES: GENERAL SERIES.
          1915–1962.   359 pieces.   [III 113].   Closed for 50 years.

The few files already open deal with the formation of the Advisory Council and its financing; there are some papers on early grants to universities and institutions, and on fellowships and grants for postgraduate research.

DSIR 18   REGISTERED FILES: ESTABLISHMENT SERIES.
          1915–1958.   48 pieces.   [III 113]

The papers deal mainly with staffing, distribution of administrative work, and appointments, to the Advisory Council.

DSIR 19   GAS CYLINDERS AND CONTAINERS COMMITTEE.
          1935–1945.   9 pieces.

The class contains minutes of the committee and sub-committee.

DSIR 20   ILLUMINATION COMMITTEE.
          1923–1941.   32 pieces.

The class contains minutes of the committee, and of sub-committees on applica-tion of illumination methods to biological problems, relation between illumination and performance in industry, the National Illumination Committee of Great Britain, 1927–1941, and the Standing Conference on Lighting in Mines, 1935.

DSIR 21   PEST INFESTATION RESEARCH COMMITTEE.
            1938–1943.   18 pieces.

The class contains minutes of the Pest Infestation Research Committee, 1938–1940, Standing Conference on Infestation of Stored Grain and Grain Products by Insects, 1939–1940, and Grain Infestation Research Committee, 1938. Transferred to Ministry of Agriculture in 1959.

DSIR 22   AERONAUTICAL RESEARCH COUNCIL: MINUTES OF MEETINGS.
            1909–1940.   98 pieces.

Minutes of the following:

1	1909–1920. Advisory Committee for Aeronautics, formed in 1909 to advise on problems of flight by aeroplanes and dirigibles, composed of scientists and representatives of Admiralty and War Office; president Lord Rayleigh, chairman Dr. Glazebrook. Papers in DSIR 23.
2–8	1920–1939. Aeronautical Research Committee.
9	1924. A.R.C. Panel on Airworthiness of Airships.
10	1932–1935. A.R.C. Panel on Servo-Control.
11	1935–1937. A.R.C. Panel on Wind Tunnel.
12	1938. A.R.C. Panel on Free Flight.
13	1938–1939. A.R.C. Panel on Navigation.
14–37	1916–1935. Sub-committees, wound up.
38–57	1917–1940. Aerodynamics Sub-Committee and Panels.
58–71	1920–1939. Engine Sub-Committee and Panels.
72–77	1920–1935. Accidents Investigation Sub-Committee.
78–83	1920–1925. Materials and Chemistry Sub-Committee and Panel.
84–85	1925–1938. Elasticity and Fatigue Sub-Committee.
86	1925–1938. Seaplane Sub-Committee.
87–88	1927–1939. Alloys Sub-Committee.
89–91	1928–1939. Stability and Control Sub-Committee and Panel.
92	1929–1937. Aircraft Noise Sub-Committee.
93–95	1930–1939. Structure Sub-Committee and Panel.
96	1935–1938. Meteorology Sub-Committee.
97	1936–1939. Oscillation Sub-Committee.
98	1939–1940. Fleet Air Arm Research Sub-Committee.

DSIR 23   AERONAUTICAL RESEARCH COUNCIL: REPORTS AND PAPERS.
            1909–1940.   8,758 pieces.

1277–7889   1919–1940. Reports and Papers in the T series nos. T. 1263–3237, and Plain number series 1–4640. Papers are arranged chronologically and deal with every aspect of the work of the A.R.C. Many have been published in the 'R and M' series. (Reports and Memoranda published by the Stationery Office.)

8148–8758   1919–1932. Internal Combustion Engine Sub-Committee, I.C.E. series 259–869. Papers arranged chronologically.

DSIR 24   AERONAUTICAL RESEARCH COUNCIL: CORRESPONDENCE.
      1909–1936.   12 pieces.

5–12   1920–1936. Files deal with design of aircraft, airships, aeroplane carrier ships, and kite balloons, and problems of fog disposal, atmospheric discharge, and measurement of upward currents in the atmosphere.

DSIR 26   LABORATORY OF THE GOVERNMENT CHEMIST: CORRESPONDENCE AND PAPERS.
      1903–1945.   17 pieces.

This laboratory was formed in 1894 by the merging of a laboratory set up in 1843 by the Board of Excise in order to analyse commodities subject to excise with the laboratory of the Board of Customs which examined commodities subject to import duty. Gradually the laboratory undertook work for many government departments, with special functions under the Food and Drugs Act and the Fertiliser and Feeding Stuffs Act. The Government Chemist was responsible to the Treasury until 1959 when the laboratory was transferred to the D.S.I.R.

The class contains papers on the staffing of the laboratory and organisation of its work.

DEVELOPMENT COMMISSION

The Development Commission and Development Fund were set up in 1909. The main object was to assist works designed to strengthen the rural economy. The Development Commission considered all applications and recommended to the Treasury what grants or loans should be made from the Fund. The Fund was at first used to finance a wide range of scientific research and also works to improve transport, particularly harbours. Many of its functions have been transferred to the Ministry of Agriculture and the Ministry of Transport.

D 1   MINUTES.
      1912–1944.   5 pieces.   [III 35]

3–4   1919–1936. Meetings of the Development Commission, 85th–204th meetings (107th missing).

D 2   REPORTS TO THE TREASURY.
      1911–1939.   56 pieces.   [III 35]

23–56   1919–1939. Reports on applications for advances from the Development Fund.

D 3   ANNUAL REPORTS.
        1911–1939.   29 pieces.   [III 35]

9–29   1919–1939. Printed reports.

D 4   CORRESPONDENCE AND PAPERS.
        1910–1935.   91 pieces.   [III 35]

The papers are grouped as follows:

1–11   Agriculture.
12–23   Compulsory purchase.
24–27   Co-operative Societies.
28–47   Development Fund Act, 1909, interpretations of.
48–49   Development Fund Act and the Government of Ireland Act.
50–60   Fishery research.
61–72   Forestry.
73–76   Harbours.
77–80   Light railways.
81   Rural Community Councils.
82–86   Rural Industries Bureau; minutes.
87–89   Scientific research in government departments.
90   Ministry of Transport Act, 1919.
91   Veterinary research.

EXPORT CREDITS GUARANTEE DEPARTMENT

In 1919 the Board of Trade was empowered to grant credits and undertake insurance 'for the purpose of re-establishing Overseas Trade'. An Export Credits Department was set up under the Department of Overseas Trade. In 1930, it became a separate department run by an Executive Committee.

ECG 1   ADVISORY COMMITTEE. MINUTES.
        1919–1939.   19 pieces.   [III 51]

1–4   1919–1925. Export Credit Committee: meetings 1–170.
4–6   1925–1926. Export Credit Advisory Committee: meetings 171–217.
7–17   1926–1937. Export Credit Guarantee Advisory Committee: meetings 1–190.
18   1936–1938. Export Guarantee Advisory Committee, miscellaneous minutes.
19   1937–1939. Export Guarantee Advisory Committee: meetings 1–13.
4

ECG 2 EXECUTIVE COMMITTEE: MINUTES.
1930–1944. 8 pieces. [III 51]

66 Meetings. Files dated.

ECG 3 ADVISORY COMMITTEE.
1931–1939. 15 pieces. [III 51]

Minutes and papers of sub-committees as follows:

1	1936. 'A' (steel for Turkey).
2	1937. Afghanistan.
3	1936–37. China.
4–6	1938–39. Informal.
7	1931–33. Medium Term Credits.
8	1939. Medium Term, New Facilities.
9	1937. Shipbuilding.
10	1939. Short Term, New Facilities.
11	1939. Transfer Policy.
12	1936–37. Turkish.
13	1937. Underwriting Transfer Risks.
14–15	1939. War Emergency.

ECG 4 MISCELLANEOUS.
1925–1944. 8 pieces. [III 51]

1	1925–26. Hills Committee on credit insurance.
2	1928–29. Niemeyer Report.
3	1931. Balancing Anglo-Russian Trade, memorandum.
4	1934. Polish State Railways, contracts.
5	1938–39. Export Guarantees Bill.
6	1939–40. Proposed changes in short-term facilities.
7	1940. Price variations in export contracts.
8	1927–44. Specimens of publicity material.

NATIONAL COAL BOARD

The National Coal Board was established following the Coal Industry Nationalisation Act, 1946, and according to the Act its records are deemed to be public records. The Board took over the assets and records of the Coal Commission set up in 1938 to acquire the fee simple in all coal and mines of coal. The papers of the Coal Commission and those concerned with statutory selling schemes are to be found in this group; records of Government policy and control of the coal mining industry exercised in the past by the Home Office and Mines Department of the Board of Trade are in the POWER group.

Papers of individual collieries formerly deposited as COAL 1 and 2 have been transferred to the County Record Offices of Derbyshire, Lancashire, and Staffordshire.

COAL 4   DISTRICT SCHEMES (COAL MINES ACT, 1930): SOUTH WALES.
        1930–1946.   44 pieces.   [II 219]

Minute books of the Executive Board and committees. Most volumes are indexed.

COAL 7   COAL COMMISSION: CENTRAL AND REGIONAL VALUATION BOARDS: MINUTES.
        1938–1944.   23 pieces.

The inter-war material is with papers which extend to 1942.

COAL 8   COAL COMMISSION: CENTRAL AND REGIONAL VALUATION BOARDS: CORRESPONDENCE AND PAPERS.
        1938–1944.   10 pieces.

3   1938. Central Valuation Board; sub-committee on rules.

COAL 9   COKING INDUSTRY: ASSOCIATIONS AND COMMITTEES.
        1919–1966.   24 pieces.

1–3   1919–1934. National Association of Coke and Bye-Product Plant Owners; minutes of general meetings. Indexed.

MINISTRY OF POWER

The Ministry of Fuel and Power was set up in 1942, taking over from the Board of Trade its functions relating to mines, petroleum, gas, hydraulic power, and electricity. In 1957 it took over control of iron and steel and was renamed the Ministry of Power.

The earliest papers deal with the coal mining industry; inspectors of mines were appointed by the Home Office in 1850. Economic aspects of coal mining were the concern of the Board of Trade, and in 1920 a separate Mines Department of the Board of Trade was established which took over the responsibility of the Home Office for mines.

Since 1859 the Board of Trade had control over private gas companies. Gas undertakings by local authorities were supervised by the Local Government Board which was absorbed in 1919 by the new Ministry of Health. The following year control of municipal gas undertakings was transferred to the Board of Trade.

The Electric Light Act, 1882, was administered by the Board of Trade, first by the Railway Department and then by the Harbour Department (MT 10). The Ministry of Munitions exercised some control over electric power during the 1914–1918 war, and in 1919 its functions were transferred to the Board of Trade. The Electricity (Supply) Act, 1919, set up the Electricity Commission, a separate department responsible to the new Ministry of Transport which took over the Board of Trade's functions concerning electricity. Responsibility for electricity returned to the Board of Trade in 1941.

Interest in petroleum began in 1913 when the British Government acquired a majority holding in the Anglo-Persian Oil Company. In 1916 the Board of Trade set up a Petrol Control Committee, later a department, to control distribution of petrol for civil and industrial purposes. In 1917 the Colonial Secretary, Walter Long, formed the Petroleum Executive to co-ordinate the work of various bodies concerned with petrol supply. In 1919 it was renamed the Petroleum Department, working with the Ministry of Munitions which had been empowered to license and promote searches for home supplies of petroleum. The Ministry of Munitions was abolished in 1921, and the following year the work of the Petroleum Department was taken over by the Board of Trade. In September 1939 powers relating to petrol and petroleum products under the Essential Commodities Reserves Act, 1938, were transferred to the Ministry of Supply. Other powers of the Board of Trade were concentrated in a new Petroleum Department formed in May 1940.

The Ministry of Supply was set up in August, 1939, taking over functions and controls from the Board of Trade and the War Office. Control of iron and steel, non-ferrous and light metals remained with the Ministry of Supply until 1955, when it was transferred to the Board of Trade, and from there to the Ministry of Power in 1957.

The Ministry of Power was absorbed by the Ministry of Technology in 1969, and this ministry was merged with the Board of Trade in 1970 to form the Department of Trade and Industry.

POWER 1   MINERS' WELFARE COMMITTEE AND COMMISSION.
           1921–1951.   51 pieces.   [III 106].   No restriction on access.

The Miners' Welfare Committee was set up in 1921 to administer the Miners' Welfare Fund.

1–16	1921–1951. Minutes.
17–44	1921–1951. Agenda papers.
45	1921–1933. Miners' Welfare Fund circulars.
46	1922–1931. Conference papers of District Committee.
47–50	1921–1939. Annual reports.
51	1921–1949. Legal opinions.

POWER 2   BOARD OF TRADE: INDUSTRIAL POWER AND TRANSPORT DEPARTMENT; WATER POWER RESOURCES COMMITTEE.
           1906–1925.   52 pieces.   [III 106]

1–3	1918–1920. Committee papers.
4–24	1918–1920. Minutes of evidence: water power in England, Wales, and Scotland, proposed schemes; water power in other countries; fishery aspects.
25–40	1911–1920. Memoranda and papers: surveys, proposals, statistics, costs, legislation, etc.
41–43	1920–1925. Severn Tidal Power (see also pieces 19, 21, and 31).
44	1919. Irish sub-committee.
45–48	1919–1921. Commonwealth developments.

50–52   1918–1919. Water Power Committee of the Conjoint Board of Scientific Societies, reports.

POWER 4   HOME OFFICE: MINES AND QUARRIES: OUT-LETTERS.
            1873–1920.   72 pieces.   [III 106]

62–64   1918–1920. General out-letters. Home Office control of mines and quarries was transferred to Board of Trade Mines Department in 1920. The letters are to government departments, inspectors of mines, collieries, companies, Miners' Federation, and other organisations and individuals. Each volume is indexed.

POWER 5   MINISTRY OF SUPPLY: IRON AND STEEL CONTROL; REGISTERED FILES.
            1930–1949.   111 pieces.   [III 106–107]

The Ministry of Supply was formed in 1939, taking over the Supply Organisation of the Board of Trade, and the Principal Supply Officers Committee of the Committee of Imperial Defence. Control of metals was transferred in 1957 to the Ministry of Power. This class contains some pre-war material as follows:

43–47   1930–1940. Ferro-alloys, supply position.
62; 64–65   1938–1939. Iron ore, supply position and purchases from abroad.
70–71   1938–1940. Pig iron, stocks and purchases from India.

POWER 6   HOME OFFICE: MINES AND QUARRIES; REGISTERED FILES.
            1887–1920.   87 pieces.   [III 107]

Selected files to illustrate work of this department of Home Office. See POWER 4 above. The only inter-war material is as follows:

7   1919. New Glynen Colliery, Llanelly; explosion, report, and prosecution.
71–72   1920. Petroleum Executive's reports and proposed bill.

POWER 7   ANNUAL REPORTS OF INSPECTORS OF MINES.
            1850–1968.   94 pieces.   [III 107].   No restriction on access.

Inspectors of mines were first appointed in 1850 and reported first to the Home Office, then to the Secretary for Mines, and then to the Minister of Power.

53–72   1919–1938. Annual reports. From 1921–1938, these include annual reports of the Secretary of Mines.
73   1939–1946. Report, instead of annual reports which were suspended during the war.

POWER 8   SAFETY AND HEALTH DIVISION AND INSPECTORATE OF MINES AND QUARRIES.
            1876–1964.   315 pieces.   [III 107]

The class contains papers from the Home Office and Board of Trade. The files are arranged in sections on accidents, accident prevention, health, inspection, labour and unions, legal actions, mine equipment, organisation, pit ponies, quarries and slagheaps, regulations, rescue, and there are papers of the Committee on Occupational Diseases among Mine Workers, 1922–23, the Health Advisory Committee, 1929–39, and the International Labour Office Committee of Experts on Safety in Coal Mines, 1936–39.

POWER 10   ESTABLISHMENTS DIVISION: CORRESPONDENCE AND PAPERS.
            1887–1963.   297 pieces.   [III 107]

This class contains papers from the Home Office and Board of Trade. As well as establishment matters, there are papers on departmental organisation, transfers of functions, government policy in relation to the coal mining industry, 1922, and files concerned with the National Emergency, 1926. There is a description of the class and list of contents at the beginning of the class list.

POWER 11   ELECTRICITY COMMISSION: MINUTES.
            1920–1948.   32 pieces.

The Electricity (Supply) Act, 1919, set up the Electricity Commission, a non-departmental body, for promoting, regulating, and supervising, the supply of electricity. It was dissolved in 1948 on nationalisation.

1–27   1920–1939. Minutes.

32   Index to the minutes (incomplete).

POWER 12–14   ELECTRICITY DIVISION

POWER 12   ELECTRICITY COMMISSION: CORRESPONDENCE AND PAPERS.
            1919–1953.   888 pieces.

POWER 13   ELECTRICITY: MINISTRY OF TRANSPORT: CORRESPONDENCE AND
            PAPERS.
            1892–1945.   134 pieces.   [III 107]

POWER 14   ELECTRICITY DIVISION: CORRESPONDENCE AND PAPERS.
            1902–1963.   26 pieces.

As there is considerable overlap between these classes, the material has been grouped under the same headings in each class to facilitate cross reference.

Section headings:

1. Administration and legislation.

2. Electric lighting companies and responsible authorities.

3. Electricity distribution and charges, metering, etc.

4. Financial arrangements (Power Companies, etc.).

5. Legal matters.

6. Overhead lines; wayleaves, special orders, etc.

7. Power stations and generating plant (case files).

POWER 12 and 13 only:

8. Water resources: barrage schemes.

Power 14 was intended for papers originating in the Ministry of Fuel and Power and its successor; the early papers were re-registered on transfer from the Ministry of Transport and the Electricity Commission.

POWER 15 ELECTRICITY: REGISTERS OF CONSENTS AND SPECIAL ORDERS.
1899–1907; 1921–1964. 39 pieces.

Registers of applications for consent to purchase and use land for new generating stations, extensions to existing stations, and erection of overhead transmission lines, and special orders made by the Electricity Commissioners.

POWER 16 COAL DIVISION: EARLY CORRESPONDENCE AND PAPERS.
1896–1897; 1911–1953. 528 pieces.

This class contains papers from the Board of Trade Mines Department and the Ministry of Fuel and Power, and is non-accruing. There are selected files on various aspects of coal mining: production, labour relations, marketing, drainage and subsidence, formation of the Coal Utilisation Research Association, and papers of the Royal Commission on the Coal Industry, 1925–1926. There are also some files on metalliferous mining.

There is an account of the class and list of contents at the beginning of the class ist.

POWER 17 COAL DIVISION: EMERGENCY SERIES: CORRESPONDENCE AND PAPERS.
1937–1958. 62 pieces.

Files of the Board of Trade Mines Department and the Ministry of Fuel and Power relating to the price, control, supply, demand, and distribution, of coal, coke, anthracite, etc.

POWER 20 COAL DIVISION: CORRESPONDENCE AND PAPERS; LABOUR AND LABOUR RELATIONS.
1883–1958. 104 pieces.

Class contains papers from other departments, Board of Trade, Ministry of Labour, Home Office. Papers deal with wages, hours, international labour conventions, pit-head baths, historical account of the Miners' Federation, correspondence on nationalisation of coal royalties, and on various mining acts. There is one file on the Metalliferous Mines Bill, 1924.

POWER 21 COAL DIVISION: CORRESPONDENCE AND PAPERS; MINES DEPARTMENT: WAR BOOK AND ASSOCIATED MATTERS.
1936–1959. 65 pieces.

The inter-war material from the Board of Trade Mines Department deals with capacity of the coal industry and arrangements made to control supplies during war.

POWER 22   COAL DIVISION: CORRESPONDENCE AND PAPERS: PRODUCTION.
            1913–1963.   214 pieces.

Until 1942 the class contains papers from the Board of Trade Mines Department
grouped as follows:

Administration and legislation, action taken under various Coal Acts.
Coal and mineral rights, royalties.
Fuels other than coal, mainly peat, oil boring, and methane.
Labour relations.
Metalliferous mining.
Mining subsidence and drainage schemes.

POWER 23   BOARD FOR MINING EXAMINATIONS: MINUTES.
            1919–1949.   7 pieces.

The Board was set up in 1911 and in 1950 was superseded by the Mining Qualifica-
tion Board.

POWER 25   CHIEF SCIENTIST'S DIVISION: CORRESPONDENCE AND PAPERS.
            1921–1963.   161 pieces.

The pre-war material from the Board of Trade Mines Department deals with
hydrogenation of coal in Germany.

POWER 26   'A' FILES.
            1902–1960.   454 pieces.

Until 1942 these files are from the Board of Trade Mines Department, arranged
chronologically; they deal with strikes, coal bills, petroleum, trade negotiations, and
International Labour Office Conventions. There are papers of committees, including
the Metalliferous Mining Industry Advisory Committee, 1921–1934, the Coal
Advisory Committee, 1922–1928, the Mineral Transport Standing Committee,
1927–1939, and the Interdepartmental Committee on the Coal Mining Industry,
1934–1937. The subjects covered also occur in other POWER classes.

POWER 29   GAS DIVISION: REGISTERED FILES.
            1877–1959.   90 pieces.

The Board of Trade was responsible for control of gas undertakings under the
Sale of Gas Act, 1859, Gas Regulation Act, 1920, and Gas Undertakings Acts,
1929–1934. Control was transferred to the Ministry of Fuel and Power in 1942.
When the gas industry was nationalised in 1948, the Gas Division became responsible for policy and for liaison with the Gas Council and Area Boards. The inter-war
papers in this class derive from the Board of Trade.

12–15   1919–1920. Harbour Department: Standards Division, files on
           gas works, and production of benzole.

16–39   1920–1939. Industries and Manufactures Department, Standards
           Division: bill papers, files on metering, and powers of local
           authorities.

POWER 30   GAS DIVISION: SPECIAL PRESCRIPTIONS.
　　　　　1921–1948.　51 pieces.

The Gas Regulation Act, 1920, appointed three Gas Referees for England, Wales, and Scotland, to prescribe when, where, and how, gas was to be tested. In 1934 their functions were transferred to the Board of Trade and carried out by the Gas Testing Boards. Files are arranged chronologically, indexed to 1925.

POWER 31   GAS DIVISION: GAS REFEREES' MINUTE BOOKS.
　　　　　1872–1938.　10 pieces.

Gas referees were first appointed for the Metropolitan area and until 1920 were concerned only with London gas undertakings. (*See above,* POWER 30.)

3–10　　　　　1900–1930. Minute Books.

POWER 32   GAS DIVISION: NOTIFICATIONS AND INSTRUCTIONS TO GAS
　　　　　EXAMINERS.
　　　　　1869–1920; 1923–1934.　8 pieces.

Gas examiners were appointed either by local authorities or by quarter sessions to test gas in the particular locality. This class contains instructions issued to gas examiners on the methods to be used, and on approved measuring instruments.

6　　　　　1910–1920.
8　　　　　1923–1934.
　　　　　Piece 7 covering the years 1920–1923 is wanting.

POWER 33   PETROLEUM.

Records of Government dealings with petroleum became concentrated in the Ministry of Power. Although the ministry was absorbed by the Ministry of Technology in 1969 and is now part of the new Department of Trade and Industry, the petroleum records up to the end of 1939 will be transferred to the P.R.O. in 1971 as POWER 33.

MINISTRY OF TRANSPORT

The Ministry of Transport was established in 1919 for the purpose of improving transport facilities. It took over the powers of the Board of Trade relating to railways, tramways, canals, waterways and inland navigation, harbours, docks, and piers, all functions of the Road Board, which was abolished, and from the Ministry of Health powers relating to highways which had previously been exercised by the Local Government Board. Later in 1919, the Electricity Supply Act set up the Electricity Commission and transferred all powers concerning electricity to the Ministry of Transport.

The Board of Trade's Railway Department was established in 1840 to supervise railways, light railways, tramways, and later electricity, gas, and water undertakings which in 1896 and 1903 were transferred to the Harbour Department. A special Light Railway Commission was formed in 1896; the Board of Trade appointed the Commissioners and had to confirm their provisional orders. The Commission was absorbed by the Ministry of Transport in 1921.

The Road Board was set up following the Development and Road Improvement Fund Act, 1909, and was empowered to build new roads and make grants to local authorities for improvement of existing roads. The Local Government Board was created in 1871 and the following year took over the Home Office's powers relating to highways. The Board became the highway authority for each county, and was given powers under the Motor Car Act, 1903, to regulate road traffic. A Road Research Station was established in 1930; it was transferred to the Department of Scientific and Industrial Research in 1933, and returned to the Ministry of Transport in 1965. In 1937 the preparation of annual returns of road accidents was transferred from the Home Office to the Ministry of Transport.

The Board of Trade was responsible for nautical questions such as pilotage and light dues, and after 1846 for inspection of passenger steamers. The Mercantile Marine Act, 1850, gave the Board of Trade executive duties concerning merchant seamen and merchant shipping and the Marine Department was formed. In 1863 the Board took over the functions of the Harbour Department of the Admiralty, and the following year formed its own Harbour Department. In 1917 the Ministry of Shipping was established to control use of ships in support of the war effort and it absorbed the functions of the Admiralty's Transport Department. When this Ministry was dissolved in 1921, all its functions passed to the Board of Trade and the Marine Department was renamed the Mercantile Marine Department. In 1922 responsibility for the coastguard service was transferred to the Board of Trade from the Admiralty. In 1939 all the functions of the Board of Trade relating to shipping were transferred to the new Ministry of Shipping.

In 1941, the Ministry of Transport and the Ministry of Shipping combined to form the Ministry of War Transport, and powers relating to electricity were returned to the Board of Trade. The Ministry was renamed the Ministry of Transport in 1946. Between 1953 and 1959, the Ministry of Transport and the Ministry of Civil Aviation were combined. The functions connected with civil aviation were transferred to the Ministry of Supply, renamed Ministry of Aviation in 1959. The new Ministry of Transport took over from the Admiralty statutory functions relating to construction and repair of ships. All functions relating to merchant shipping returned to the Board of Trade in the years 1965 to 1969.

In 1970 the Ministry of Transport became part of the new Department of the Environment.

MT 1   LONDON PASSENGER TRANSPORT: ARBITRATION TRIBUNAL.
      1933–1936.   20 pieces.   [II 281]

The tribunal was set up by the London Passenger Transport Act, 1933, to determine compensation and other matters arising. The class contains awards and other papers.

MT 2   ADMIRALTY AND BOARD OF TRADE (HARBOUR DEPARTMENTS): OUT-
      LETTERS.
      1848–1919.   458 pieces.   [II 278]

452–455   1919. Out-letters arranged alphabetically.

456   1919. Out-letters to Admiralty, Commissioners for Northern Lights, Commissioners for Irish Lights, Trinity House, and circulars.

MT 4   BOARD OF TRADE MARINE DEPARTMENT: OUT-LETTERS.
        1851–1939.   1,424 pieces.   [II 279]

755–1424   1919–1939. In 1919 these are either letter books to individual
            departments and other named recipients, or general books
            arranged alphabetically. From 1926 most letters are divided into
            sea transport, general, and until 1932, pensions. From 1930 there
            is a section each year on foreshores and wrecks.

MT 6   RAILWAYS: CORRESPONDENCE AND PAPERS.
        1840–1963.   3,446 pieces.   [II 280]

The files for the period up to 1919 originated in the Board of Trade Railway
Department and were transferred to the Ministry of Transport. They are arranged
chronologically.

2524–2594   1884–1919. Great Britain.

2599–2600   1918–1919. United Kingdom, tramways, provisional orders.

2603–3446   1903–1963. The files of the Railway Department of the Ministry
             of Transport, from 1919, are listed by subject; there is a list of
             headings at the beginning of this section of the class list. Within
             each group the order is haphazard. The subject headings include:
             accidents, compensation, conditions of service, Exchequer pay-
             ments, light railways, signals, staff, and train control; also papers
             of committees and of the Royal Commission on Transport, 1928–
             1933. (See also MT 42.)

For Railway Assessment Authority, see IR 32.

For Railway and Canal Commission, see J 75 and LCO 2.

MT 7   BOARD OF TRADE RAILWAY DEPARTMENT: INDEXES AND REGISTERS OF
        CORRESPONDENCE.
        1840–1919.   324 pieces.   [II 280]

321–324   1919. Indexes and registers to MT 6.

MT 9   MARINE DEPARTMENT: CORRESPONDENCE AND PAPERS.
        1854–1959.   2,688 pieces.   [II 279].   Piece 1735 is closed for 50
                                                    years.

The Marine Department of the Board of Trade was formed in 1850, and changed
its name to the Mercantile Marine Department in 1921 when it took over the functions previously exercised by the Ministry of Shipping and the Admiralty Transport
Department. In 1939 all the functions of the Board of Trade relating to shipping were
transferred to the new Ministry of Shipping, and hence to the Ministry of War
Transport and Ministry of Transport. They returned to the Board of Trade in the
years 1965 to 1969.

From 1903 onwards, the papers are grouped in sections under the following
headings; sections with no inter-war material are omitted.

Aliens. 1915–1926.
Armaments. 1914–1933.

Awards. 1903–1936.
Boiler explosions. 1907–1928.
Boilers. 1919–1928.
British Empire Exhibitions. 1923.
Cargoes, coal. 1912–1937.
Carriage of dangerous goods. 1902–1938.
Certificates of Competency. 1891–1938.
Chamber of Shipping. 1904–1938.
Channel Islands. 1906–1933.
Coastguard. 1906–1933. *See also* ADM 175.
Collisions. 1905–1937.
Communications. 1907–1938.
Compensation. 1890–1933.
Conditions of Service. 1910–1937.
Contraband. 1907–1934.
Deaths. 1901–1936.
Detention of Ships. 1898–1921.
Discipline. 1906–1937.
Dues and Charges. 1906–1948.
Emigration. 1905–1933.
Ferry Boats. 1907–1934.
Fires. 1906–1938.
Fisheries. 1905–1937.
Foreshores. 1885–1938. *See also* CREST 37 and 42.
Freight. 1902–1938.
Hong Kong. 1905–1934.
Imperial Merchant Service Guild. 1917–1919.
Imperial Shipping Committee. 1923–1937.
Imperial Shipping Conference. 1925–1932.
International Mercantile Marine Company. 1915–1934.
League of Nations. 1925–1936.
Life Saving Apparatus. 1886–1937.
Lloyd's Register of Shipping. 1915–1933.
Marine Insurance. 1908–1937.
Maritime Law. 1905–1936.
Mercantile Marine. 1916–1939.
Mercantile Marine Offices. 1901–1936.
Merchant Shipping Acts. 1883–1940.
Merchant Shipping Advisory Committee. 1908–1934.
Meteorology. 1914–1935.
Ministry of Shipping. 1916–1955. (Ambatielos Case 1917–1955. *See also* MT 53.)
National Insurance Acts. 1911–1932.
National Maritime Board. 1918–1938.
Navigation. 1904–1937. (Harbour and dock bye-laws, lights, river, signals.)
North Atlantic Ice Patrol. 1912–1934.
Oil Pollution. 1917–1938.
Petroleum. 1902–1929. (Carriage by Woolwich Free Ferry.)
Pilotage. 1910–1947.
Pleasure Boats. 1913–1937.
Prisoners of War. 1914–1930.
Prizes of War. 1913–1921.

Provisions. 1916–1923.
Registry of Seamen. 1910–1929.
Registry of Shipping. 1904–1955.
Requisitioning. 1914–1924.
Royal Naval Reserve. 1903–1921.
Salvage. 1905–1937.
Seamen, abroad. 1891–1950.
Seamen, home. 1905–1938.
Seamen's lodging houses. 1901–1934.
Shipbuilding. 1915–1937.
Shipping Liquidation Board. 1923–1924.
Shipping losses. 1915–1933.
Sight tests. 1906–1931.
Signals. 1885–1937.
Survey, Ships. 1902–1937. (International Loadline Convention, etc.)
Thames Passenger Service. 1932–1934.
Wages. 1910–1937.
War Risks Compensation Scheme. 1918–1923.
War Risks Insurance. 1899–1931.
Wireless. 1907–1936.
Workmen's Compensation Acts. 1903–1925.
Wrecks. 1903–1940.

There is an index to all places and ships named in these records from 1856 to 1937.

MT 10   HARBOUR DEPARTMENT: CORRESPONDENCE AND PAPERS.
        1864–1920.   2,076 pieces.   [II 278]

The Harbour Department of the Board of Trade was formed in 1864 and the
following year combined with the Lighthouse Department. In 1896, it took over
responsibility for electric lighting from the Railway Department and in 1903 duties
connected with gas and water works. The department was dissolved in 1919; its
port and harbour duties were transferred to the Ministry of Transport and other
functions were divided between the Marine and the Industries and Manufactures
Departments of the Board of Trade. Later correspondence and papers are in MT 48.

2015–2074   1919. Papers deal with coastal communications, laying of cables,
             foreshores, gas, harbours, lights, pilotage, and wrecks; and there
             are orders and private bills concerned with these.

2076   1917–1920. Draft Liverpool pilotage order.

MT 14   LIGHT RAILWAY COMMISSION: OUT-LETTERS.
        1896–1922.   20 pieces.   [II 280]

The Light Railway Commission was set up in 1896, responsible to the Board of
Trade. It was absorbed by the Ministry of Transport in 1921. *See also* MT 17 and 18.

20   1919–1922. Out-Letters; those for 1920 are missing.

MT 15   CONSULTATIVE MARINE: CORRESPONDENCE AND PAPERS.
        1867–1958.   833 pieces.   [III 121]

The Consultative Marine Branch of the Marine Department of the Board of Trade dealt with surveys of ships, checking their hull construction, machinery, and equipment. The Ministry of Shipping, set up 1917, absorbed the Admiralty's Transport Department and became responsible for the merchant shipbuilding programme. When it was dissolved in 1921, its functions were transferred to the Board of Trade. In 1940, the Board of Trade's responsibilities for shipping were taken over by the new Ministry of Shipping, and they eventually returned to the Board of Trade in the years 1965–1969.

The papers are listed by subject, and the list of subject headings is given at the beginning of the class list.

MT 17 LIGHT RAILWAY COMMISSION: REGISTERS OF IN-LETTERS.
1896–1922. 7 pieces. [II 280]

7   1915–1922. Registers of In-Letters. The in-letters have not survived. Registers have columns for date of receipt, name of sender, very brief note of subject of letter, and disposition. Arranged chronologically. *See also* MT 14 and 18.

MT 18 LIGHT RAILWAY COMMISSION: INDEXES TO IN-LETTERS.
1896–1922. 14 pieces. [II 281]

7   1915–1922. Index to In-Letters. The in-letters have not survived. The letters are indexed alphabetically by name of sender, and given a reference number. *See also* MT 14 and 17.

MT 21–22 RAMSGATE HARBOUR

MT 21 DEEDS, EVIDENCES, AND PLANS.
1613–1939. 465 pieces. [II 281]. Open after 5 years.

MT 22 ACCOUNTS, CORRESPONDENCE, MINUTES, ETC.
1749–1937. 65 pieces. [II 281]

The Board of Trade took over the administration of this harbour from trustees in 1863. It was transferred to the Ministry of Transport in 1919, and to the Corporation of Ramsgate in 1934.

MT 25 MINISTRY OF SHIPPING: CORRESPONDENCE AND PAPERS.
1914–1926. 88 pieces. [II 280]

26–77   1919–1926. These papers cover most aspects of the work of the Ministry. They include files on: blockade of Fiume and Islands of Arbe and Veglia, convoys, the Manning papers, national shipyards, policy statements, repatriation and evacuation of troops, Russian general papers regarding Murman railways and port of Archangel, scheme for power from the Severn Estuary, and war losses sustained by the Allies. There are also papers of the following: Armistice Shipping Commission, 1919; Allied Supreme Council of Supply and Relief, 1919; Enemy Tonnage Conference, 1919; Maritime Service Reparation Commission, 1920–21;

Neutral Tonnage Conference, 1918; re-delivery of neutral and demised vessels, 1920; and Conference at Spa, 1919.

78–88   1914–1925. Proceedings of the Oversea Prize Disposal Committee, accounts of British merchant and fishing vessels sunk or damaged by enemy action; report on shipping control, 1914–18, and insurance on Greek vessels sunk during war.

MT 26   LOCAL MARINE BOARDS.
     1850–1923.   34 pieces.   [II 279]

These papers came from the Board of Trade Marine Department. Only the Sunderland Marine Board has minutes extending to 1919, and there is an agenda book for Greenock Marine Board until 1923.

MT 27   VARIOUS: HOLYHEAD AND SHREWSBURY ROAD.
     1789–1951.   197 pieces.   [II 282]

In 1840, the Shrewsbury and Holyhead Road was placed in the care of the Office of Woods and Works. After 1884 the road was transferred to the charge of the county authorities. The inter-war files are concerned with maintenance of the Menai Bridge, responsibility for which was transferred from the Office of Works to the Ministry of Transport in 1919.

MT 29   RAILWAY INSPECTORATE: REPORTS.
     1840–1930.   85 pieces.   [II 281]

79–85   1917–1930. Copies of inspectors' reports; originals can usually be found in MT 6. All but last volume are indexed.

MT 30   RAILWAY INSPECTORATE: INDEXES.
     1871–1928.   13 pieces.   [II 281]

12–13   1913–1928. Indexes to reports in MT 29.

MT 33   ROAD TRANSPORT: CORRESPONDENCE AND PAPERS.
     1916–1954.   417 pieces.   [III 121]

Selected files are concerned with various functions of the Ministry in relation to road transport. Papers are listed by subject and list of headings is at beginning of the class list. Early files originated with the Local Government Board.

MT 34   ROAD TRAFFIC AND SAFETY: CORRESPONDENCE AND PAPERS.
     1879–1961.   386 pieces.

Selected files deal with traffic and safety problems, including licensing, insurance, pedestrian crossings, penalties for driving offences, speed limits, the Highway Code, road signs and signals, and street playgrounds. Early files originated with the Local Government Board.

MT 36   COMMITTEES AND COMMISSIONS: ADVISORY COMMITTEE ON LONDON TRAFFIC.
     1919–1925.   13 pieces.   [III 121]

This class contains papers of the committee and technical sub-committees, also a report on financial position of London transport undertakings, 1919, proposal for a London Traffic Authority, and draft London Traffic Bill.

MT 37   COMMITTEES AND COMMISSIONS: LONDON AND HOME COUNTIES
         TRAFFIC ADVISORY COMMITTEE.
         1924–1963.   60 pieces.   [III 122]

This committee was established under the London Traffic Act, 1924, to advise the Minister of Transport on the improvement of traffic regulation in the London Area. In 1933 the Committee was reconstituted so that it could act as liaison between the new London Passenger Transport Board and the travelling public. It was disbanded in 1963. The class contains minutes of the committee and sub-committees, annual reports, and other papers.

MT 38   ROAD BOARD: CORRESPONDENCE AND PAPERS.
         1909–1928.   47 pieces.   [III 121]

The Road Board was set up under the Development and Road Improvement Funds Act, 1909, with powers to construct new roads and to make grants to local authorities for road improvement. It was absorbed by the Ministry of Transport in 1919. A few files continue into the 1920's, including one on the Birmingham ring road, 1913–1925, and Irish Free State claims on the Road Fund to 1928.

MT 39   MINISTRY OF TRANSPORT: HIGHWAYS: CORRESPONDENCE AND PAPERS.
         1862; 1904–1965.   651 pieces.

A few early files originated with the Local Government Board, and piece 30 contains papers of the Ministry of Reconstruction with proposals for post-war road construction, strengthening of bridges for railways and other traffic, a memorandum on shipping freights, and a memorandum on roads by Beatrice Webb.

The papers are listed by subject, full list of headings at the beginning of the class list. The headings include aerial surveys, archeology, horticulture, report on German motorways 1937–1938, operation of the Restriction of Ribbon Development Act, 1935, proposed Severn barrage, statutory declarations, determinations, and orders, and proposals to alleviate unemployment.

MT 40   SEA TRANSPORT: CORRESPONDENCE AND PAPERS.
         1903–1962.   164 pieces.

The Transport Department of the Admiralty was transferred to the Ministry of Shipping in 1917, and in 1921 to the Board of Trade, where it became the Sea Transport Division of the Mercantile Marine Department. In 1939, it was transferred to the new Ministry of Shipping. Much early material is in files that continued in use after 1940 and will be open in 1972.

MT 42   ROYAL COMMISSION ON TRANSPORT.
         1928–1931.   79 pieces.

1   1928–1931. Membership, general procedure.

2–29   1928–1930. Agenda and minutes of 28 meetings.

30–75   1928–1931. Views and evidence; most files preserved in this
             section contain material not used in the reports.

76–79   1929–1930. Interim and final reports.

See also MT 6.

MT 43   TRANSPORT ADVISORY COUNCIL.
         1934–1944.   84 pieces.

This Council was set up in 1934 following the Road and Rail Traffic Act, 1933,
and recommendations of the Royal Commission on Transport. Its purpose was to
assist the Minister with the discharge of his functions in relation to facilities for
transport and their co-ordination, improvement, and development. It was replaced
in 1947 by the Central Transport Consultative Committee.

1–29   1934–1939. Agenda and minutes of 29 meetings.

50–82   1934–1939. Papers of committees and sub-committees.

MT 44   ROAD TRAFFIC CENSUS.
         1922–1953.   36 pieces.

The first general traffic census was held in 1922. These papers are mainly summarised particulars for each census point, which were not shown separately in the
published reports. The returns are for trunk roads, Class I, and Class II roads. Some
records for the census of 1931, 1935, and 1938 are in files extending to 1953 and are
open, as they were available for public inspection before transfer to the P.R.O.

MT 45   ESTABLISHMENT AND ORGANISATION: CORRESPONDENCE AND PAPERS.
         1906–1960.   249 pieces.

The files are listed by subjects, and there is a key to arrangement at the beginning
of the class list. The sections include: civil emergency measures, dealing mainly
with the General Strike, 1926; transfers of functions and powers; and the Ways and
Communications Bill, 1919.

MT 46   CO-ORDINATION OF LONDON PASSENGER TRANSPORT: CORRESPONDENCE
         AND PAPERS.
         1926–1948.   145 pieces.

This class contains the papers relating to the preliminary discussions and negotiations that led to the London Passenger Transport Act, 1933, and the formation of
the London Passenger Transport Board.

MT 47   FINANCE: CORRESPONDENCE AND PAPERS.
         1910–1953.   344 pieces.

The selected papers deal mainly with government control of transport in time
of war, and exercise of control over railways in peacetime. There is a section on the
financing of the Road Fund, a statistical section which contains returns of road

accidents, 1936–39, and a section on tunnels. The papers are listed by subject and there is a key to arrangement at the beginning of the class list.

MT 48 PORTS: CORRESPONDENCE AND PAPERS.
      1919–1953.   141 pieces.

These papers relate to docks, harbours, piers, and ferries, after responsibility for them had been transferred to the Ministry of Transport in 1919 from the Harbour Department of the Board of Trade (MT 10).

The papers are listed by subject, and there is a key to arrangement at the beginning of the class list. There is a section on grants, including some from the Unemployment Grants Committee, on unemployment relief, on a proposed Thames barrage, and Thames passenger services.

MT 49 GEDDES PAPERS.
      1919–1922; 1940.   210 pieces.

Sir Eric Geddes as Minister without Portfolio was responsible for drafting the Ministry of Ways and Communications Bill, and became the first Minister of Transport in 1919. His main task was the amalgamation of the numerous railway companies into four groups, and settlement of their claims on the government on account of wartime control. The papers are arranged as follows:

1–94	Railways. One file of 1940 contains correspondence with Geddes' executors.
95–119	Ports, canals, and ferries.
120–145	Roads.
146–169	Traffic and vehicles.
170–210	Miscellaneous: papers dealing with electricity, strikes, appointments, etc.

MT 50 DEFENCE PLANNING.
      1919–1946.   113 pieces.

These papers include defence measures prepared before the Second World War by senior officers of the Ministry of Transport concerned with recommendations of various Cabinet Committees. The pre-war papers are arranged as follows:

1–20	1924–1939. Minutes of the Interdepartmental Committee on Co-ordination of Requisitioning, and of the Departmental Committee on Control of Road Transport in Time of War. Papers on fuel and power resources, protection of electricity supply, comments on passive defence measures, and progress report in 1938 on departmental defence plans.
21–34	1938–1940. Defence (Transport) Council: minutes, progress reports, report on defence measures taken at time of Munich crisis, 1938, papers on evacuation of civilians from London and Middlesex, and London emergency ambulance service.
60–78	1938–1940. Road Transport Control: observations by Traffic Commissioners, papers on civilian evacuation, electricity supply, etc.

| 79–82 | 1939–1943. Air Raid Precautions (Civil Defence) Bill: use of underground parking places, precautionary measures. |

104–113   1919–1940. Ports: draft schemes for diversion of shipping, papers of the Headlam Committee on Distribution of Imports in Time of War. Files transferred from the Board of Trade.

MT 51   MINISTRY OF TRANSPORT COUNCIL.
         1919–1922.   39 pieces.

The Council, a non-statutory body consisting of heads of departments, was formed to assist the Minister with the many problems with which the newly established Ministry had to deal, in particular restoring the railways to peacetime use. It was disbanded in August 1922.

1–38   1919–1922. Agenda, minutes, and memoranda, of 38 meetings of the Council.

39   Subject index of meetings.

MT 52   INLAND WATERWAYS.
         1917–1950.   55 pieces.

1–9   1917–1920. Canal Control Committee; minutes of meetings, reports and memoranda on future policy.

10   1919. Thames Conservancy; transfer of powers to Ministry of Transport from the Board of Trade.

11–42   1919–1940. Committee on Inland Waterways; papers of Neville Chamberlain's Committee; various proposals for improvement or abandonment of canals; recommendation on canals of Royal Commission on Transport.

43–50   1939–1940. Canals (Defence) Advisory Committee; appointment, terms of reference, agenda and minutes of first seven meetings.

MT 53   AMBATIELOS CASE.
         1917–1956.   66 pieces.

The papers in this class are concerned with a dispute over payment for ships purchased by N.E. Ambatielos, a Greek shipowner, from the Ministry of Shipping in 1919. The dispute was taken to the International Court of Justice and settled by an International Arbitration Commission in 1956. The early papers deal with the nine ships concerned, surveys, log books, etc.

MT 55   EMERGENCY ROAD TRANSPORT ORGANISATION: CORRESPONDENCE AND PAPERS.
         1937–1953.   475 pieces.

This organisation was set up in September, 1939, having been planned by the Road Transport (Defence) Committee appointed in 1938. The few pre-war papers are concerned with its formation, circulars to regional transport commissioners, petrol rationing, evacuation schemes, and road safety in blackout.

MT 56 · RATES AND CHARGES.
1927–1956.   307 pieces.

This class contains papers of the Rates and Charges division of the ministry set up in 1939 when the Minister was given powers under the Defence (General) Regulations to control all charges made by inland transport undertakings. There is very little inter-war material.

LAND

MINISTRY OF AGRICULTURE, FISHERIES, AND FOOD

The Board of Agriculture was established in 1889, taking over the functions of the Land Commissioners, who dealt with legislation on inclosures, copyholds, and tithes, and the Agricultural Department of the Privy Council, which administered the Contagious Diseases (Animals) Acts and issued annual agricultural statistics. Other functions were transferred to the new Board such as the Ordnance Survey from the Office of Works, and in 1903 it was made responsible for fisheries and renamed the Board of Agriculture and Fisheries.

In 1911 a separate Scottish Board of Agriculture was set up. In 1919 the Board was changed into a Ministry. An Agricultural Advisory Committee was formed, with Councils of Agriculture for England and Wales; these were dissolved in 1947. Duties concerned with forestry and tithe redemption were transferred to independent commissions in 1919 and 1936 respectively. In 1955 the Ministry absorbed the Ministry of Food, and assumed its present name.

Many of the functions of the Ministry to do with land, including regulation and protection of commons, and apportionment and redemption of rentcharges, were transferred to the new Ministry of Land and Natural Resources in 1965. When that Ministry was dissolved in 1967, these functions passed to the Ministry of Housing and Local Government.

Papers dealing with applications under the Agricultural Credits Acts, 1923, are in PWLB 7.

MAF 1   LAND TENURE: INCLOSURE AWARDS.
         1847–1936.   1,134 pieces.   [II 36].   No restriction on access.

Inclosure awards were made under Inclosure Acts, 1845–1868 and awards of inclosure and regulation made under the Commons Act, 1876. The last inclosure act was in 1914 and the last award in 1918. The inter-war documents are amendments of awards. Awards are arranged by county.

MAF 2   LAND TENURE: VARIOUS AWARDS AND ORDERS.
         19th C.–1961.   259 pieces.   [II 36].   No restriction on access.

These awards and orders have been made under Inclosure Acts, the Land Clauses Consolidation Act, 1845, the Commonable Rights Compensation Act, 1882, and the Copyhold Act, 1894. They include boundary awards, orders and awards dealing with compensation money, and drainage awards.

They are arranged in numerical order, and by county.

MAF 3   LAND TENURE: COMMONS: DECLARATIONS AND LIMITATIONS.
         1925–1964.   186 pieces.   [II 37].   No restriction on access.

Deeds of Declaration and Orders of Limitation made under s.193 of the Law of Property Act, 1925, regulate public access to common land for recreational purposes. They are arranged by county.

Deeds and Orders made after 5.2.1965 are in HLG 59.

MAF 4   LAND TENURE: COMMONS: SCHEMES OF REGULATION (METROPOLITAN).
1867–1956.   36 pieces.   [II 36].   No restriction on access.

Schemes of regulation made under Metropolitan Commons Acts, 1866–1898, and City of Norwich Act, 1867; arranged by county: Kent, Middlesex, Norfolk, Surrey.

MAF 8   LAND TENURE: LONDON (CITY) TITHES: CERTIFICATES OF REDEMPTION
AND MISCELLANEOUS DOCUMENTS.
1880–1947.   23 pieces.   [II 38].   No restriction on access.

The documents include certificates of redemption of tithe rentcharge, agreements for commutation, declarations of merger, etc., and are arranged by parish.

MAF 9   LAND TENURE: DEEDS AND AWARDS OF ENFRANCHISEMENT.
1841–1925.   369 pieces.   [II 37].   No restriction on access.

Under the Copyhold Acts, 1841–1894, copyhold land could be enfranchised either voluntarily by deed, or by an award of the Copyhold Commissioners. These documents are arranged by county under the name of the manor concerned. This procedure was ended in 1925, by the Law of Property Act, 1922, *see* MAF 13. Registers of these deeds and awards are in MAF 76.

MAF 10   CORN RETURNS.
1799–1959.   369 pieces.   [II 40].   No restriction on access.

Registers of weekly and monthly returns of the quantities and average prices of corn in the several returning markets, and abstracts and summaries of returns.

MAF 11   LAND TENURE: ORDERS OF EXCHANGE UNDER INCLOSURE ACTS.
1846–1964.   1,041 pieces.   [II 37].   No restriction on access.

The orders are arranged by county.

MAF 13   LAND TENURE: EXTINGUISHMENT OF MANORIAL INCIDENTS UNDER THE
LAW OF PROPERTY ACTS, 1922 and 1924.
1926–1944.   16 pieces.   [II 38].   No restriction on access.

Manorial incidents had to be extinguished within ten years from 1st January, 1926. This class contains copies of compensation agreements arrived at voluntarily, and copies of certificates issued by the Minister when agreement was not reached. The papers are arranged by county under the name of the manor concerned. Most compensation agreements after 1935 are in MAF 27. Registers of these agreements and certificates are in MAF 76.

MAF 14   LAND TENURE: AWARDS OF EXCHANGE OF GLEBE LANDS.
1841–1935.   139 pieces.   [II 38].   No restriction on access.

Awards made by the Tithe Commissioners of exchange of glebe lands for other land. Arranged by county.

MAF 15   REGISTERS OF MARKET PRICES.
1896–1939.   312 pieces.   [II 40].   No restriction on access.

Registers of weekly prices of cattle, sheep, pigs, foreign animals, dead meat, feedingstuffs, fertilisers, seed, straw, grain, fruit, and vegetables.

MAF 16   LAND TENURE: VICAR'S RATE IN HALIFAX ACT, 1877: CERTIFICATES OF REDEMPTION OF RENTCHARGE AND RATE BOOK.
1873–1926.   3 pieces.   [II 39].   No restriction on access.

Redemption of special rate levied on several townships in the parish of Halifax; arranged by township. Registers of these certificates are in MAF 76.

MAF 17   LAND TENURE: ORDERS OF APPORTIONMENT OF RENTCHARGE UNDER INCLOSURE ACT, 1854, S.10–14, LAW OF PROPERTY ACT, 1925, S.207, AND LANDLORD AND TENANT ACT, 1927, S.20.
1854–1965.   92 pieces.   [II 37].   No restriction on access.

These orders apportion a rentcharge where a piece of land bearing such a charge is divided. The rents may be a rentcharge on freehold land, including fee farm rents, chief rents, and other annual or periodic payments of a fixed amount, and rents reserved by leases. If the rentcharge after apportionment is £2 or less, there may be an order that the charge should be redeemed. Most orders in this class concern leasehold land.

The orders are arranged by county. Orders made after 5.2.1965 are in HLG 61.

MAF 19   LAND TENURE: CERTIFICATES OF APPORTIONMENT OF RENTCHARGE UNDER THE LAW OF PROPERTY ACT, 1925, S.191.
1926–1965.   65 pieces.   [II 38].   No restriction on access.

These certificates deal mainly with apportionment of rentcharge on freehold land. The rents may be a quit rent, chief rent, or other annual or periodic sum issuing out of land, or a rent reserved on a sale or made payable under a grant or licence for building purposes, or a compensation rentcharge created on extinguishment of manorial incidents. There may be orders for redemption of the rentcharge.

The certificates are arranged by county. Certificates issued after 5.2.1965 are in HLG 62.

MAF 21   LAND TENURE: ORDERS OF PARTITION OF LAND UNDER THE INCLOSURE ACTS.
1849–1924.   115 pieces.   [II 37].   No restriction on access.

Orders dividing land owned in undivided shares by two or more persons. Arranged by county.

MAF 22   LAND TENURE: CERTIFICATES OF REDEMPTION OF RENTCHARGES UNDER THE CONVEYANCING, ETC. ACT OF 1881.
1882–1925.   1 piece.   [II 38].   No restriction on access.

The certificates are arranged by county. After 1925, redemption of rentcharges came under the Law of Property Act, 1925, and certificates are in MAF 26.

MAF 23   WHITE FISH COMMISSION.
         1938–1939.   7 pieces.   [II 40]

Papers of the commission set up following the Sea Fish Industry Act, 1938.

MAF 25   LAND TENURE: COMMONS: CORRESPONDENCE AND PAPERS.
         1800–1956.   259 pieces.   [II 37]

The class contains material on inclosure and regulation of commons and greens, amendment of awards, schemes of management, stints, apportionment of compensation money, exchange of land, etc. Arranged by county in three alphabetical sections which overlap chronologically.

MAF 26   LAND TENURE: CERTIFICATES OF REDEMPTION OF RENTCHARGE UNDER THE LAW OF PROPERTY ACT, 1925, S.191.
         1926–1965.   502 pieces.   [II 38].   No restriction on access.

The certificates are arranged chronologically, and by county; full description at beginning of class list. Before 1926 redemption of rentcharges was effected under the Conveyancing Act, 1881, see MAF 22. Certificates issued after 5.2.1965 are in HLG 63.

MAF 27   LAND TENURE: CERTIFICATES OF DETERMINATION OF COMPENSATION UNDER THE LAW OF PROPERTY ACTS, 1922 and 1924.
         1936–1957.   6 pieces.   [II 38].   No restriction on access.

If compensation for the extinguishment of manorial incidents (see MAF 13) had not been decided before 1.1.1936, application could be made to the Minister to ascertain the amount payable. The certificates are arranged by county. Registers of these certificates are in MAF 76.

MAF 28   LAND TENURE: CERTIFICATES OF REDEMPTION OF CORN RENTS UNDER THE KENDAL CORN RENT ACT, 1932.
         1937–1964.   42 pieces.   [II 39].   No restriction on access.

In 1834, an act commuted the tithes and dues payable to the rectors and vicar of Kendal for a corn rent. The 1932 act allowed this corn rent to be redeemed. Certificates of redemption are arranged chronologically, by township. Certificates issued after 5.2.1965 are in HLG 64.

MAF 29   SEA FISH COMMISSION.
         1934–1936.   21 pieces.   [II 39]

The class contains the papers of this commission set up by the Sea Fishery Industry Act, 1933, its constitution, evidence taken, and copies of the Herring Report, and two reports on the White Fish Industry. See MAF 23.

MAF 30   LAND TENURE: SCHEMES OF REGULATION UNDER THE COMMONS ACT, 1899.
         1900–1966.   266 pieces.   [II 36].   No restriction on access.

Schemes of regulation of commons made by local authorities, arranged by county.

MAF 31   LIVESTOCK COMMISSION.
          1933–1946.   57 pieces.   [II 40]

Papers of the Cattle Emergency Advisory Committee, 1934, the Cattle Committee, 1934–1937, and the Livestock Commission and sub-committees; also papers on general legislation. *See also* MAF 91.

MAF 33   AGRICULTURAL EDUCATION AND RESEARCH: CORRESPONDENCE AND PAPERS.
          1891–1963.   890 pieces.   [II 41]

1–57   Universities, colleges, and institutes.

58–78   Miscellanea.

79–389   Universities, colleges, and institutes.

390–890   Miscellanea.

The miscellaneous sections cover agricultural education, science, and training, committees, grants, scholarships, etc. All four sections are arranged in roughly alphabetical order. The papers of the first two sections tend to be earlier than those of the last two, but there is considerable overlap.

MAF 34   AGRICULTURAL MARKETING: CORRESPONDENCE AND PAPERS.
          1918–1957.   915 pieces.   [III 9].   Various files are closed for
                                                 50 years.

This class contains the papers of various committees and schemes which operated under the following acts:

Agricultural Produce (Grading and Marketing) Act, 1928, amended 1931.
Agricultural Marketing Acts, 1931, 1933.
Bacon Industry Act, 1938, amended 1939.
British Sugar (Subsidy) Act, 1925.
British Sugar Industry (Assistance) Act, 1931.
Sugar Industry (Reorganisation) Act, 1936, amended 1942.

These are fully described at the beginning of the class list, and there is a list of contents.

MAF 35   ANIMAL HEALTH: CORRESPONDENCE AND PAPERS.
          1876–1963.   593 pieces.   [III 12]

This class deals with various animal diseases and legislation and orders designed to control them, import and export regulations, veterinary surgeons, inspectors, laboratories and research stations, etc. There is a list of contents at the beginning of the class list.

MAF 36   COMMERCIAL CONTROL: CORRESPONDENCE AND PAPERS.
          1893–1957.   309 pieces.   [II 41]

This class deals with action taken under the following acts:

Fertilisers and Feedingstuffs Acts, 1893, 1906, 1926. *See also* MAF 79.

Seeds Act, 1920, and Seed Regulations, 1921, amended 1925 and 1935. *See also* MAF 78.

Merchandise Marks Acts, section dealing with produce of agriculture, horticulture, and the fishing industry.

Food and Drugs Act, 1899.

Milk and Dairies Acts.

Poisons and Pharmacy Act, 1908.

Sale of Food (Weights and Measures) Act, 1926.

These are fully described and there is a list of contents at the beginning of the class list.

MAF 37   CROP PRODUCTION: CORRESPONDENCE AND PAPERS.
1932–1958.   132 pieces.   [III 9]

1–32	1932–1940. Wheat Act, 1932, papers and orders of the Wheat Commission. *See also* MAF 61.
33–58	1937–1945. Wheat Acts, 1932 and 1939, regulations and orders.
64–73	1932–1958. Wheat Commission.
74–82	1934–1939. Standard Price Committee.
83–86	1930–1935. Flour: quota scheme, Flour Millers' Corporation.
113	1939. Brewing and distilling in wartime, report by Interdepartmental Committee.
115	1939. Ministry's representation on Cereals Advisory (Defence) Committee.
128	1936. Storage of wheat in stack.

MAF 38   STATISTICS AND ECONOMICS: CORRESPONDENCE AND PAPERS.
1866–1960.   476 pieces.   [III 9]

The class deals with agricultural investigations, prices, price indexes, returns, and surveys; and contains the papers of many committees and conferences. List of contents at beginning of class list.

MAF 39   ESTABLISHMENT AND FINANCE: CORRESPONDENCE AND PAPERS.
1839–1960.   324 pieces.   [III 9]

The class includes files on the history of the department and papers of departmental and other committees.

MAF 40   TRADE RELATIONS AND INTERNATIONAL AFFAIRS: CORRESPONDENCE AND PAPERS.
1919–1948.   168 pieces.   [III 13]

Papers relating to the following organisations:

1–4	1919–1932. International Institute of Agriculture.
5–9	1927–1934. League of Nations.
10–14	1933–1935. World Economic Conferences.

15–45	1923–1938. Imperial Economic Conferences.
46–51	1933–1939. Imperial Economic Committee.
52–57	1932–1937. Import Duties Advisory Committee.
58–168	1923–1948. Import Duties, tariffs, and quotas, for a range of products, arranged alphabetically.

MAF 41 FISHERIES DEPARTMENT: CORRESPONDENCE AND PAPERS.
 1839–1960. 1,308 pieces. [II 39]. Various files are closed for 50 years.

This class contains papers dealing with the regulation of sea-fishing, nationally and internationally, and with the conservation of inshore, salmon, and freshwater fisheries. A full account of the relevant legislation is given at the beginning of the class list with a list of contents.

Maps and plans relating to these records are in MAF 71.

MAF 42 FOOD PRODUCTION DEPARTMENT: CORRESPONDENCE AND PAPERS.
 1916–1920. 8 pieces. [II 41]

1–7	1917–1920. Circulars and memoranda, bound volumes.
8	1916–1919. Box of miscellaneous files dealing with the Women's Land Army, Women's War Agricultural Committee, etc. *See also* MAF 59.

MAF 43 HORTICULTURE: CORRESPONDENCE AND PAPERS.
 1896–1959. 96 pieces. [III 10]. No restriction on access.

This class contains the papers of the Horticultural Advisory Council, orders and regulations dealing with destructive insects and pests, and material on bees, bulbs, fruit, grass and fodder crops preservation, hops, and willow growing. Contents at beginning of class list.

MAF 44 INFESTATION CONTROL: CORRESPONDENCE AND PAPERS.
 1893–1960. 62 pieces. [III 10]

This class is concerned with the work of the Ministry under the following acts:

Rats and Mice (Destruction) Act, 1919.
Destructive Imported Animals Act, 1932.
Prevention of Damage by Rabbits Act, 1939.
Wild Birds Protection Acts, 1880–1939.
Protection of Animals Acts, 1911–1927.
Pharmacy and Poisons Act, 1933.

There is a full description of the work at the beginning of the class list.

MAF 45 INFORMATION AND PUBLICITY: CORRESPONDENCE AND PAPERS.
 1926–1955. 6 pieces.

Papers on the Cowan Memorial Library, the Journal, and Growmore Bulletin.

MAF 46   ROYAL BOTANIC GARDENS, KEW: CORRESPONDENCE AND PAPERS.
1861–1955.   85 pieces.

Papers on the administration, land, buildings, and staffing, at Kew. The main records relating to the collections at Kew are preserved at the Herbarium and Library there under s.4(1) of the Public Records Act, 1958.

MAF 47   LABOUR AND WAGES: CORRESPONDENCE AND PAPERS.
1900–1959.   140 pieces.   [III 10]

This class contains inter-war material on the economic position of agriculture, conditions of employment, housing of seasonal workers, migration of workers from agriculture to government projects, unemployment, and unemployment insurance; and from 1938 onward on reserved occupations and the effect on agricultural organisation of evacuation of urban populations. *See also* MAF 62, 63, and 64.

MAF 48   LAND: CORRESPONDENCE AND PAPERS.
1837–1958.   591 pieces.   [III 10]

This class contains bill papers and other material concerning smallholdings and allotments, with files on settlement arising from the Special Areas (Development and Improvement) Act, 1934, commons, copyhold enfranchisement and extinguishment of manorial incidents, with variations in scale of compensation and precedent cases, glebe lands with precedent cases, land improvement with schemes for alleviation of unemployment, rural housing, orders under the Defence of the Realm Regulations and Corn Production Acts, universities and college estates, and a miscellaneous section including agricultural rates, Lloyd George's proposals for agriculture, fuel allotments, proposals for county war agriculture executive committees. List of contents at beginning of the class list.

MAF 49   LAND DRAINAGE AND WATER SUPPLY: CORRESPONDENCE AND PAPERS.
1861–1957.   1,930 pieces.   [III 10]

This class is concerned with the administration of several Land Drainage Acts, The material is arranged according to catchment boards, listed alphabetically. There is an index to drainage authorities and catchment boards at the beginning of the class list.

MAF 51   LIME AND FERTILISERS: CORRESPONDENCE AND PAPERS.
1919–1966.   345 pieces.   Pieces 211–225 are closed for 50 years.

1–29   1935–1963. Supply of fertilisers in wartime.

30–324   1919–1961. Land Fertility and Agricultural Lime Schemes.

329   1919–1920. Limestone grinding plants eligible for Development Commission grants.

Full description of class at beginning of class list.

MAF 52   LIVESTOCK AND DAIRYING: CORRESPONDENCE AND PAPERS.
1891–1963.   242 pieces.

This class deals with legislation to improve livestock, milk standards, and methods of marketing milk. There is a full account at the beginning of the class list and two lists of contents, one for the first 19 pieces, and another for pieces 20–242.

MAF 53   SECRETARIAT AND PARLIAMENTARY BRANCH: CORRESPONDENCE AND PAPERS.
1890–1947.   117 pieces.

This class contains weekly reports of the department, reports of deputations, reports for Minister's conference, agricultural policy papers, comments on bills, and report and evidence of the Royal Commission on Agriculture, 1920.

MAF 54   POULTRY AND SMALL LIVESTOCK: CORRESPONDENCE AND PAPERS.
1914–1956.   117 pieces.

This class deals with the activities of the Ministry to assist the production of poultry, eggs, goats, and rabbits. Full description and list of contents at beginning of class list.

MAF 55   SUBSIDIES AND GRANTS: CORRESPONDENCE AND PAPERS.
1936–1950.   54 pieces.

11–38   1936–1942. Subsidies on barley, oats, and rye.

43–47   1939–1940. Ploughing grants.

MAF 56   TEMPORARY COMMISSIONS AND ORGANISATIONS: CORRESPONDENCE AND PAPERS.
1932–1937.   14 pieces.   [II 40]

This class contains the papers of Reorganisation Commissions for: eggs, poultry, milk, pigs, and fatstock, and also of the Technical Committee on Abattoir Design.

MAF 58   AGRICULTURAL MACHINERY: CORRESPONDENCE AND PAPERS.
1920–1960.   176 pieces.   [III 10]

The few pre-war papers deal with an advisory committee appointed in 1920, and a testing committee in 1925, files on tractors, and a few in the miscellaneous section. Full description and list of contents at beginning of the class list.

MAF 59   WOMEN'S LAND ARMY.
1916–1950.   23 pieces.   [III 11]

1–3   1916–1918. Women's Land Army during the First World War.

4–25   1938–1950. Women's Land Army during the Second World War. All files extend beyond 1940, most will be open in 1972.

See also MAF 42.

MAF 60   MINISTRY OF FOOD, AND FOOD DEPARTMENTS OF THE BOARD OF TRADE.
1914–1939.   568 pieces.   [III 12].   Closed for 50 years, some files 100 years.

Most of the records in this class are still closed, but there are files dealing with the work of the Ministry of Food and the Food Departments of the Board of Trade which do not extend beyond 1920. These include papers of various committees, on control of commodities, imports and exports, rationing, price regulation, organisation of the Ministry of Food, diaries of the Permanent Secretaries for 1918 and 1920, report on the work of the National Kitchens, and some papers of the Royal Commission on Wheat Supplies, also:

162–173	1918–1920. Food Council documents; each volume is indexed.
372–373; 378	1917–1920. Industrial unrest and the railway strike, 1919.
397, 399, 402, 404	1919–1920. Industrial unrest; milk supply.
530–542	1919. Railway Strike; reports.
562	1914–1918. Food statistics.
565–568	1917–1920. Reports of action taken and food position.

There is a full description and subject index at the beginning of the class list.

MAF 61   WHEAT COMMISSION.
          1932–1957.   69 pieces.   [III 11]

This class contains papers of the commission set up under the Wheat Act, 1932, and of committees appointed by the Wheat Commission. There are also legal opinions on deficiency and quota payments, and proceedings of the law suit, Wheat Commission v. R. W. Paul, Ltd., 1934–1936. *See also* MAF 37.

MAF 62   AGRICULTURAL WAGES BOARD: CORRESPONDENCE AND PAPERS.
          1917–1947.   52 pieces.   [III 11]

1–5	1917–1918. First Agricultural Wages Board, regulations and minutes.
6–12	1924–1934. Second Agricultural Wages Board, duties and powers.
14–29	1925–1940. Second Agricultural Wages Board, annual reports.
30–31	1918–1921. First Agricultural Wages Board, gazette and orders.
32	1925–1930. Second Agricultural Wages Board, report of proceedings under the Agricultural Wages (Regulation) Act, 1924.
33–45	1924–1937. Second Agricultural Wages Board, orders.

See also MAF 47, 63, and 64.

MAF 63   AGRICULTURAL WAGES BOARD: MINUTES.
          1924–1945.   20 pieces.   [III 11]

Minutes of 215 meetings. *See also* MAF 47, 62, and 64.

MAF 64   AGRICULTURAL WAGES COMMITTEES.
          1924–1963.   210 pieces.   [III 11]

This class contains minutes of meetings of county committees and permit sub-committees, arranged alphabetically in two lists, and also proposals for new wage rates made under the Agricultural Wages (Regulation) Act, 1924. *See also* MAF 47, 62, and 63.

MAF 66 LAND IMPROVEMENT: REGISTERS OF LOANS.
          1851–1942.   12 pieces.   [III 11].   Various files are closed for 50 years.

11   1864–1940. Loans advanced under the Improvement of Land Act, 1864.

12   1870–1924. Loans advanced under the Limited Owners Residences Act, 1870.

There is a full description at the beginning of the class list.

MAF 68 AGRICULTURAL RETURNS: PARISH SUMMARIES.
          1866–1957.   4,598 pieces.   [III 12].   Access restricted.

Summaries of annual returns of livestock and crop acreages in England and Wales. These are available without restriction until 1917. For piece numbers after 1917, application must be made to the officer in charge of the search rooms, and a special undertaking has to be signed concerning use of the material.

MAF 69 ROYAL COMMISSION ON FOOD PRICES; AND FOOD COUNCIL.
          1924–1939.   100 pieces.   [III 12]

1–5   1924–1925. Royal Commission on Food Prices, chairman Sir Auckland Geddes; minutes of private meetings and circulars.

6–100   1925–1939. Food Council: minutes, circulars, and reports on bread, bacon, cocoa, dairy products, fish, meat, sugar, tea, vegetables.

Full description at beginning of class list.

MAF 70 WELSH DEPARTMENT: CORRESPONDENCE AND PAPERS.
          1912–1949.   186 pieces.   [III 13]

This class contains papers of the Council of Agriculture for Wales, the County Agricultural Executive Committees, and papers on agricultural education and research, improvement of livestock, land drainage, smallholdings, and miscellaneous sections which include agricultural industry, apprenticeships, land settlement, tithes, action taken under the Special Areas Act, 1934, and government investigation into derelict areas in South Wales. There is a full description of the work of the Welsh Department and list of contents at the beginning of the class.

MAF 71 FISHERIES DEPARTMENT: MAPS AND PLANS.
          1852–1947.   376 pieces.   [III 9]

Maps and plans relating to records in MAF 41, arranged as follows:

Salmon and freshwater fisheries: fishery district areas, and fish passes, gauges, gratings, and weirs.

Sea fisheries: fishery district areas and shell fish areas.

Harbours.

MAF 72   BOARD OF TRADE FOOD (DEFENCE PLANS) DEPARTMENT: RECORDS.
1935–1953.   721 pieces.   Closed for 50 years.

MAF 74   MINISTRY OF FOOD: CORRESPONDENCE AND PAPERS: CENTRAL REGISTRY.
1937–1955.   368 pieces.   Closed for 50 years.

MAF 76   LAND TENURE: REGISTERS.
1841–1957.   16 pieces.   [III 9]

Registers to records of enfranchisement and extinguishment of manorial incidents, found in MAF 9, 13, and 27, and records of redemption of the Halifax rentcharge in MAF 16.

MAF 78   SEEDS: CORRESPONDENCE AND PAPERS.
1918–1961.   63 pieces.

Most of the records in this class belong to the Seeds Branch set up after 1939; the few inter-war files supplement the material concerning work arising from the Seeds Act, 1920–1925 to be found in MAF 36.

MAF 79   ANIMAL FEEDING STUFFS: CORRESPONDENCE AND PAPERS.
1937–1954.   60 pieces.

The only inter-war file is of the scheme for control of animal feeding stuffs of the Food (Defence Plans) Department. For earlier papers, *see* MAF 36.

MINISTRY OF FOOD: SUPPLY DEPARTMENT

The following departments were set up to deal with the procurement, distribution, and processing, of various commodities during war time. In each class there are some early papers which are already open.

MAF 84   CEREALS GROUP.
1938–1962.   892 pieces.   Various files closed for 50 years.

MAF 85   DAIRY PRODUCE AND FATS GROUP.
1939–1959.   604 pieces.   Various files closed for 50 years.

MAF 86   FISH AND VEGETABLE GROUP.
1938–1956.   450 pieces.   Various files closed for 50 years.

MAF 87   GROCERIES AND SUNDRIES GROUP.
1939–1957.   315 pieces.

MAF 88   MEAT AND LIVESTOCK GROUPS.
1937–1958.   598 pieces.

MAF 89   GENERAL DIVISION: CORRESPONDENCE AND PAPERS.
1921–1946.   13 pieces.

This class contains papers of the Council of Agriculture for England, 1921–1940, the British Empire Producers' Conference, 1938–1939, and on insurance against war risks.

MAF 91   CATTLE MARKETS: CORRESPONDENCE AND PAPERS.
          1892–1954.   110 pieces.

This class contains files concerned with the development and regulation of cattle markets. A general section deals with legislation and papers of the Livestock Commission (*see also* MAF 31), followed by papers on individual markets arranged by county.

MAF 900   SPECIMENS OF CLASSES OF DOCUMENTS DESTROYED.

This class includes one box of routine correspondence of the Essex County Agricultural Executive Committee, 1917–1919.

CROWN ESTATE COMMISSIONERS

The Commissioners manage those portions of the hereditary estates of the Crown in England, Wales, Scotland, and Northern Ireland, the revenues of which have since 1760 been surrendered to Parliament under provisions of the Civil List Acts. At first the land revenues were managed by a Surveyor General of Land Revenues, and a Surveyor General of Woods, Forests, Parks, and Chases. In 1832 the Office of Woods, Forests, and Land Revenues was combined with that of Works; when the Offices were separated in 1851 the Office of Woods was left in the charge of two commissioners. In 1906 the President of the Board of Agriculture was made an *ex officio* commissioner. In 1924 the management of most Crown woods and forests was transferred to the Forestry Commission, and the Commissioners were renamed Commissioners of Crown Lands.

In 1956 an Act established a new board of eight Crown Estate Commissioners, responsible to the Lord Privy Seal and the Secretary of State for Scotland. In 1959 responsibility was transferred from the Lord Privy Seal to the Chancellor of the Exchequer.

Responsibility for most foreshores was transferred to the Board of Trade in 1866 and returned to the Commissioners of Crown Lands in 1950. During the 1939–1945 war these functions had been exercised by the Ministries of Shipping and War Transport, and later by the Ministry of Transport.

By law between 1832 and 1961 deeds of Crown lands had to be deposited at the Land Revenue Record Office. Other records selected for preservation were also deposited at this office, but in 1961 these were reclassified in CREST classes.

CREST 3   OFFICE ESTABLISHMENT.
           1731–1923.   21 pieces.   [II 100]

17   1911–1923. Quit Rent Office, accommodation.

21   1914–1921. Quit Rent Office, staff.

See also CREST 21.

CREST 4   WINDSOR ESTABLISHMENT: FILES.
           1766–1948.   20 pieces.   [II 100]

Most files deal with establishment matters in the nineteenth century, but a few files continue into the inter-war period. There is some information on rates of pay in 1919 and on other allowances up to 1922.

5

CREST 5   COURT ROLLS AND OTHER MANORIAL DOCUMENTS.
1441–1937.   479 pieces.   [II 100]

These documents are arranged under the name of the manor or lordship. Many court rolls and some rentals extend into the inter-war period.

1–173   English manors; arranged alphabetically.

174–271   Welsh manors: arranged alphabetically.

272–362   English manors; additional documents arranged alphabetically.

365–479   English manors; additional documents.

CREST 9   ENGLAND AND COUNTRY: LETTER BOOKS AND TREASURY REPORT BOOKS.
1802–1919.   165 pieces.   [II 101]

165   1914–1919. Bound volumes of letters to the Treasury, in chronological order. Letters in 1919 cover various transactions relating to Crown estates at Egham, Eltham, Esher, Hainault, Osborne, and Windsor. Letters also deal with leasing of mines in Cornwall, Cumberland, and Kent, sporting rights at Askrigg, coastal land in Durham, and at Scarborough, and also with tithes on agricultural land and exemption of staff from contributions under National Health Insurance Act. Some copies of Treasury replies are included.

CREST 18   AGRICULTURAL DEPARTMENT: TREASURY REPORT BOOKS.
1907–1919.   5 pieces.   [II 102]

5   1915–1919. Bound volumes of letters to the Treasury, in chronological order, with some replies. The letters set out proposals for leases, sales, purchases, repairs needed, and other matters of farm management. 1919 letters end in April; one letter describes fully the case for commuting tithe charges on Crown agricultural lands.

CREST 21   OFFICE ESTABLISHMENT: ESTABLISHMENT BOOKS.
1851–1923.   8 pieces.   [II 103]

8   1914–1923. Book containing particulars of each member of staff of the Office of Woods, giving date of appointment, rank, age, salary, increments, particulars of life insurance, and of war service. Ends in 1923 when information was transferred to cards. See also CREST 3.

CREST 30   WARRANT BOOKS.
1803–1925.   28 pieces.   [II 104]

17   1910–1925. General entry book of Royal and Treasury Warrants to the Commissioners of Woods.

CREST 34   REGISTERED FILES: OLD ESTATES.
1685–1961.   337 pieces.   [III 33]

Files of estates sold before 1941, except for those of a few small estates which are in CREST 35. The files are arranged by county, alphabetically. The class contains information on conveyances, licensing, fines, tithes, rentcharges, mineral rights, disafforestation, and commutation of manorial incidents.

CREST 35   REGISTERED FILES: ESTATES.
           1706–1965.   749 pieces.

Files dealing with the management of Crown properties, arranged by county, alphabetically.

CREST 37   REGISTERED FILES: FORESHORES.
           1815–1963.   372 pieces.

This class after 1866 contains records relating to the foreshores that were not transferred to the Board of Trade in that year. The following remained with the Office of Woods:

1. Foreshores in front or adjacent to Crown lands and land belonging to government departments.
2. Coal and minerals in or under the foreshore.
3. Foreshores of the Thames, Tees and County Palatine of Durham, already covered by Acts in 1857 and 1858.

There is a two-volumed index to these records giving number of each file, and a numerical list showing the piece numbers of the file numbers. *See also* CREST 42.

CREST 38   TITLE DEEDS, ETC.
           13th C.–1964.   2,219 pieces.   [III 33]

Deeds are arranged by county in England, followed by Ireland, Isle of Man, and Wales. The class contains leases, conveyances, and other documents which passed to the Crown when the properties concerned were acquired.

CREST 40   MISCELLANEOUS BOOKS.
           1570–1961.   128 pieces.

The following pieces contain inter-war material:

99   1845–1929. Office of Woods, entry book of warrants and appointments. Indexed.
108   1900–1948. Land Tax contract book, certificates for redemption of. Indexed.
113–126   1914–1935. Registers of assignments of Crown leases. Indexed.
127   1906–1928. Registers of probate of wills with details of settlements of property; since 1913 include letters of administration.

CREST 42   FORESHORES (BOARD OF TRADE) FILES.
           1920–1935.   12 pieces.

These records originated in the Board of Trade Mercantile Marine Department, and most are concerned with applications for permission to use foreshores. Five relate to the transfer of management of foreshores in Northern Ireland to the Land Purchase Commission. *See also* CREST 37 and MT 9.

FORESTRY COMMISSION

An Interim Forest Authority was formed in 1918, and was replaced under the Forestry Act of 1919 by the Forestry Commission, charged with the duty of promoting the interests of forestry and the production and supply of timber in the United Kingdom. It was empowered, under Treasury direction, to acquire and hold land, buy and sell timber, make grants or loans, advise on management of privately owned woods, establish woodland industries, and promote timber production in the British Empire. The powers of the Board of Agriculture and of the Scottish Board of Agriculture in relation to forestry were transferred to the Forestry Commission, and in 1924, it took over most of the woods previously controlled by the Commissioners of Woods.

The Forestry Commission was reorganised in 1945, when its powers to acquire and hold land were rescinded, and land required for forestry was vested in the Ministry of Agriculture or the Secretary of State for Scotland.

F 1   MINUTES.
       1918–1964.   12 pieces.   [II 166]

1   1918. Minutes of the Interim Forest Authority.

2–5   1919–1938. Minutes of the Forestry Commission, each volume covers five years.

DIRECTOR OF FORESTRY FOR ENGLAND   [II 166]

Correspondence and papers relating to the following forests, each file is named and dated.

F 3   DEAN FOREST.   1786–1957.   1,556 pieces.

F 4   ALICE HOLT FOREST.   1816–1946.   146 pieces.

F 5   BERE FOREST.   1791–1947.   52 pieces.

F 6   CHOPWELL FOREST.   1823–1949.   43 pieces.

F 8   DELAMERE FOREST.   1819–1945.   121 pieces.

F 9   DYMOCK FOREST.   1913–1946.   52 pieces.

F 10   NEW FOREST.   1666–1953.   499 pieces.

F 11   PARKHURST FOREST.   1815–1945.   52 pieces.

F 12   SALCEY FOREST.   1831–1945.   61 pieces.

F 13   WOOLMER FOREST.   1846–1940.   49 pieces.

F 16   DEAN FOREST: DEPUTY SURVEYOR'S OFFICE.
       1662–1935.   71 pieces.   [II 166]

58   1928–1935. Memoranda and correspondence on effect of Property
        Acts, 1922 and 1924, on extinguishment of manorial incidents.

F 17   DIRECTOR OF FORESTRY FOR ENGLAND: MAPS, PLANS, AND DRAWINGS.
        1608–1943.   439 pieces.   [III 155]

Most of these maps and plans were drawn in the eighteenth and nineteenth
centuries; they are arranged by name of forest, grouped under Division or Conservancy, as follows:

Dean Forest Division.
New Forest Division: New Forest, Parkhurst Forest.
North-West Conservancy: Delamere Forest.
North-East Conservancy: Chopwell Forest.
East Conservancy: Hazelborough Forest, Salcey Forest.
South-East Conservancy: Alice Holt Forest, Bere Forest, Woolmer Forest.
South-West Conservancy: Bentley Forest, Dymock Forest.
Lands Disafforested: Hainault, Whittlewood, Wychwood.
Miscellaneous Maps.

F 18   HEAD OFFICE: REGISTERED FILES.
        1912–1960; 1967.   270 pieces.   [III 72]

Files are arranged under the following headings:

Acquisitions.
Administration and organisation, including section on transfer of responsibilities
    to Forestry Commission.
Commissions, committees, and conferences, including files on consultative
    committees for England, Wales, Scotland, and Ireland, Development Com-
    mission, imperial and international conferences, the Agricultural Tribunal of
    Enquiry, the National Home Grown Timber Council, the Rural Industries
    Intelligence Bureau, and report of Committee on Crown Woodlands.
Establishment, including section on unemployment relief schemes.
Finance.
Forest and estate management.
Grants.
Miscellaneous, including file on Forest Products Research Board.
Private forestry.

F 19   DIRECTOR OF FORESTRY FOR ENGLAND: GENERAL AND VARIOUS.
        1913–1960.   51 pieces.   [III 72]

Files include: Forestry Commission Housing Policy, National Forest Parks,
research, transfer of Crown lands to the Forestry Commission, Experimental Work
Committee, Conference on Private Forestry, and comments on Forestry Acts, 1919
and 1921, Ribbon Development Act, 1935, and the Coal Act, 1938.

F 20   DIRECTOR OF FORESTRY FOR ENGLAND: MISCELLANEOUS BOOKS.
        1660–1963.   92 pieces.   [III 72]

The only inter-war material is as follows:

28–34   1914–1939. Dean Forest, conveyances.

90–92   1918–1921. Sub-accountants' Abstract Books; forests and woodlands.

F 21   RESEARCH DIVISION: CORRESPONDENCE AND PAPERS.
       1925–1961.   9 pieces.

1–8   1930–1961. Advisory Committee on Forest Research.

9   1925–1939. Bedgebury Pinetum Committee.

Files on research also in F 18 and F 19.

F 24   NEW FOREST: DEPUTY SURVEYOR'S OFFICE: CORRESPONDENCE AND PAPERS.
       1720–1939.   153 pieces.

The inter-war material is as follows:

59   1918–1920. Accounts book. Indexed.

60–71   1918–1924. Letter books. Indexed.

133   1906–1932. Avon and Stour Fishery, Crown's right to fish.

134   1910–1919. Finance Act, 1909–1910, duties on land values.

136   1915–1924. Abstracts of accounts.

137   1930. Sales and exchanges.

138   1932–1939. Charcoal kilns and production.

F 27   MEETINGS OF DIVISIONAL OFFICERS AND CONSERVATORS: MINUTES.
       1925–1945.   4 pieces.

1–3   Minutes for the years 1925, 1929, and 1934.

F 29   UNPUBLISHED ANNUAL REPORTS.
       1939–1944.   6 pieces.   No restriction on access.

These are typewritten reports produced during the war instead of the usual printed reports.

F 31   CONSERVANCIES FILES.
       1923–1950.   5 pieces.

Files on acquisition of land:

1   1923–1926. Hemsted Estate, Bedgebury Forest.

2   1936–1945. Inholmes Wood and Stoughton Down, Slindon Forest.

3   1937–1947. Transfer of Crown Land in Bedgebury to Forestry Commission.

4   1937–1950. Fitzalan-Howard Estate, Arundel Forest.

5   1938–1939. Preservation of South Downs in Friston area.

To date only these records of the South East Conservancy have been transferred.

F 32   SECRETARIAT: LAW FILES.
       1920–1964.   10 pieces.

This class contains papers on the transfer of Forestry Commission property to the Irish Free State, transfer of Crown Woods to the Forestry Commission, on the Forestry Act, 1927, application of the Town Planning Act, 1925, to land owned by the Forestry Commission, and on the Access to Mountains Act, 1939.

LAND REGISTRY

The Land Registry was set up by an Act of 1862 following recommendations of a Royal Commission. Its purpose is 'to give certainty to the title to real estates and to facilitate the proof thereof, and also to render the dealing with land more simple and economical'. At first it was on a voluntary basis; landowners who wished to do so could submit their title to land for examination and if approved their title would be registered. The Land Transfer Act in 1897 introduced compulsory registration on sale in certain areas; this compulsory principle was first applied in the County of London, and has gradually extended to the main urban areas of England and to the Home Counties.

The Land Registry was at first confined to England; it now covers England and Wales. It is administered by the Chief Land Registrar, responsible to the Lord Chancellor.

LAR 1   CORRESPONDENCE AND PAPERS.
      1825–1967.   245 pieces.

This class contains papers dealing with the general administration of the office, including the administration of the Land Charges Act, 1925.

LAND REVENUE RECORDS AND ENROLMENTS OFFICE

This office was established in 1832 to take over the enrolling and record keeping duties of the Auditors of the Land Revenue. In 1902 the Deputy Keeper of the Public Records was appointed Keeper of the Land Revenue Records; the records were then kept at the P.R.O. and enrolments were made there until 1961. In that year the Crown Estate Act abolished enrolment in the Land Revenue Records Office, those documents which by law had to be enrolled at the office remained but ceased to accrue. Other records were re-classified as belonging to the Crown Estate Commissioners and are to be found in the CREST classes.

LRRO 1   MAPS AND PLANS.
      1560–1953.   4,641 pieces.   [II 204]

These are arranged by county, each additional set of records starting a new alphabetical list. The alphabetical list of counties starting at piece 3784 contains many maps and plans of Crown estates drawn during the inter-war period.

LRRO 12   ACCOUNTS: RENTALS.
      1832–1955.   2,100 pieces.   [II 204]

The estates are described at the beginning of the class list, and the way in which they are grouped and the changes in the grouping are set out. During this century the rentals are usually for one year, and each year begins with London and Middlesex and ends with Scotland. Rentals for 1918–1919 start with London and Middlesex, piece 746.

LRRO 14 ENROLMENTS BY BOOKS: OFFICE OF WORKS.
1852–1943. 8 pieces. [II 203]

4–7 1907–1939. These are mainly licences to use pieces of freebord beside Bushey, Hyde, and Richmond Parks, and Longford River; also licensing of encroachments, and use of parks for sporting activities.

LRRO 18 ENROLMENTS BY DEPOSIT: FORESTRY COMMISSION.
1924–1926. 3 pieces. [II 203]

These deeds are mainly leases for land in the Forest of Dean and the New Forest; many of the former are for mines and quarries.

LRRO 22 SUB-ACCOUNTANTS' ABSTRACT BOOKS.
1849–1925. 76 pieces. [II 204]

70–76 1919–1925. Accounts with agents, rates and taxes paid, rents and royalties of mines, payments for repairs, emergency afforestation, etc.

LRRO 23 CASH ABSTRACT BOOKS.
1848–1927. 79 pieces. [II 204]

71–77 1919–1925. Cash abstract books of the Office of Woods, contain receipts from sales of land, of unimprovable rents (mainly quit rents), enfranchisement of copyholds, fines, interest, royalties, etc., and payments for purchase of estates, rates and taxes, imprests, repairs, salaries, etc.

78–79 1925–1927. Account abstract books of the Commissioners of Crown Lands contain debit and credit accounts with agents, analysis of receipts and expenditure, etc.

LRRO 24 JOURNALS.
1832–1925. 90 pieces. [III 158]

84–90 1919–1925. Monthly accounts showing cash receipts and payments.

LRRO 64 ENROLMENTS: REGISTERS AND INDEXES TO ENROLMENTS.
1832–1962. 42 pieces. [III 158]

11–13 1912–1947. General Register of deeds and documents enrolled and deposited. These relate to enrolments in LRRO 13–18 and 20.

The following classes are closed for 100 years:

LRRO 13 ENROLMENTS BY BOOKS: OFFICE OF WOODS 1833–1961.

LRRO 15 ENROLMENTS BY BOOKS: BOARD OF TRADE 1873–1945.

LRRO 16   Enrolments by Deposit: Office of Woods 1852–1961.

LRRO 17   Enrolments by Deposit: Board of Trade 1868–1939.

LRRO 20   Enrolments by Deposit: Ministry of Shipping and Ministry of Transport 1939–1950.

LANDS TRIBUNAL

The Land Values Reference Committee for England and Wales, responsible to the Lord Chancellor, was set up by the Acquisition of Land (Assessment of Compensation) Act, 1919, and after 1925 it appointed arbitrators who dealt with applications under s.84(1) of the Law of Property Act of that year. This work and the relevant records passed to the Lands Tribunal when it was created in 1949.

LT 3   Law of Property Act, 1925: Case Files.
       1926–1962.   46 pieces.

1–37   1926–1940. Files are numbered and arranged by year. They relate to applications under s.84(1) of the Act for orders to discharge or modify restriction on holding land. Files of successful cases contain a copy of the official arbitrator's order.

LT 4   Law of Property Act, 1925: Register of Cases.
       1926–1949.   7 pieces.

1–6   1926–1939. The registers are indexes to the caes files in LT 3, arranged by name of applicant.

ORDNANCE SURVEY

The Ordnance Survey arose out of the hindrance to operations in 1745–46 against the Young Pretender because of the absence of reliable maps. The Survey was formally established in 1791 to continue the trigonometrical survey begun in 1784 and to prepare, chiefly for military purposes, a one-inch map of England and Wales.

The Ordnance Survey Act, 1841, provided for the survey of the whole of Great Britain and the Isle of Man under the direction of the Board of Ordnance. After the abolition of the Board in 1855, responsibility for the Survey passed successively to the War Office, the Office of Works, and the Board of Agriculture. In 1965 the Survey was taken over by the newly created Ministry of Land, and when that Ministry was abolished in 1967, the Survey passed to the Ministry of Housing and Local Government which is now merged in the Department of the Environment.

OS 1   Correspondence and Papers.
       1831–1967.   204 pieces.   [II 224]

The class consists mainly of the records of the Ordnance Survey Department, after the dissolution of the Board of Ordnance. It consists of administrative, technical, and scientific matters, and special maps and surveys.

OS 2 OLD TRIANGULATION: RECORDS.
       1813–1945.   698 pieces.   [III 100]

These are books recording the exact positions of the Tertiary Triangulation
Stations used for the Old Triangulation, which was superseded by the New Triangulation begun in 1935 and completed in 1962. They contain the calculated
distances between adjacent stations. The records are listed by counties, and are the
survivors of a collection much of which was destroyed in a war-time fire.

OS 3 MISCELLANEA.
       1756–1939.   28 pieces.   [III 100]

   14–15   Plans of the Palestine Exploration Fund.

   24–27   1939. Revision of County Series: specimen items of base material.
            (25″ map.)

OS 4 AREA DOCUMENTS: COUNTY SERIES: PARISH ACREAGE LISTS.
       1870–1966.   171 pieces.   [III 100].   Open after 5 years.

These books were compiled as each county revision of the survey was completed.
The books list the total area of land, inland water, saltmarsh, and tidal water, in
each parish, with parish and county totals. They form the authoritative documents
from which area statistics were obtained for official purposes. They are listed by
county.

OS 5 MAPS AND PLANS.
       1777–1938.   20 pieces.

This class contains a collection of miscellaneous original maps which have been
considered worthy of permanent preservation. The inter-war maps are of the Isle
of Man, 1920, and plans of the Ordnance Survey Office, Southampton, 1938.

OS 6 MAGNETIC SURVEYS.
       1914–1933.   12 pieces.

These books contain locating details for the Magnetic Survey Stations, computa-
tions to find the geographical co-ordinates, azimuths for the stations, and calculations
to obtain the magnetic variations of various points in Great Britain.

SOCIAL SERVICES

The main subjects covered include the health services, the national schemes of insurance, dependants' allowances, pensions, and assistance, and on the 'environmental' side, housing, local government, town and country planning, public health, and related matters. Also referred to are the administration of war pensions and the care of war pensioners, and the central government's responsibility for the care of children deprived of a normal home life.

Before 1945, each service grew up separately, in response to different social and political pressures, and applied only to particular sections of the community. The work of each service was administered separately but not necessarily by one department. For this reason the boundaries between the P.R.O. groups reflect the somewhat complicated administrative history of the period, rather than any sharp division of subject matter.

The method followed in this section is to describe the situation in relation to the social services in 1918, then to trace interchanges and additions of functions thereafter in a chronological list.

In 1918 unemployment insurance was in the hands of the Ministry of Labour, which had been established in 1916 and which took over this function from the Board of Trade. The scheme was administered through labour exchanges, and trade unions were permitted in certain circumstances to handle the benefits. Unemployed persons who had no insurance rights at all were supported by the poor law guardians, in 1918 still responsible to the Local Government Board. The latter was not only the poor law authority, it also had powers in respect of local administration of the great mass of public health legislation which had been one of the main achievements of the nineteenth century. These included a code of sanitary law, slum clearance, town planning, and also personal health services such as the isolation and treatment of sufferers from infectious diseases, public vaccination, and quarantine administration. The Local Government Board also had powers in relation to the registration of births, deaths, and marriages, supervision of local sanatoria in connection with health insurance, and old age pensions appeals.

Since 1905, the Board of Education and local authorities had developed a very considerable interest in the health of children and maternity and child welfare. An Act of 1907 made the medical inspection of all school children compulsory in England and Wales, and a School Medical Service grew up, adminstered by the local authorities with the help and under the eye of the Board of Education. The Privy Council had certain powers in relation to the governing body of the medical profession, the General Medical Council, and was also responsible through the Central Midwives Board for regulating the practice of midwifery in England and Wales.

The Home Office also had some health and welfare responsibilities, notably in connection with factory and mines legislation, shop hours, and the protection of children, lunatics, and mental defectives. It also exercised a general oversight of the scheme of workmen's compensation for industrial injury.

In 1908 a non-contributory pensions scheme was introduced for persons of seventy or more years who had limited means. The Treasury was responsible for these old age pensions, but delegated the execution of the scheme to the Board of Inland Revenue which had local offices used for the collection of excise duties. In 1909, the excise and pensions work was transferred to a new Board of Customs and Excise. Appeals on decisions of local pension committees were made to the Local Government Board.

Health insurance legislation was passed in 1911; in return for contributions manual and lower paid non-manual employees were eligible to receive medical attention and money benefits when they were sick and could not work, and the scheme also included special provisions for maternity and sanatorium benefits. The Government farmed out the routine work of collecting contributions and making payments to a large number of friendly societies, trade unions, medical aid societies, and industrial assurance companies. These organisations, so far as their health insurance activities were concerned, were henceforward called 'approved societies'. Four Insurance Commissions, one for each of the four countries of the United Kingdom, were set up and a Joint Committee was established to deal with matters of policy and finance. The Treasury was the 'parent' department of all these bodies but the main responsibility for administering the scheme fell on the chairman of the Joint Committee and the chairmen of the four Commissions.

The state assumed little responsibility for dependants of sailors and soldiers who were killed or disabled on service until the Boer War. The Royal Patriotic Fund Commission set up during the Crimean War provided benefits for the disabled and the dependants of those killed or disabled in that war and subsequent colonial wars. In 1903 it was reorganised as the Royal Patriotic Fund Corporation and supplemented the dependants' allowances given by the War Office (whose allowances were paid through Chelsea Hospital) and by the Admiralty. In 1915 a Statutory Committee of the Royal Patriotic Fund Corporation assisted by local committees was set up to deal with the problems arising from the scale of the fighting. Voluntary contributions were inadequate and the Treasury was forced to provide money. This led to the formation in 1917 of a Ministry of Pensions which took over administration of disablement pensions and allowances from the Admiralty and War Office, except officers' wounds pensions. The Statutory Committee was brought under the control of the Ministry and in September ceased to exist, its functions being taken over by the Ministry with the exception of its judicial work which passed to an independent Grants Committee.

The following chronological list gives transfers affecting the functions of the Ministry of Health, the Ministry of Housing and Local Government, the Ministry of Pensions and National Insurance, and the National Assistance Board; that is the MH, HLG, PIN, and AST groups. Transfers to and from the Ministries of Education and Labour, and the Home Office are only referred to in connection with these departments; under the respective entries of ED, LAB, and HO, other transfers are listed.

CHRONOLOGICAL LIST OF CHANGES AFFECTING THE SOCIAL SERVICE MINISTRIES 1918–1970

1919   Ministry of Pensions to Ministry of Labour, powers relating to training and employment of disabled servicemen, and the dependants of deceased servicemen.

Ministry of Health established. Assumed all the powers of the Local Government Board, the English and Welsh Insurance Commissioners, and the powers of the Privy Council under the Midwives Acts, 1902 and 1918. Welsh Board of Health set up.

Board of Education to Ministry of Health, powers relating to expectant and nursing mothers and to children under five.

Home Office to Ministry of Health, powers of supervising the administration of Children Act, 1908, relating to infant life protection.
Board of Education to Ministry of Health, powers relating to medical inspection and treatment of young persons.

1920   Home Office to Ministry of Health, powers and duties under the Anatomy Acts and the Lunacy and Mental Deficiency Acts.
Ministry of Health to Board of Education, powers and duties in relation to public libraries, museums, and gymnasia.
Admiralty to Ministry of Pensions, certain mercantile marine pensions.
Ministry of Pensions to Ministry of Labour, further powers concerning the training and employment of disabled officers and men, widows and dependants, and nurses.

1921   Ministry of Health to Home Office, powers relating to registration of electors and the conduct of parliamentary elections.
Ministry of Pensions to Service departments, all powers relating to disablement pensions and allowances, except powers relating to disablement or death resulting from service in 1914–18 War and pensions already awarded in respect of disablement in former wars.
Service Departments to Ministry of Pensions, officers' wounds pensions.

1922   Ministry of Agriculture and Fisheries to Ministry of Health, powers under Rats and Mice (Destruction) Act, 1919, in relation to port sanitary districts and vessels.

1925   Board of Education to Ministry of Health, administration of grants for the training of midwives and health visitors.

1929   Boards of guardians and poor law unions were abolished and their functions were transferred to county and county borough councils, which became the local public assistance authorities in England and Wales.

1931   Transitional payments scheme introduced. Until 1929 unemployed persons who were outside the insurance scheme were supported by the poor law guardians (who were responsible to the Ministry of Health) and after 1929 by the public assistance committees of the county and county borough councils (also responsible to the Ministry of Health). The transitional payments scheme administered by the public assistance authorities from Exchequer grants assisted unemployed persons whose benefits were exhausted. The Ministry of Labour was responsible for the scheme, using the services of the Poor Law Division and the General Inspectors of the Ministry of Health in its dealings with the public assistance committees.

1934   Two Commissioners for Special Areas set up, one for England and Wales appointed by the Minister of Labour, one for Scotland appointed by the Secretary of State.
Unemployment Act provided for the establishment of the Unemployment Insurance Statutory Committee. Part II of the Act set up the Unemployment Assistance Board with responsibility for the care of the able-bodied unemployed who were without resources or whose resources including unemployment benefit were inadequate. Functions were transferred to the new Board from the local public assistance committee

in two instalments: in 1935 it took over responsibility for persons qualified for benefit but having exhausted it, and in 1937 for others.

Home Office to Ministry of Health, powers of confirming bye-laws for regulating the business and proceedings of Metropolitan Borough Councils.

1937   Home Office to Ministry of Health, organisation of base hospitals for civil defence.

1938   Home Office to Ministry of Health, responsibility for Emergency Hospital Service and responsibility for preparation of first aid posts, ambulance services, and evacuation scheme for civil defence purposes.

1939   Ministry of Pensions given responsibility for the administration of pensions and grants on account of disablement or death arising out of service after 2nd September, 1939 and also for the Personal Injuries (Civilians) Scheme for which Unemployment Assistance Board acted as agents.

1940   Unemployment Assistance Board renamed Assistance Board. It took over the duty of supplementing the incomes of old age pensioners and widow pensioners of 60 years of age or over from local public assistance authorities.

1941   Board of Trade responsible for war damage claims. Advances were made by the Customs and Excise where loss caused undue hardship, and by the Assistance Board where there was immediate need. From June 1940 war damage payments had been paid by the Assistance Board at Treasury instance but without statutory authority.

1942   Ministry of Health to Ministry of Works, renamed Ministry of Works and Planning, town and country planning powers.

Beveridge Report on Social Insurance and Allied Services published.

1943   Board of Customs and Excise to Assistance Board, responsibility for payment of non-contributory old-age pensions to pensioners whose pensions were being supplemented by the Board. Decisions as to whether or not a pension should be awarded and the amount of any pension awarded were still made by local pension committees. Assistance Board responsible on behalf of Board of Trade for issue of permits for purchase of utility furniture (transferred to Board of Trade in 1945).

To Assistance Board from local public assistance authorities, responsibility for supplementing the pensions of widows under 60 years with children.

Ministry of Health to Ministry of Food, power to regulate labelling and composition of food. Catering Wages Commission recommended Wages Boards, later set up.

1945   Ministry of National Insurance established, taking over powers and duties of the Ministry of Health relating to health insurance and pensions, of the Ministry of Labour and National Service relating to unemployment insurance and assistance, and of the Home Office relating to workmen's compensation. Provision was made that previous functions of the Ministry of Labour and National Service should continue to be carried out through the local organisation of that department on behalf of the new department.

Local Government Boundary Commission for England and Wales set up. Minister of Health given power of making regulations prescribing general principles by which Commissioners were to be guided.

Family Allowances Act, 1945; functions given to Ministry of National Insurance.

1946   Assistance Board responsible on behalf of Ministry of Food for investigating circumstances of applicants for free welfare foods and determining eligibility for and authorising free supplies.

1947   Home Office to Ministry of Town and County Planning, regulation of advertisements.

Customs and Excise to Assistance Board, responsibility for payment of non-contributory old age pensions to pensioners not receiving supplementary pensions (thus completing transfer of functions, see 1943). Decisions as to award and amount of pension still remained with local pension committees.

Board of Control (lunacy and mental deficiency) to Ministry of Health, all powers except those of a quasi-judicial nature.

Ministry of Health to Home Office, functions relating to the care of children deprived of a normal home life.

Ministries of Health and Food to Ministry of Agriculture and Fisheries, functions relating to the control of rats, mice, and food pests transferred in 1922, except for the powers of the Ministry of Health in respect of vessels.

1948   National Health Service established. Comprehensive system of national insurance and industrial injuries benefit introduced.

Home Office to Ministry of Health, management and buildings of Broadmoor Institution; control of admission and discharge of patients remaining with the Home Secretary.

Ministry of Health to Home Office, functions relating to the regulation of markets and fairs.

Assistance Board renamed National Assistance Board on taking over functions from local public assistance authorities. Local authorities remained reponsible for providing institutional accommodation, central oversight remaining with the Minister of Health, but the Board was made responsible for providing reception centres for the provision of temporary board and lodging for persons without a settled way of living. Local pension committees were dissolved and the National Assistance Board became responsible for deciding questions relating to the award and the amount of non-contributory old age pensions with the assistance of its local advisory committees. The Minister of National Insurance was to answer for the Board in Parliament and have regulation-making functions analogous to those previously exercised by the Minister of Labour and the Minister of Health.

Establishment of Central Youth Employment Executive under Employment and Training Act, 1948.

1950   Legal Aid Scheme brought in. General administration in hands of English and British Law Societies. National Assistance Board responsible for investigating and determining resources of applicants. The Lord Chancellor became the minister responsible for scheme.

1951	Ministry of Town and Country Planning (set up in 1943) became the Ministry of Local Government and Planning. In addition to the planning functions, it took over from the Ministry of Health functions relating to local government finance, environmental health services, including water supply, sewerage and sewage disposal, and housing, land, rent control, burials, coast protection, and certain civil defence services. The Ministry of Health continued to be responsible for personal health services, mostly under the National Health Service Acts, including the services provided by local authorities, the National Assistance welfare and accommodation services of local authorities, and health aspects of food and nutrition. Ministry of Local Government and Planning to Ministry of Transport, functions concerned with authorisation of compulsory purchase of land by a county council for the improvement of highways. Ministry of Local Government and Planning renamed Ministry of Housing and Local Government.
1953	Ministries of Pensions and National Insurance amalgamated. Certain functions relating to medical and surgical treatment and the provision of appliances, etc., transferred to Ministry of Health.
1954	Ministry of Transport and Civil Aviation to Ministry of Pensions and National Insurance, functions relating to the award of pensions to merchant seamen and fishermen disabled in the war of 1914–18 and to dependants of those men who died as a result of injuries sustained in that war.
1955	Ministry of Agriculture and Fisheries and Ministry of Food amalgamated; primary responsibility for food hygiene transferred to Ministry of Health.
1956	Ministry of Health to Ministry of Housing and Local Government, certain civil defence functions.
1960	Board of Control (lunacy and mental deficiency) abolished; personnel absorbed into Ministry of Health.
1964	Ministry of Housing and Local Government to Ministry of Public Building and Works, functions with respect to bye-laws and regulations relating to building control and certain related ancillary functions. Ministry of Housing and Local Government and Scottish Office to Ministry of Labour, functions concerning bye-laws as to means of escape from fire in factories. Ministry of Land and Natural Resources set up; took from Ministry of Housing and Local Government responsibility for water, national parks, and access to countryside.
1966	Ministry of Pensions and National Insurance and National Assistance Board merged to form Ministry of Social Security. Ministry of Works to Ministry of Housing and Local Government, building control and responsibility for historic buildings.
1967	Ministry of Land and Natural Resources abolished; most functions transferred to Ministry of Housing and Local Government.
1968	Ministries of Health and Social Security merged, under a Secretary of State for Social Services.

1969   Secretary of State for Local Government and Regional Planning appointed, to have general direction over the Ministry of Housing and Local Government and Ministry of Transport.

1970   Department of the Environment created by integrating three existing departments, the Ministry of Housing and Local Government, the Ministry of Transport, and the Ministry of Public Building and Works, under the Secretary of State for the Environment.

Ministerial responsibility for child care services in England and Wales transferred from the Home Secretary to the Secretary of State for the Social Services in respect of England, and to the Secretary of State for Wales in respect of Wales.

MINISTRY OF HEALTH

The Ministry of Health was set up in 1919 taking over the powers and duties of the Local Government Board and the National Health Insurance Commissioners for England and Wales, together with certain functions of other Government departments concerned with health services. In 1968 it merged with the Ministry of Social Security to form the Department of Health and Social Security. There is an index in the search rooms to the whole MH group, it gives class and piece references to subjects shown in sub-headings in the class lists.

MH 8   WORLD WAR I: WAR REFUGEES COMMITTEE.
        1914–1919.   93 pieces.   [II 176]

These are the records of the voluntary committee which administered relief from public funds. They include correspondence, allocation cases, hostel lists, files on Serbian refugees, general record books, minutes, accounts, and Belgian case history cards, the last being arranged alphabetically by name.

MH 9   POOR LAW: REGISTERS OF PAID OFFICERS.
        1837–1921.   37 pieces.   [II 173].   Records are open after 5 years.

These are records of appointments made by the boards of guardians to the staff of institutions under their control; they show the date of appointment and date and cause of resignation or dismissal, etc. The volumes are arranged alphabetically by unions.

MH 10   POOR LAW: CIRCULAR LETTERS.
        1834–1919.   85 pieces.   [II 173].   Records are open after 5 years.

These are circulars from the Local Government Board and its predecessors to Local Government Board auditors and other local officials. The arrangement is chronological.

84–85   1919. Each volume is indexed.

MH 11   LEAGUE OF MERCY.
        1899–1947.   58 pieces.   [II 176].   Records are open after 5 years.

The League was established in 1899 by charter, to promote the welfare of hospitals generally, and to institute the 'Order of Mercy' awarded for good personal service. It was dissolved in 1948 after the National Health Act, and the Ministry of Health took over its records. The class contains the Roll of the Order, minute books, and reports.

MH 15 POOR LAW: INDEX OF SUBJECTS.
1836–1920. 107 pieces. [II 173]

These are subject indexes to the correspondence and papers in the MH 12, 19, and 30 classes which contain the correspondence of the Poor Law Commission, the Poor Law Board, and the Local Government Board with poor law unions, county authorities, and government departments. However, although the index extends to 1920, the papers after 1900 to which they refer were largely destroyed by enemy action. The indexes are included here because they give the subject, and a short précis of the letters, which cover the whole field of poor law and (after 1871) local government and public health administration. The indexes for 1910–1920 cover twelve volumes, arranged alphabetically.

MH 20 POOR LAW: GOVERNMENT OFFICES: REGISTERS OF CORRESPONDENCE.
1837–1920. 85 pieces. [II 174]

These relate to the papers in the MH 19 class, but again the records for the period 1909–1920 have not survived. Each register covers correspondence from one or more government departments arranged chronologically. There are also volumes devoted to special subjects, for example, plague, cholera.

MH 31 POOR LAW: COUNTY REGISTER: REGISTERS OF CORRESPONDENCE.
1867–1920. 134 pieces. [II 175]

The registers refer to the originals in MH 30 but again, the papers after 1900 (1904 for London), have not survived. The registers give the subject and a précis of the letters.

MH 35–46 GENERAL NURSING COUNCIL FOR ENGLAND AND WALES

These classes comprise microfilms of the General Register of Nurses and other registers and indexes, kept by the General Nursing Council. In some classes the time-span has not yet been ascertained.

MH 35 GENERAL REGISTER OF NURSES.
1920–1965. 88 pieces. [II 176]

MH 36 REGISTER OF MENTAL AND MENTAL DEFECTIVE NURSES.
1921–1962. 8 pieces. [II 176]

MH 37 REGISTER OF SICK CHILDREN'S NURSES.
1921–1960. 3 pieces. [II 176]

MH 38 REGISTER OF FEVER NURSES.
1921–1950. 5 pieces. [II 177]

MH 39   REGISTER OF MALE NURSES.
    1922–1950   1 piece.   [II 177]

Each of the above is arranged chronologically following the sequence of registration numbers.

MH 41   KARDEX CARDS OF REGISTERED NURSES.
    4 pieces.   [II 177]
    Arranged alphabetically.

MH 42   PANEL OF EXAMINERS WHITE AND COLOURED CARDS.
    2 pieces.   [II 177]

MH 43   KARDEX CARDS FOR TRAINING SCHOOLS.
    1 piece.   [II 177]

The London group comes first, then towns in alphabetical order.

MH 45   STATE ENROLLED ASSISTANT NURSES: KARDEX CARDS.
    2 pieces.   [II 177]
    Arranged alphabetically.

MH 46   PANEL OF ASSESSORS.
    1 piece.   [II 177]

MH 47   MILITARY SERVICE TRIBUNALS, 1916–1918.
    1915–1922.   161 pieces.   [II 176].   Closed for 100 years.

MH 48   PUBLIC HEALTH AND POOR LAW SERVICES: LOCAL AUTHORITY SERIES: FILES OF CORRESPONDENCE, SERIES I.
    1868–1935.   523 pieces.   [II 176]

This class contains the surviving papers relating to public health and poor law services which have been selected for preservation. They are files of the Local Government Board inherited by the Ministry of Health in 1919. Papers relating to functions which have been passed to the Ministry of Housing and Local Government are in HLG group. The class consists of correspondence with local authorities, joint hospital boards and committees, asylum boards, and port sanitary authorities; and is concerned with particular cases rather than general policy. A continuation of this series after 1922 is MH 52; only a few pieces extend beyond 1920.

MH 49   WELSH INSURANCE COMMISSION.
    1911–1949.   33 pieces.   [III 81]

The functions of the Welsh Insurance Commission, established under the National Insurance Act of 1911, were transferred to the Ministry of Health in 1919, and were exercised thereafter by the Welsh Board of Health. The records of the Commission proper therefore end in 1919, but the class also contains registered files dealing with Medical Aid Societies in Wales, 1913 to 1948, when they ceased under the National Insurance Act, 1946.

8   1919. Minutes of meetings of the Commission.

9–33   1911–1949. Files for named Medical Aid Societies. The files are arranged under the relevant society. They include accounts, applications for the approval of societies, complaints, banking arrangements. Most of the files end before 1940.

See note to PIN 2.

MH 50-51   LUNACY COMMISSIONERS AND BOARD OF CONTROL

Under the Mental Deficiency Act, 1913, the Lunacy Commission was merged in a Board of Control, subject to regulations to be made by the Secretary of State for the Home Department. Under the Ministry of Health Act, 1919, responsibility for making these regulations passed to the Ministry of Health. The Board was dissolved in 1959.

MH 50   MINUTES.
        1845–1938.   69 pieces.   [III 81]

46–67   1918–1938. Minutes of Board of Control, arranged in annual volumes indexed to 1931 only.

MH 51   CORRESPONDENCE AND PAPERS.
        1845–1960.   242 pieces.   [III 81]

87–89   . 1919–1921. Research grants: allocation of yearly grant.

208–235   1932–1935. Departmental Committee on Sterilisation: report, minutes, correspondence and papers including evidence submitted to the committee and returns. *See also* MH 58.

239–241   1914–1940. Circular letters.

MH 52   PUBLIC HEALTH AND POOR LAW SERVICES: LOCAL AUTHORITY SERIES: FILES OF CORRESPONDENCE, SERIES II.
        1919–1962.   410 pieces.   [III 80]

This class contains records of the Ministry of Health relating to public health and poor law services, functions which were taken over from the Local Government Board in 1919. The topics covered include appointments, administration of hospitals, welfare schemes, handling of epidemics. Included in this class are references to interpretations of many acts dealing with public health matters, particularly the Local Government Act, 1929. Local authorities are grouped under the following headings.

1–141   County Councils.

142–208   Corporation of City of London and Metropolitan borough councils.

209–365   Boroughs, county boroughs, and urban district councils.

366–401   Rural district councils.

402–410   Port Health Authorities: Grimsby, Dover, Hayle, and Penzance only.

MH 53   PUBLIC HEALTH AND POOR LAW SERVICES: LOCAL GOVERNMENT ADMINISTRATION AND FINANCE.
        1910–1913; 1919–1950.   103 pieces.   [III 79]

This class contains papers on public health acts and other bills, Exchequer grants and conditions of service, and duties of public health staff. The class list is headed by an alphabetical list of subjects. The references to bills are not exhaustive, other classes must be consulted also.

MH 54 LOCAL GOVERNMENT ACT, 1929; ADMINISTRATIVE SCHEMES AND REGULATIONS.
1929–1947. 7 pieces. [III 80]

This Act was passed to amend the law relating to the administration of poor relief, registration of births, deaths, and marriages, highways, town planning, and local government. The class includes the administrative schemes prepared by the county and county borough councils for the Ministry of Health for the discharge of functions transferred to them under the Act. It also includes regulations for domiciliary assistance to blind persons under the Blind Persons Act, 1920. There are references to the Local Government Act in other classes also: see particularly MH 52.

MH 55 PUBLIC HEALTH AND POOR LAW SERVICES: ADMINISTRATION AND SERVICES.
1883–1884; 1900–1950. 879 pieces. [III 79]

These are general subject files relating to the administrative side of public health. It is difficult to draw a distinction between MH 53 and this class. Briefly MH 53 contains general papers relating to public health, public assistance staff, and related legislation, and MH 55 deals with the administration of public health services, and includes staffing.

An alphabetical list of subjects precedes the class list. The following references are cited because they are perhaps not obvious from the title to the class.

285	Children and Young Persons Bill, 1933.
322B	Workmen's Compensation Act, 1935: spirochaetal jaundice.
350–355	Health of Mercantile Marine and Navy.
444–481	Nurses and nursing; training, conditions of service, and reconstitution of General Nursing Council.
583–619	Blind welfare.
620–621	Deaf, deaf-dumb, and deaf-blind, activities of county associations.
688–695	Children, day nurseries, and nursery schools.
696	Birth control: Contraceptives Bill, 1934.

MH 56 PUBLIC HEALTH AND POOR LAW SERVICES: FOODS.
1900–1937. 172 pieces. [III 79]

Responsibility for the supervision of hygienic food conditions was vested in the Ministry of Health during this period. The class includes files of the Departmental Committee on Food Law, 1929–1935, regulations governing preservatives in food, imported foods, contamination of foodstuffs, and food poisoning. The files are arranged chronologically under general headings. At the beginning of the class list is an alphabetical subject index.

MH 57 PUBLIC HEALTH AND POOR LAW SERVICES: PUBLIC ASSISTANCE.
1907–1935. 204 pieces. [III 79]

These are general subject files relating to the administration of public assistance. There is no subject index but the pieces are listed under the following headings:

General: poor law and public assistance administration, reports on conditions in provinces and Wales.
Conferences: Public Assistance Conference, 1931, General Inspectors' Conferences.
Transitional payments.
Institutions.
Boarding out children.
Training and employment of children.
Removal of children from institutions, childrens' associations, homes, etc.
Emigration.
Vagrancy.
Departmental Committee on the Relief of the Casual Poor, 1929.
Relief: includes applications by strikers.
Assignment of functions.
Orders.
Poor Law Reform.

An additional set of papers starts at piece 175 and also includes pieces on the prevention and relief of distress arising from World War I and the administration of the Unemployed Workmen Act, 1905.

MH 58   PUBLIC HEALTH AND POOR LAW SERVICES: GENERAL HEALTH QUESTIONS.
    1910–1954.   398 pieces.   [III 79]

These are files of correspondence and minutes on policy and individual cases. The class list is headed by the following alphabetical index. Here a brief description of the category has been added where possible.

Aliens: employment in hospitals, etc.
Anaesthesia: administration of.
Anatomy: interpretation of Anatomy Acts.
Beauty culture establishments: control of.
Chiropodists: Registration Bill, 1928–1929; government recognition.
Dangerous drugs: regulations, drug addiction.
Dentistry: treatment, Dentists Act, 1921, Dental Board.
Drugs and medical supplies: artificial limbs; Departmental Committee on Supply of Drugs to Insured Persons, 1920–1922; Advisory Committee on Definition of Drugs, 1929–1932.
General Series: People's League of Health, Insurance Practitioners' Medical Research Scheme, hydrology, Medical Research Council, euthanasia.
International Labour Office: invalidity, old age, widows' and orphans' pensions insurance.
League of Nations: Health Committee and Health Organisation.
Lunacy: Royal Commission on Lunacy and Mental Disorder, 1924–1928, Cobb Committee on Administration of Public Mental Hospitals, 1922–1923, Medical Committee on Drug Addiction, 1923–1926, minutes and evidence.
Medical Education: postgraduate hospitals, medical schools and courses, Postgraduate Medical Education Committee, 1925–1930, Athlone Committee on postgraduate education, 1920–1921, proposed international academy, report of 7th Congress of Far Eastern Association of Tropical Medicine, 1928.

Medical Herbalists: Bill, 1923.

Medical Research Council.

Medicines: related bills, medicine stamp duty.

Mental deficiency: related bills, institutions, Advisory Committee on Scientific and Ancillary Mental Health Services, 1936–1939.

Military Training Act, 1939: statistical records and Opticians Central Emergency Committee.

Opticians: Bill, 1927, Departmental Committee on.

Osteopaths: Bill, 1931–1936.

Poisons and Pharmacy: Act, 1933, Departmental Committee on.

Population: health of rural population, population trends; Agricultural Policy Committee, 1930.

Public Medical Services: co-ordination, sundry proposals from British Medical Association, etc.

Radium: supply and distribution, National Radium Trust.

Registration: medical and dental in Irish Free State.

Sterilisation of mental defectives: Departmental Committee on Sterilisation. *See also* MH 51.

Therapeutic substances: Act, 1925, and regulations.

Tropical diseases: schools and hospitals.

Voluntary hospitals: Commission, 1921–1928, Sankey Commission of Enquiry, 1935–1938, administration of finances, co-operation with local authorities, Lord Nuffield's Provincial Hospitals Trust.

MH 59   METROPOLITAN WATERWORKS: REGISTERS OF CORRESPONDENCE.
       1873–1919.   6 pieces.   [III 82]

These are listed chronologically but no correspondence exists after 1902. The registers give a précis of the letters received and the replies of the Metropolitan Water Board which was established in 1902.

MH 60   MISCELLANEOUS: REGISTERS OF CORRESPONDENCE.
       1899–1920.   32 pieces.   [III 82]

Most of the correspondence has not survived. The volumes of registers are arranged chronologically. They include two volumes on the Local Government (Emergency Powers) Act, 1916. The registers give a précis of each letter and reply; topics covered include tenancies, application for posts, sanctioning of allowances.

MH 61   COMMISSIONER FOR SPECIAL AREAS: FILES OF CORRESPONDENCE.
       1934–1948.   82 pieces.   [III 82]

The Special Areas (Development and Improvement) Act, 1934, provided for the appointment of two Commissioners (one for England and Wales and the other for Scotland) whose functions were to assist and co-operate with government departments, local authorities, voluntary organisations, etc. in improving the areas, particularly by providing work. The Commissioner for England and Wales was appointed by the Ministry of Labour, with the consent of the Treasury, and most of the files in this class were created in the Ministry of Labour. The Ministry of Health worked closely with the Commissioner's staff to secure the provision of adequate medical services, to encourage hospital building, and to alleviate problems of local administration. The class list is preceded by a table of Treasury grants under the various Acts. The finance file for each subject (prefixed F) where it exists is listed with the main file. The files are arranged as follows:

1–3	1934–1945. General: definitions and provisions of assistance.
4–12	1934–1939. Medical services and public health: includes files on birth control clinics.
13–19	1934–1944. Work schemes: wages and working conditions, supply of skilled labour for housing schemes, local authority schemes.
20–82	1934–1948. Individual schemes: sewerage, clinics, hospitals and housing, includes housing schemes of Durham Aged Mine Workers' Associations.

See also LAB 23.

MH 62   NATIONAL HEALTH INSURANCE: ADMINISTRATION: SERIES II.
1912–1937.   227 pieces.   [III 81]

Early files are those of the English National Health Insurance Commissioners and the Secretariat of the Joint Committee of the four National Health Insurance Commissions. After 1919 the files are those of the Ministry of Health and its Insurance Department. The files are arranged in sections as follows:

Administration.
Additional benefits.
Chemists.
Dental Benefit Council.
Dental service, regional.
Doctors:
  capitation fee.
  excessive prescribing.
  general: includes British Medical Association insurance proposals.
  medical records.
  medical services.
  offences.
  remuneration.
  unregistered practitioners.
Drugs and appliances: Advisory Committee on Definition of Drugs and Medicines.
General.
Medical benefit.
Medical services, regional.

See also MH 81 *and* note to PIN 2.

MH 63   CENTRAL (UNEMPLOYED) BODY FOR LONDON.
1906–1907; 1919–1930.   10 pieces.   [III 82]

This body was set up under the provisions of the Unemployed Workmen Act, 1905, which empowered the Local Government Board to set up distress committees, and central bodies to co-ordinate them. The duties of the Central Body for London included the establishment of labour exchanges until 1910, the maintenance of registers of unemployed, and the collection of relevant information. It could also find temporary work for the unemployed, help them to move to another area, or to emigrate. During the 1914–18 War many of the distress committees throughout the country gradually ceased to function and by 1919, the only duty of the London Committee was to elect representatives to the Central (Unemployed) Body which was concerned exclusively with administering Hollesley Bay Colony. This was a farm acquired in 1906 and used until 1915 as a training centre for agricultural workers. From 1915 to 1919 it was commandeered for war purposes, but it reverted to the Central Body in 1919. In 1930 the Central Body was formally dissolved; its assets, including the Colony, passed to the London County Council.

MH 64   POOR LAW INSTRUMENTS.
        1916–1932.   28 pieces.   [III 79]

This class comprises copies of poor law authorisations, issued by the Local Government Board until 1919 and then by the Ministry of Health. The instruments gave official sanction for:

Expenditure to assist emigration of poor persons.

Alterations to union institutions.

Raising of loans.

Acquisition and sale of property, etc.

The pieces are listed chronologically but are not described.

MH 65   NATIONAL HEALTH SERVICE: LONDON EXECUTIVE COUNCIL.
        1912–1948.   113 pieces.   [III 81]

This class contains the agenda and minutes of the London Insurance Committee and its sub-committees, appointed under National Insurance Act, 1911. In 1948 on the setting up of the National Health Service, local executive councils were established and the insurance committees dissolved. The title of the class is somewhat of a misnomer since executive council minutes have not yet been transferred. *See* note to PIN 2.

MH 66   LOCAL GOVERNMENT ACT, 1929: PUBLIC HEALTH SURVEY.
        1930–1943.   1,055 pieces.   [III 79]

This Act empowered the Minister of Health to withhold grants from local authorities if they were not providing efficient health services. The survey was undertaken to satisfy the Minister that the services were efficient. The files in this class are arranged under local authorities. Subjects covered include survey reports, reports on welfare services for the blind, co-ordination of the health services, and some annual reports of the medical officers of health. General policy files on the survey are in MH 55.

MH 67   PUBLIC HEALTH AND POOR LAW SERVICES: JOINT HOSPITAL BOARDS.
        1903–1938.   135 pieces.   [III 80]

This class consists of correspondence and minutes of selected joint hospital boards.

MH 68 POOR LAW AUTHORITIES.
        1904–1933.   425 pieces.   [III 80]

This class consists of the files of the Local Government Board relating to poor law administration inherited by the Ministry of Health in 1919, and of the Ministry of Health until 1929 when responsibility for the relief of the poor passed from the boards of guardians to the local authorities. Very few files in this class date later than 1930; for other relevant files, see also MH 52. The files are arranged by unions under county headings. The subject matter in the main is a specific aspect of administration and finance, not general policy. The class also includes sections on joint poor law committees, the Metropolitan Asylums Board, and Poplar and Stepney Sick Asylum District.

MH 69 NATIONAL HEALTH SERVICE: EXECUTIVE COUNCILS.
        1912–1966.   136 pieces.

This class is to contain minute books and other specimen records of selected executive councils and the insurance committees which preceded them. So far only records of insurance committees have been transferred. Some volumes are indexed. The selected areas are:

Bedfordshire and Luton.
Birmingham.
Eastbourne.
Kingston-upon-Hull.
Merioneth.
Middlesex.
Newcastle-upon-Tyne.
Salford.

To date no records for Eastbourne have been transferred. For the records of the London Insurance Committees, *see* MH 65. *See* note to PIN 2.

MH 70 GOVERNMENT LYMPH ESTABLISHMENT.
        1898–1946.   19 pieces.   [III 80]

Selected volumes and files on the production and testing of vaccine. *See also* MH 78 for staffing arrangements.

MH 71 COMMITTEES.
        1927–1939.   49 pieces.   [III 82]

1–3   1929–1931. Donoughmore Committee: selected papers. *See also* PIN 4 and LCO 2.

4–9   1927–1935. Advisory Committee on Medical Questions: minutes, correspondence, co-ordination of British policy at international conferences.

11–17   1936–1939. Interdepartmental Committee on Rehabilitation of Persons Injured in Accidents (Home Office, Ministry of Health, Scottish Office): evidence, correspondence, papers, and minutes of sub-committees.

18–30	1937–1939. Interdepartmental Committee on Abortion (Ministry of Health, Home Office): evidence, circulated papers, and report.
31–49	1935–1939. Interdepartmental Committee on Nurses and Nursing (Ministries of Health and Education): constitution, minutes, evidence, reports.
50–54	1936–1940. Advisory Committee on Medical Questions: minutes, representations.
55–56	1939–1941. Cancer Sub-Committee: constitution, proceedings.

MH 73 PUBLIC HEALTH AND POOR LAW SERVICES: CONSULTATIVE COUNCILS.
1918–1926. 49 pieces. [III 80]

The Ministry of Health Act, 1919 provided for the establishment by Order in Council of consultative councils in England and Wales to advise and assist the Minister. Four Councils were formed for England to cover respectively medical and allied services, national health insurance (replacing the Advisory Committee of the National Health Insurance Joint Committee), local health administration, and general health questions. One Council to cover the four functions was set up for Wales but was discontinued after 1924. The Council on National Health Insurance was transferred in 1945 to the Ministry of National Insurance. The Councils were purely advisory but had power to initiate proposals as well as make reports to the Minister.

This class contains minutes, reports, and papers of the Councils on Medical and Allied Services, Local Health Administration, and General Health Questions, and records of the Welsh Consultative Council. Similar records of the Council on National Health Insurance, its committees, and sub-committees, are in PIN 5. Both classes also contain correspondence and papers of the Ministry of Health relating to the constitution of these councils and consideration of their reports and proceedings.

MH 74 ANATOMY ACTS OF 1832 and 1871: REGISTERS AND FILES OF CORRESPONDENCE.
1832–1963. 45 pieces. [III 82]

The Anatomy Act of 1832 (amended in 1871) was intended to end the illegal methods previously used to procure bodies for medical research. The Home Secretary was responsible for the granting of licences, etc., until 1920 when his powers and duties were transferred to the Ministry of Health. Inter-war material which is open, includes certificates of licences to practice anatomy, quarterly reports of inspectors, and correspondence with the Anatomy Office and between the Anatomy Office and boards of guardians.

MH 75 WELSH NATIONAL MEMORIAL ASSOCIATION.
1912–1941. 36 pieces.

The Association was incorporated in 1912 to promote the prevention and eradication of tuberculosis and other diseases. The records cover correspondence, finance, and reports.

MH 76 EMERGENCY MEDICAL SERVICES.
1935–1961. 495 pieces.

Most files deal with the period 1939 to 1945, but there are some pre-war pieces which are open covering: plans for first aid posts, extension of hospitals, evacuation from London, air-raid precautions, and correspondence with local authorities on war preparations. There is a subject key.

MH 78 ESTABLISHMENT AND ORGANISATION FILES.
      1870–1961.   160 pieces.

This class contains papers on establishment matters and on the organisation of the Ministry of Health, strikes, and co-ordination of work with the General Register Office.

MH 79 100,000 SERIES FILES.
      1914–1961.   633 pieces.

This class contains registered files with a restricted circulation. There are papers on most topics dealt with by the Ministry of Health. They include papers of sub-committees set up to prepare for the 1939 war, several of which were sub-committees of the Committee of Imperial Defence. Subject index is available in search rooms.

MH 80 BILL PAPERS.
      1885–1939.   20 pieces.

This class so far contains papers for the following bills: Dentists, 1921; Poor Law, 1925–1927; Mental Deficiency, 1926–1927; Sale of Food and Drugs, 1927; Nursing Home Registration, 1927–1928; Mental Treatment, 1928–1930; Midwives, 1935–1936; Cancer, 1936–1939; Food and Drugs, 1931–1938.

MH 81 NATIONAL HEALTH INSURANCE: ADMINISTRATION: SERIES I.
      1912–1949.   119 pieces.

This series includes constitutions of selected local medical committees; minutes and papers of the National Association of Insurance Committees; files of conferences with and deputations from the British Medical Association; papers dealing with the early organisation and financing of the Medical Research Council; and files on the Friendly Societies Medical Associations and the Insurance Committees.

MINISTRY OF HOUSING AND LOCAL GOVERNMENT

This Ministry was formed in 1951 as the Ministry of Local Government and Planning, combining the Ministry of Town and Country Planning and certain functions of the Ministry of Health. Later in the year it was renamed the Ministry of Housing and Local Government. In 1970 the ministry was absorbed into the Department of the Environment. Most of the records in this group have been taken over from the departments whose functions were transferred to this ministry, nearly all the inter-war records came from the Ministry of Health which is the department referred to in descriptions of the class lists below.

Many classes in this group contain correspondence and returns from local authorities; these are usually arranged in the following way:

1. County councils.
2. Metropolitan borough councils.
3. County borough councils, borough councils, and urban district councils.
4. Rural district councils.
5. Miscellaneous.

The arrangement within each section is alphabetical.

HLG 1   'O' FILES. LOCAL AUTHORITY SERIES.
         1852–1927.   1,539 pieces.   [II 194]

These are registered files of departmental correspondence transferred from the Ministry of Health in 1951. Most of the files are for the period 1901 to 1919 and consist of papers instituted prior to 1919 by the Local Government Board. The few papers subsequent to 1919 are continuations of papers begun earlier. The 'O' denotes old papers.

The subject matter covers the whole field of environmental services. 'O' files relating to general policy and procedure are in HLG 46. A subject index given at the beginning of the class list can be used to find the subjects indicated by the code figures although the index was compiled for other purposes.

HLG 4   PLANNING SCHEMES: FILES.
         1905–1951.   4,021 pieces.   [III 85]

These resulted from the various Housing and Town Planning Acts which enabled local authorities to prepare schemes for land in course of development or likely to be used for building purposes. The working plans of individual schemes are either associated with the original file, or will be found in HLG 5. The pieces are arranged in local authority order.

HLG 5   PLANNING SCHEMES: MAPS AND PLANS.
         1905–1951.   3,671 pieces.   [III 85].   No restriction on access.

These are maps and plans relating to the schemes in HLG 4, and they are listed in the same way.

HLG 6   MAPS AND PLANS: MISCELLANEOUS.
         1800–1919.   2,068 pieces.   [III 85]

These are plans and drawings of schemes submitted by local authorities to the Local Government Board and the Ministry of Health for approval, either for loans, or deposited in connection with Bills. The pieces are dated and listed under local authorities.

HLG 7   SPECIAL WAR-TIME FUNCTIONS.
         1925–1954.   1,047 pieces.   [III 85]

These are files and registers dealing exclusively with certain war-time functions which have no parallel in peace-time. They include defence areas, manpower, war damage, evacuation, care of the homeless, etc. The period covered in the main is

1938–1945. There is much material on the period immediately preceding the outbreak of war, 1938 to 1939. Listed below are the main topics covered:

1	1939. Military Training Bill.
14	1938. Committee of Imperial Defence: man-power sub-committee.
15	1939–1940. War Cabinet: schedule of reserved occupations.
36	1938–1939. Census of 1941.
37, 38, 42	1935–1939. Air raid precautions.
46	1939. Compensation (Defence) Bill.
59–330	1938–1950. Evacuation: regional organisation, co-ordination with other departments, finance, requisitioning, expectant mothers, schools, children.
441–444	1925–1939. War deaths and burials.
890	1936. War Emergency Water Committee.

HLG 8   ROYAL COMMISSION ON LOCAL GOVERNMENT.
          1922–1929.   116 pieces.   [III 88]

This Commission was appointed to enquire into the existing law and procedure relating to the extension of county boroughs, the creation of new county boroughs in England and Wales, and the effect of such extensions and creations on the administration of the other local authorities, to investigate the relations between these local authorities, and to make recommendations as to their constitution, areas, and functions. The Commission published three reports: Cmd. 2006 in 1925, Cmd. 3213 in 1928, and Cmd. 3436 in 1929.

The records in this class consist of material submitted in evidence by various bodies, papers circulated to members, and minutes of private meetings. *See also* HO 45.

HLG 9   ROYAL COMMISSION ON LONDON GOVERNMENT.
          1921–1922.   46 pieces.   [III 89]

This was appointed in 1921 to enquire into the local government system of the administrative county of London and surrounding districts. The report was published in 1922, Cmd. 1830. With the exception of certain published material this class includes a complete set of papers circulated to the members of the Commission, submissions and evidence, and the minutes of meetings and private meetings.

HLG 10   ROYAL COMMISSION ON LONDON SQUARES.
           1927–1928.   7 pieces.   [III 89]

The conversion of Mornington Crescent and Endsleigh Gardens for building purposes in the early 1920's, together with similar threats to other London squares, led to the appointment of this Commission in 1927, to enquire into and report on the squares and similar open spaces in the administrative county of London, and the desirability of their preservation as open spaces. The Commission's report was published in 1928, Cmd. 3196. Some of its recommendations were incorporated in a Bill promoted by the London County Council, which became the London Squares

Preservation Act, 1931. The class contains unpublished material, papers circulated to members, and minutes of evidence heard at private meetings. *See also* HO 45.

HLG 11 ROYAL COMMISSION ON LOCAL GOVERNMENT IN THE TYNESIDE AREA.
1935–1937. 40 pieces. [III 89]

This Commission was appointed in 1935 on the recommendation of the Commissioner for Special Areas. The report was published in 1937, Cmd. 5402. This class contains unpublished material, minutes of evidence, and statements by local authorities and individuals. *See also* HLG 30/14 *and* HO 45.

HLG 12 ROYAL COMMISSION ON THE LOCAL GOVERNMENT OF MERTHYR TYDFIL.
1935–1936. 11 pieces. [III 89]

This Commission was appointed in 1935 to investigate whether Merthyr Tydfil should continue as a county borough. The report was published in 1936, Cmd. 5039. This class consists of minutes of meetings and a summary of evidence none of which was published. *See also* HLG 30/14 *and* HO 45.

HLG 13 HOUSING: INSTRUMENTS AND CONSENTS.
1910–1955. 219 pieces. [III 85]

Housing authorities were required under the Housing of the Working Classes Act in 1903, and subsequent legislation, to seek approval for action proposed by them. This class contains instruments and consents in connection with the sale, exchange, and lease of land, the purchase and appropriation of land, and the construction of sewers and new street works for housing purposes. The registers for the class are in HLG 14, and are dated volumes arranged by local authorities.

HLG 15 LOCAL AUTHORITIES: INSTRUMENTS AND CONSENTS TO FINANCIAL TRANSACTIONS.
1850–1871; 1899; 1908–1925. 19 pieces. [III 86]

These are instruments and consents to loans raised by local authorities to enable them to enforce statutory provisions of such Acts as the Public Health Act, 1875, the Small Dwellings Acquisition Act, 1890, and the Housing Acts, 1890–1919. Since 1871 only a sample has been preserved; related files of correspondence which have been retained up to 1920 may be found in 'O' Files, HLG 1, and possibly in the poor law union papers of the Ministry of Health. The volumes cover a range of years and relate to particular acts. The registers to this class are in HLG 16 and are volumes arranged chronologically and grouped by local authorities.

HLG 17 MUNICIPAL CORPORATIONS ACT, 1882; INSTRUMENTS AND CONSENTS.
1899–1934. 52 pieces. [III 86]

These are instruments and consents relating to the sale or transfer of corporate lands of boroughs. The pieces are dated and there are registers up to 1926 consisting of local authorities arranged alphabetically.

HLG 18 LOCAL GOVERNMENT ACT, 1888: INSTRUMENTS AND CONSENTS.
1889–1934. 60 pieces. [III 86]

These relate to the approval of transactions, including the raising of loans, sales, appropriations and leases of corporate property, the purchase of land, the application or investment of money raised from the sale of land, and the appropriation of the proceeds of the transfer of Government stock or annuities. The pieces are listed chronologically and until 1924 can also be found by consulting a register of local authorities.

HLG 19   MISCELLANEOUS INSTRUMENTS AND CONSENTS.
         1853–1937.   89 pieces.   [III 86]

These are various types of consent covering loans and land transactions given under the Acts set out below:

Local Government Acts, 1858, 1894, and 1933.
Public Health Act, 1875.
Burial Acts, 1853 and 1900.
London Government Act, 1899.
Public Works Loan Act, 1881.
Education Acts, 1909 and 1921.
Ministry of Health Act, 1919.
Land Settlement (Facilities) Act, 1919.

The list gives the dates of pieces only and there are registers in HLG 20. The latter are both nominal and chronological and grouped by local authorities.

HLG 21   BURIAL ACTS, 1852–1900: INSTRUMENTS AND CONSENTS.
         1901–1936.   18 pieces.   [III 86]

These relate to the opening of new burial grounds, which were controlled by the Local Government Board and its successor the Ministry of Health. Some papers relating to burials for the period 1901 to 1920 were destroyed by enemy action. Files relating to loans in respect of burial grounds and cemeteries and those relating to the Burial Acts for 1901 to 1919 which were not destroyed by enemy action are in HLG 1. The class list gives the date of pieces only. *See also* HLG 45.

HLG 23   SEALED PLANS: MISCELLANEOUS.
         1923–1937.   21,238 pieces.   [III 87]

Plans relating to orders and schemes made later than March, 1923 by the Ministry of Health. The orders are in Legal Branch Orders, HLG 26; and in some cases the plans are kept with the orders. Registers and indexes to these plans are in HLG 66.

HLG 24   REHOUSING SCHEMES OF STATUTORY UNDERTAKERS: SEALED PLANS AND
         SCHEMES.
         1890–1939.   438 pieces.   [III 87]

The Local Government Board and the Ministry of Health approved schemes for providing accommodation for persons displaced from working class dwellings under powers conferred by local acts, railway acts, and provisional orders confirmation acts. This power was later executed under section 3 of the Housing of the Working Classes Act, 1903, and subsequent housing legislation. Most of the schemes have plans attached. The pieces are dated and refer to both the area and statute. They are listed chronologically.

HLG 25   LOCAL AUTHORITY BYE-LAWS.
            1872–1940.   1953–1954.   667 pieces.   [III 87]

This class contains bound volumes of bye-laws which had to be approved by the Local Government Board and later the Ministry of Health. Pieces covering the inter-war period are:

314–657   1919–1939. Local authority bye-laws.
662–667   1935–1939. Local authority bye-laws, supplementary.

For each year local authorities are listed alphabetically. *See also* HLG 58.

HLG 26   LEGAL BRANCH ORDERS.
            1842–1952.   1,005 pieces.   [III 87]

The Poor Law Board, the Local Government Board, and the Ministry of Health were empowered by various statutes to make orders on a wide variety of subjects relating to local administration, such as: assessment areas, transfer of investments of boards of guardians, town planning schemes, and preservation of historic buildings.

HLG 27   ROYAL COMMISSION ON THE DISTRIBUTION OF THE INDUSTRIAL
            POPULATION, 1937–1940.
            1937–1940.   128 pieces.   [III 89]

The Commission was appointed in 1937 under the chairmanship of Sir Montague Barlow. The Commission's report (Cmd. 6153) recommended the decentralisation of industry from congested areas, and proposed a central national authority to deal with the problem. The class consists of submissions and evidence to the Commission. The set of papers is incomplete; it is uncertain whether files were weeded or destroyed by enemy action. *See also* BT 64, HLG 52/1004–1005, HLG 68/50, HO 45, *and* LAB 10.

HLG 29   PUBLIC HEALTH AND LOCAL GOVERNMENT LEGISLATION: BILLS AND
            PAPERS.
            1840–1939.   235 pieces.

This class consists of bound volumes of papers concerned with the passage through Parliament of bills sponsored by the Local Government Board and the Ministry of Health. The volumes contain legislative proposals, consultations with government departments, local authorities, and others, draft bills, notes on clauses, amendments, and various correspondence. A wide range of bills is cited, including:

Rating and Valuation Bill, 1925.
Local Government Bill, 1929.
Housing Bill, 1930.
Town and Country Planning Bills, 1931, 1932.
Housing Bill, 1936.
Public Health Act, 1936.
Tithe Bill, 1936. *See also* Tithe group.
Emergency Legislation, 1939.

6

260–262   1906–1927. Bound volumes of papers collected when the transfer of poor law functions to local authorities was being considered. The volumes include bill papers, cabinet and departmental memoranda, correspondence, committee reports, and papers on the administration of poor law and public health services.

HLG 30 UNEMPLOYMENT: SPECIAL AREAS.
1920–1939.   65 pieces.   [III 87]

These records comprise registered files taken over from the Ministry of Health dealing with legislation, financial questions, commissions and committees relating to schemes of unemployment relief in the Special Areas. The main topics covered are given below:

I   1933. Ernest Bevin's plan for 2,000,000 workless.

2–11   1920–1938. Unemployment Bills, 1920, 1933, and 1934, Special Areas (Amendment) Bill, 1936–1937, Compulsory Purchase Order Bill, 1938.

12–24   1925–1938. Commissions: include appointment and reports of Commissioner for Special Areas, leading to Royal Commissions on Tyneside and Merthyr Tydfil. See HLG 11, HLG 12, and HO 45.

25–26   1925–1928. Sir W. H. N. Goschen's Committee: schemes of assistance.

27–30   1929–1931. Chelmsford Committee on Regional Development.

31   1937. Interdepartmental Committee on Special Areas (Ministries of Health and Labour).

32   1923–1924. Interdepartmental Conferences on Unemployment and Poor Law.

33–34   1929–1937. Policy on acquisition of land for public purposes.

35–37   1933–1936. Setting up of Unemployment Assistance Board.

38–46   1932–1939. Finance grants.

47–51   1928–1934. Investigations and surveys.

52–59   1924–1932. Schemes.

60–65   1928–1937. Representations: includes draft bill to prohibit hunger marches; Lancashire Industrial Development Council; deputations from mining areas.

See also LAB 23.

HLG 31 HOUSING NOTES AND INSTRUCTIONS.
1919–1921; 1925–1939; 1944–1957.   24 pieces.   [III 87]

The class includes memoranda issued to the housing commissioners by the Housing Department of the Local Government Board and the Ministry of Health, various handbooks and manuals of instructions for the guidance of housing staff, legal decisions, and High Court cases.

HLG 32 LOCAL GOVERNMENT FINANCIAL STATISTICS.
1862–1945.   3,838 pieces.

The statistics in this class are supplementary to those published in Local Government Financial Statistics. The class contains epitomes of accounts, which are the forms used for the financial returns made by local authorities from 1920–1921, and tabulation sheets, on which the returns of the epitomes were tabulated to show the several services against the various authorities. The tabulation sheets have been prepared yearly since 1933–1934. The class also contains other unpublished statistical material on rates and rateable values and also poor law returns. The introductory note to the class describes the forms used.

Tabulation Sheets:

15–2784	1934–1945. Accounts of county councils, county borough councils, borough councils, urban district councils, and rural district councils, including trading accounts (water, estates, cemeteries, harbours, transport, electricity, gas, markets, airports) and special funds.
2785–2901	1931–1939. Accounts of parish councils, including joint committees.
2902–2903	1938–1940. Accounts of metropolitan boroughs.
2909–2969	1936–1940. Miscellaneous accounts including: joint hospital boards, harbour authorities, joint sewerage boards, joint gas, electricity, transport, and tramway boards, sea fisheries committees, burial boards, joint town planning committees, joint water boards, Welsh education authorities, assessment committees.
3038–3043	1934–1940. Grand summaries of all local authorities. Sheets for year 1938–1939 are wanting.

Valuations:

3049–3081	1921–1935. Gross estimated rental: rateable value of agricultural land, buildings, government property, assessable valuations, industrial hereditaments, freight transport, and others.
3090–3108	1918–1928. Summary of the annual local taxation returns.

Poor Law Unions and Rates:

3109–3111	1927–1929. Statements for each rating area, the reduced assessable value according to the valuation lists in force, distinguishing amounts in respect of agricultural land.
3112–3114	1928–1929. Adjustment of rateable value of urban rating areas, showing for each year the sum which should be added to bring urban rateable value on to the same basis as rural rateable value.
3131–3146	1918–1934. Rates levied in various towns; also profits and losses on municipal undertakings by which rates in those towns have been reduced or increased.
3147–3229	1922–1930. Poor law returns; statements showing the average weekly cost of in-maintenance per head of persons relieved in institutions provided by boards of guardians.

Epitomes of Accounts:

3230–3247	1937–1938. Accounts of 18 county councils, including general statistics, rate fund services, special funds, aggregate rate fund account, loan and capital account, etc.

| 3248–3821 | 1938–1939. Accounts of urban district councils, including general statistics, rate fund services, housing revenue account, trading services and private works, etc. Arranged under counties in two alphabetical lists. |
| 3822–3828 | 1937–1938. Accounts of metropolitan borough councils, including general statistics, etc. |

HLG 34   Agricultural Rates Acts: Grants.
1921–1958.   37 pieces.

This class consists of general policy files and registers relating to agricultural rating and valuation. The files contain papers concerning financial and accountancy procedure, sporting rights exercised over agricultural land, calculation of grants, assessments, de-rating, valuation, and general correspondence. The registers contain records of grants payable to local authorities including boards of guardians, between 1923–1930, under the following Acts:

Agricultural Rates Act, 1923.
Agricultural Rates Act, 1929.
Local Government Act, 1929.

HLG 35   Tithe Rentcharges.
1920–1958.   28 pieces.

This class contains general policy files and registers relating to tithe rentcharges. The files consist of information about grants to local authorities, rates and rate refunds, evidence prepared by the Ministry of Health to the Royal Commission on Tithe Rentcharge, and general correspondence. The registers contain records of the payment of grants made under the Tithe Act, 1936, to local authorities.

HLG 36   Central Housing Advisory Committee: Minutes and Papers.
1935–1955.   31 pieces.   [III 89]

This committee was set up under the Housing Act, 1936, to advise the Minister and the Housing Management Commissions. The class contains minutes and papers of the committee, formation of sub-committees and papers on slum clearance and housing associations.

HLG 37   Central Housing Advisory Committee: Records of Sub-Committees.
1935–1957.   66 pieces.   [III 90]

There is a subject index, and the pieces are listed in the following groups:

1–2	1936–1939. General Purposes and Technical Sub-Committee.
4–11; 13–19	1935–1939. Housing Management Sub-Committee.
41	1936–1938. Planning Sub-Committee.
42–45	1936–1937. Rural Housing Sub-Committee.
56	1938. Sub-Committee on Demolition Procedure.
57	1938. Housing Manual Sub-Committee.
61	1938–1941. Sub-Committee on Redevelopment Areas.

HLG 40   RURAL HOUSING AND TIED HOUSES.
         1925–1955.   47 pieces.   [III 88]

These records relate to the provision of special subsidies to rural district councils for building houses and for improvement grants in agricultural areas. Topics for the inter-war period include:

1–14	1935–1940. Rural Housing Committee.
15–20	1931–1934. Rural Housing Advisory Committee.
21–25	1930–1931. Interdepartmental Committee on Tied Cottages. (Ministries of Agriculture and Health.)
30–32	1930–1938. Rural Housing, general.
38–39	1925–1927. Housing (Rural Workers) Bill.
45	1927–1928. Legal opinion on sub-letting of tied cottages.
46	1936–1938. Rural Workers Act, publicity on housing.

HLG 41   RENT CONTROL: PAPERS.
         1920–1960.   114 pieces.   [III 88]

These are the papers of various committees and other records on the control and decontrol of rent of unfurnished residential property and the prevention of eviction of tenants. The pieces are listed under the following headings:

1–13	1920. Salisbury Committee: to enquire into workings of Rent Acts.
14–27	1922–1923. Norman/Onslow Committee.
28–44	1930–1931. Marley Committee.
45–64	1937. Ridley Committee.
86	1937–1938. Cabinet Committee on Rents.
87	1938. Departmental Committee on Distress for Rent.
88	1926–1932. Rent control.
97–104	1924–1938. Legislation: Rent Restriction Bill, 1924, Increase of Rent and Mortgage Interest (Restriction) Bill, 1938, and various Acts.
109	1924–1925. Legal opinions on rent restriction.

HLG 43   LOCAL AUTHORITIES: AREAS, BOUNDARIES, AND STATUS: CORRESPONDENCE AND PAPERS.
         1888–1958.   1,067 pieces.

This class contains correspondence and papers on changes in boundaries of local authorities, the creation of new county boroughs and urban districts, following the Local Government (County Boroughs and Adjustment) Act, 1926, and the Local Government Act, 1929, which gave effect to the recommendations of the Royal Commission on Local Government (see HLG 8).

1–19	1927–1931. Local Government reform; observations on proposals.
20–73	1928–1937. Local Government Reform Bill and Act: rating relief schemes, transfer of poor law functions, etc.

74	1925–1932. Provision in local acts for alteration and extension of boundaries.
89–95	1919–1929. Representations for alterations of borough boundaries.
109–561	1929–1939. Review of English county districts.
562–906	1905–1939. Proposals for alteration of boundaries of metropolitan boroughs, English county boroughs, boroughs, urban districts, and rural districts.
907–916	1920–1937. Review of Welsh county districts.
917–940	1917–1939. Proposals for alteration of boundaries of Welsh county boroughs, boroughs, urban districts, and rural districts.
941–968	1921–1939. General papers on county review: effect of orders altering boundaries on other aspects of local government.
1019–1056	1923–1958. Proposals for alteration of boundaries of English counties, county boroughs, boroughs, urban districts, and rural districts.
1057–1063	1930–1933. First General Review of County Districts.
1064–1065	1929–1938. Proposals for alteration of county and borough boundaries.

Maps and plans of proposed alterations are in HLG 44 below.

HLG 44 LOCAL AUTHORITIES: AREAS, BOUNDARIES, AND STATUS: MAPS AND PLANS.
1894–1938.   609 pieces.   [III 88]

This class contains the maps and plans of proposed alteration in local authority boundaries found in HLG 43. They are arranged as follows:

1–494	1928–1938. County councils arranged alphabetically, with some county boroughs, boroughs, urban district, and rural district councils within each county.
495–507	1927–1936. County borough councils, arranged alphabetically.
508–551	1922–1938. Borough councils.
552–596	1922–1938. Urban district councils.
597–603	1923–1937. Rural district councils.
604–609	1920–1935. Wales.

HLG 45 BURIAL GROUNDS: CORRESPONDENCE AND PAPERS.
1854–1965.   1,400 pieces.

This class contains records concerning burial grounds, crematoria, and mortuaries. There are general papers, regulations, closing orders, extensions, consents to loans, and other transactions. The files are arranged in the usual order of local authorities for England and Wales. *See also* HLG 21.

HLG 46 'O' FILES: GENERAL POLICY AND PROCEDURE.
1852–1927.   135 pieces.

These are files opened before 1919 by the Local Government Board and its predecessors. The few papers subsequent to 1919 are continuations of files begun before. The local authority files to which these relate are in HLG 1 and in both cases the 'O' denotes old papers. Files covering the inter-war period relate to burials, coast protection, housing, allotments, borrowing powers, rating and valuation, roads, acquisition of land, and town planning.

HLG 47 Housing Orders: Correspondence and Papers.
1910–1940.   904 pieces.

This class covers measures taken under Housing Acts, 1890–1936, by Parliament, local authorities, and other bodies, to deal with the problem of slum clearance, over-crowding, and redevelopment of land for housing, and other purposes. The files contain reports of the department's inspectors, district valuers' reports, medical officers of health reports, clearance orders, objections, compulsory purchase orders, and relevant correspondence. Apart from 13 pieces under general papers, covering policy on demolition, closing orders, and slum clearance, the files are listed under local authorities and cite specific cases.

HLG 48 Housing Finance: Correspondence and Papers.
1918–1943.   905 pieces.

These are general papers relating to rents, subsidies, building societies, etc., and housing schemes listed under local authorities. An additional set of general papers and schemes starts at piece 680 and these tend to be later in date but there is considerable overlap.

HLG 49 Local Authorities: Housing: Proposals and Schemes: Correspondence and Papers.
1919–1943.   1,375 pieces.

The Housing, Town Planning, etc. Act, 1919, gave local authorities in England and Wales statutory duties regarding housing; they had to submit to the Minister of Health detailed surveys of housing conditions and needs and proposals for housing and town development. The class contains general papers and proposals listed under local authorities, these include plans, papers on acquisition of land and property, loan sanction, district valuers' and surveyors' reports.

1–11	1919–1933. General papers, including:
4	1920–1921. Building materials supply: reorganisation of department dealing with, and report of Moir Committee.
5–6	1921. Housing Building Costs Committee: appointment, reports, and papers.
7	1933. Departmental Committee on Housing: circulated papers.
10	1923–1924. Labour Party's bill to amend Housing Acts, 1890–1921.
12–870	1905–1940. Housing proposals and schemes, arranged as follows:
12–73	English counties and metropolitan boroughs.
74–495	English county boroughs, boroughs, and urban districts in one alphabetical list.

496–642	English rural districts.
643–700	Public Utility Societies.
701–870	Welsh county boroughs, boroughs, urban districts, and rural districts.
871–887	1919–1941. General papers: housing assisted schemes.
888–1375	1915–1943. Housing proposals and schemes, arranged as follows:
888–924	English counties and metropolitan boroughs.
925–1160	English county boroughs, boroughs, and urban districts, in one alphabetical list.
1161–1370	English rural districts.
1371–1375	Public Utility Societies.

HLG 50   WATER AND SEWERAGE: CORRESPONDENCE AND PAPERS.
       1905–1947.   1,986 pieces.

This class contains local authority and general policy files on water supply, sewerage, sewage disposal, river pollution, and land drainage. They consist of reports, research data, geological and water surveys, local enquiries, discussion on parliamentary bills, and related correspondence. Land drainage is the responsibility of the Ministry of Agriculture and is to be found in MAF 49. The Ministry of Housing and Local Government is concerned only where land is drained into sewers and thence into water courses. The pieces are arranged as follows:

1–140	General papers: sewerage and sewage disposal, river pollution, water supply, land drainage, and papers of the Joint Advisory Committee on River Pollution, Water Advisory Committee, Central Water Advisory Committee, Inland Water Survey Committee, and Regional Water Committee.
141–164	County councils listed alphabetically.
165–836	County borough councils, borough councils, and urban district councils, listed alphabetically.
837–1338	Rural district councils listed alphabetically.
1339–1552	Joint water committees, water boards, drainage boards, sewerage boards, river boards, catchment boards, waterworks companies, and the Port of London Authority.
1553–1639	Wales: local authorities.
1640–1858	1934–1938. Drought returns.
1859–1892	1918–1945. General papers on sewage disposal, regional water committees, and flood prevention.
1894–1986	1920–1947. Local authorities.

HLG 51   LOCAL GOVERNMENT SERVICES: CORRESPONDENCE AND PAPERS.
       1904–1945.   759 pieces.

This class consists of general policy files covering local government administration and finance and includes all subjects where the material available is not sufficient to form separate classes. The files contain Royal Commission reports, departmental committee reports, reports of the department's inspectors, district valuers' reports, orders, approvals, objections, records of loan consents, public local enquiries, and correspondence in connection with the promotion of parliamentary bills relating to a variety of local authority functions. There is some overlapping of subject matter between this class and HLG 1, and HLG 46; HLG 53 contains papers relating to particular local authorities. The general papers are concerned with provision of the following:

Baths and wash houses, and public cleansing.
Highways and private street works.
Public lighting.
Electricity and gas undertakings.
Sea defence.
Markets.
Municipal banks.
Recreation grounds.
Aerodromes.
Miscellaneous: includes Miners Welfare Fund, sailors homes, harbour and pier acts.
Privy conversion.
Local government staff: includes Departmental Committee on Recruitment, 1930–1939.

Specific schemes are listed under local authorities, grouped in the usual way. An additional set of papers starts at piece 553.

HLG 52   LOCAL GOVERNMENT ADMINISTRATION AND FINANCE: GENERAL POLICY AND PROCEDURE.
         1898–1948.   1,189 pieces.

This class consists of general policy files and committee papers, mostly relating to the period 1919–1940, concerned with local government administration and finance. It includes all subjects where the material available has not been considered sufficient to form separate classes. Related papers concerning particular local authorities are to be found in HLG 53. The following list of subjects indicates the wide range of topics covered:

Advertisements, control of.
Aerodromes.
Aged persons, provision of accommodation.
Alkali works.
Ancient monuments and historic buildings, preservation.
Architects registration acts.
Bills, 1931–1933.
Bribery and corruption.
Building and civil engineering, national programme for.
Building law and practices.
Building materials supply.
Building research.
Buildings, control and design.
Built up areas.
Canal boats.
Census.

Charities (Fuel Allotment) Bill in relation to town planning.
Committees:
  Departmental (Moyne) Committee on Housing, 1935.
  Flat Construction.
  Garden City.
  Town and Country Planning Joint Committees.
  Town Planning Advisory Committee.
Compensation and betterment.
Conferences, congresses.
Contracts.
Contributory Pensions Act.
Corporate property.
Correspondence, foreign.
Countryside, preservation of.
Court, production of documents in.
Crown lands.
Development.
Development agreements.
Dock Approaches (Improvements) Bill, 1929.
Drage returns (returns made annually to the Treasury and published as a command paper of expenditure on public social services).
Elections.
Exchequer grants.
Factories and workshops: regulations.
Fine Arts Commission.
Flats for the working classes.
Foreign correspondence.
Housing:
  associations.
  miscellaneous.
  overcrowding.
  prefabricated.
Housing Bill, 1934 and 1935.
Infestation.
Inland waterways, houseboats on.
Injuries.
Interim development (of land).
Kennet Committee, on the restoration of land affected by iron ore workings.
Land charges.
Land restoration.
Law of property.
Laws (expiring) continuance.
Legislation.
Loans.
Local bodies: expenses of members.
Local Government Act, 1929.
Local government acts consolidation.
Local government officers, superannuation and compensation of.
Local inquiries.
London regional planning, standing conference on.
Maps, preparation and reproduction.

Meston Committee on Percentage Exchequer Grants.
Mines and mining subsidences.
Municipal trading.
National economy.
National parks.
Office handbook.
Office procedure and policy.
Office regulations.
Official records.
Parliamentary questions.
Physical education (national).
Planning authorities, circulars issued to.
Planning schemes, miscellaneous.
Population: distribution and trend.
Procedure:
   general, stock forms, memoranda.
   progress reports.
Public health bills.
Public services, co-ordination.
Public works facilities.
Publicity.
Railway works.
Redevelopment schemes.
Ribbon development.
Rights of Way.
Rural amenities.
Rural Resources, National Survey of.
Safety of dams, reservoirs and embankments.
Salt.
Slaughter of animals.
Standardisation.
Stock.
Subsidies, consolidation.
Taxation.
Tents, vans, and sheds.
Town and Country planning.
Town and Country Planning Act, 1932, responsible authorities under s.2.
Town planning:
   Council for National Housing.
   policy and procedure.
Tyneside (Special Derelict Areas).
Widows' and orphans' pensions, powers of local authorities under Contributory
   Pensions Act.
Zoning, density and.

HLG 53   LOCAL GOVERNMENT ADMINISTRATION AND FINANCE: LOCAL
       AUTHORITY FILES.
         1914–1945.   264 pieces.

This class consists of local authority files relating to various functions connected
with local government administration and finance such as investments, sinking

funds, superannuation funds, borrowing powers, audits, housing schemes, loans, etc. The general policy files are in HLG 52. The period covered is mainly 1914–1940. The files are listed by groups of local authorities in the usual way. *See also* HLG 32.

HLG 54 LOCAL AUTHORITIES: BILL PAPERS.
       1913–1940.   482 pieces.

This class contains reports by various ministers, reports by the department's inspectors, objections, general comments and correspondence relating to provisional orders and bills submitted to Parliament by departments, local authorities, water undertakers, railway companies and other bodies. The bills cover a wide range of subjects and include town planning and development, water, gas and electricity supply, compulsory purchase of land and property, sewerage and sewage disposal, transport, roads, railways, fisheries, harbours, bridges, tunnels, and finance. There are general papers and papers concerned with bills arranged according to local authorities, grouped in the usual way, water boards, cemetery boards, water companies and a utility company. An additional set of papers starts at piece 440.

HLG 55 AIR POLLUTION AND SMOKE ABATEMENT: CORRESPONDENCE AND PAPERS.
       1914–1948.   37 pieces.

This class consists of general policy files dealing with smoke abatement and air pollution caused mainly by domestic and industrial smoke. The files contain reports of the Department of Scientific and Industrial Research, various proposals for smoke abatement, legal opinions, departmental conference and committee reports, medical officers of health reports, papers in connection with the promotion of various parliamentary bills and general correspondence.

HLG 56 RATING AND VALUATION: CORRESPONDENCE AND PAPERS.
       1920–1946.   864 pieces.

These are files of the Ministry of Health. They contain legal opinions, departmental and interdepartmental committee reports, district auditors' reports, representations, orders, written evidence and observations, appeals, schemes for consolidation of poor and general rates, local authority statistics, etc. The pieces are listed under the following headings:

1–8	1926–1938. Rules, orders, and forms.
9–26	1920–1940. Railways.
27–32	1924–1937. Sporting rights.
33	1930. Playing fields.
34–61	1923–1939. Rating of Machinery Committee.
62–123	1928–1946. Rating and Valuation (Apportionment) Act, 1928.
124–153	1924–1925. Interdepartmental Committee on the Rating of Plant and Machinery. (Ministry of Health and Secretary for Scotland.)
154–170	1938–1939. Departmental Committee on Valuation for Rating.
171–209A	1926–1934. Rating reform: local statistics, arranged under county councils.
209B	1925–1938. Schemes under the Rating Valuation Act, 1925, listed alphabetically by local authorities.

HLG 57 LOCAL AUTHORITIES, AUDIT OF ACCOUNTS: CORRESPONDENCE AND
        PAPERS.
        1919–1941.   302 pieces.

This class consists of local authority and general files relating to the work of
District Audit between 1919 and 1940. The files contain instructions to auditors,
auditors' reports and decisions, appeals against auditors' decisions, legal opinions,
papers relating to various parliamentary bills, and correspondence dealing with
many aspects of local government expenditure. Files have been kept only from
selected local authorities. An additional set of papers starts at piece 290.

HLG 58 LOCAL AUTHORITY BYE-LAWS: CORRESPONDENCE AND PAPERS.
        1915–1940.   139 pieces.

This class consists of correspondence and papers (including model bye-laws)
relating to the bye-laws deposited in HLG 25. There are a number of general papers
and the rest of the pieces are listed by local authorities. An additional set of papers
starts at piece 119.

HLG 66 SEALED ORDERS AND SEALED PLANS: REGISTERS AND INDEXES.
        1835–1952.   56 pieces.

This class consists of registers and indexes relating to Legal Branch Orders
(HLG 26) and Sealed Plans (HLG 23).

HLG 68 100,000 SERIES FILES.
        1919–1945.   72 pieces.

These papers were originally registered with security classification. They cover a
wide variety of functions and supplement papers contained in other HLG classes.
The class list is preceded by an index. The topics covered are:

Building laws and regulations.
Civil defence.
Defence programme: acquisition of land.
Distress: prevention and relief of, including Interdepartmental Committee on
    Relief in Kind in Wartime (Food (Defence Plans) Department, Ministries of
    Health, Labour and Pensions, Unemployment Assistance Board, and the
    Treasury). See also AST 11.
Highway administration: including Restriction of Ribbon Development Bill,
    1935.
Housing:
    1920–22, closing down of Addison Scheme.
    1933–34, proposals for legislation.
    1936, Rent Restrictions Bill.
Landlord and tenant: 1919–21, Select Committee on Business Premises.
Legislation:
    1929–1930, Local Authorities (Enabling) Bill on municipal trading.
    1930, Land Drainage Bill.
    1933–34, housing proposals.
    1934–37, proposed programme of legislation.

1936, Tithe Bill.

1937, Population statistics: proposed legislation to obtain from census.

1938–1939, local government emergency legislation.

1938–1939, war-time legislation, sub-committee.

Local Government, includes:

1920–26, enforcement of trade unionism.

1936–1940, issue of stock to local authorities.

1923, poor law reform; organisation and function of local authorities.

1926, proposal for quaternary elections.

1926–1927, strike levy of trade unions.

National expenditure: 1921 and 1931 proposed reductions.

National parks, 1937–1939: Exchequer grant.

National physical education, 1936–1938.

Poor law reform, 1923–1927.

Poor law unions, 1922–1928.

Population: Royal Commission on Geographical Distribution of Industrial
   Population, 1937–1940, establishment and terms of reference. *See also* HLG 27.

Rating reform, 1927–1928.

Rating and valuation, 1937–1938.

Silver jubilee medal, 1935.

Town and country planning, 1931.

Welwyn Garden City, special investigation, 1929.

HLG 70   RATING AND VALUATION: ASSESSMENT COMMITTEES AND LOCAL
   VALUATION PANELS AND COURT MINUTES.
   1926–1956.   59 pieces.

This class contains records relating to valuation of hereditaments for the general
rate. Assessment committees were established in 1925 to hear objections to the
draft valuation list and revise it accordingly. Sample areas only are included, and
only the records of West Middlesex and Manchester fall within the inter-war period.

NATIONAL ASSISTANCE BOARD

The Board was originally established as the Unemployment Assistance Board in
1934, and was renamed the Assistance Board in 1940 and the National Assistance
Board in 1948. In 1966 its functions were divided between the newly formed
Ministry of Social Security and the Supplementary Benefits Commission.

AST 1   ASSISTANCE AND PENSIONS: REPRESENTATIVE CASE PAPERS.
   1935–1969.   56 pieces.   [II 217].   Closed for 100 years.

AST 3   LOCAL PENSION COMMITTEES: REPRESENTATIVE MINUTE BOOKS AND
   REGISTERS.
   1908–1948.   47 pieces.   [II 217].   Closed for 100 years.

The local pension committees were set up under the Old Age Pensions Act, 1908,
and were successively supervised by the Local Government Board, the Ministry of
Health, and the Ministry of National Insurance, until 1948 when they and their

records were transferred to the National Assistance Board. This class contains a representative selection of minute books and registers of claims.

AST 4   OLD AGE PENSION APPEALS: REPRESENTATIVE CASE PAPERS.
          1911–1946.   1 piece.   [II 218].   Closed for 100 years.

A representative selection of case papers on appeals against decisions of the local pension committees dealt with by the central pension authority under the Old Age Pensions Acts, 1908 and 1936, and the Blind Persons Acts, 1920 to 1938.

AST 5   ADVISORY COMMITTEES: REPRESENTATIVE MINUTES.
          1936–1945.   4 pieces.   [II 218].   Closed for 100 years.

Minutes of selected advisory committees set up under the Unemployment Act, 1934. The work of the committees was extended by the Old Age and Widows Pensions Act, 1940, and the National Assistance Act, 1948.

AST 7   GENERAL FILES.
          1910–1958.   683 pieces.

This class consists of files covering a wide variety of subjects which do not fall easily into any other class. The papers relate to the administration of the Unemployment Assistance Scheme, explaining the origin and constitution of the Unemployment Assistance Board set up under Part II of the Unemployment Act 1934. The early files deal with the non-contributory pensions scheme.

The files are listed in chronological order and there is a comprehensive subject index.

AST 8   VAGRANCY FILES.
          1925–1950.   44 pieces.

These records were transferred from the Ministry of Health to the Board in 1948. The files mainly relate to the administration of casual wards and reception centres in selected parts of England. The files are arranged chronologically in the following groups:

1–18   1932–1948. London County Council.

19–23   1931–1950. Berkshire, Buckinghamshire, and Oxfordshire Joint Vagrancy Committee.

24–28   1934–1948. Midlands and Northern Home Counties Joint Vagrancy Committee.

29–32   1931–1947. South Eastern Counties Joint Vagrancy Committee.

33–36   1925–1947. Miscellaneous: report on visit to Germany, complaints, co-operation with the Forestry Commission.

AST 9   ESTABLISHMENT.
          1933–1951.   100 pieces.

Apart from normal establishment matters, the following files are of more general interest:

16	1937. Old Age Pensions (non-contributory): administration by Customs and Excise.
25	1939. Memorandum on Board's work prepared for Royal Commission on Workmen's Compensation.
92–96	1935. Reports from district officers on relations between Board's officers and applicants.

AST 10 TRAINING.
1934–1946. 49 pieces.

These records relate to the activities of the Board in carrying out duties under the Unemployment Assistance Act, 1934, to prepare applicants for entry into, or return to, regular employment. Before 1948, the Board utilised existing training facilities provided by voluntary organisations, local authorities, and government departments, particularly those of the Ministry of Labour. The files refer both to particular schemes and general policy. The class contains papers of the Committee of Enquiry into schemes of land settlement for the unemployed, 1938–1940, and also those of the Land Settlement Association.

AST 11 WARTIME FUNCTIONS.
1914–1954. 217 pieces.

These records relate to additional relief duties undertaken by the Board in wartime. Except for the following references, all concern the 1939–1945 War.

1–5	1926–1938. Wartime organisation for the prevention and relief of distress: proceedings of Interdepartmental Conference, October 1936, and papers of the Interdepartmental Committee (Ministries of Labour, Pensions, and Health, Scottish Office, Unemployment Assistance Board, Treasury, and War Office). *See also* HLG 68.
29–30	1938–1939. Evacuation: refugees, homeless persons.
57–61, 94, 122	1914–1939. The Forces: policy and procedure on dependants' allowances.
129	1935–1939. Territorial Army proficiency grant: treatment in assessing need.
130	1937. Service in the Forces: 'normal occupation' qualifications.

AST 12 BOARD PAPERS.
1934–1946. 51 pieces.

This class contains memoranda, minutes, district officers' reports, and papers of sub-committees of the Unemployment Assistance Board and the Assistance Board.

1–12	1934–1940. Board's memoranda.
15–24	1934–1940. Minutes of meetings of Unemployment Assistance Board.
26–28	1935–1939. Annual Reports and background papers.
33–43	1937–1939. District officers' reports for selected areas.
44–47	1934–1935. Committees: standing committee and sub-committees, minutes, correspondence, and papers.

50	1935–1941. Conference of regional officers.
131–132	1939. Military Training Act and Reserve Auxiliary Forces Act, 1939: dependants' allowances.
218–224	1938–1940. Civil defence and assistance to persons in need.

AST 13   CODES OF INSTRUCTIONS AND CIRCULARS.
           1934–1967.   11 pieces.

These were issued to local offices and cover unemployment assistance, supplementary and old age pensions, special wartime assistance, national assistance, legal aid, and work undertaken as an agency for other government departments. The papers are bound in volumes, there is no index but some volumes are headed by a list of titles. The volumes are grouped as follows:

1	1934–1936. Assistance circulars.
2	1937–1939. Assistance circulars.
3	1939. Defence procedure: assistance circulars.

AST 14   SOLICITOR'S FILES.
           1925–1941.   75 pieces.

The Solicitor of the Unemployment Assistance Board for 1934 to 1940 was the Solicitor of the Ministry of Labour. Files in this class contain correspondence of the Assistant Solicitor of the Unemployment Assistance Board and the Assistance Board relating to the interpretation of legislation, together with copies of legal opinions on individual cases and points of general policy referred to the Solicitor.

MINISTRY OF PENSIONS AND NATIONAL INSURANCE

A Ministry of Pensions was set up in 1917 to deal with disablement pensions and allowances for the armed forces. After the war it was decided that the Ministry should deal only with pensions awarded for service during the war of 1914–1918 and earlier wars; administration of disablement pensions arising out of service in peace-time prior to the war and subsequent to September, 1921, was transferred back to the Service Departments to be handled in conjunction with other service pensions based on years of service, good conduct, etc. The administration of officers' wounds pensions was transferred to the Ministry of Pensions which thus assumed responsibility for all disablement pensions and allowances awarded for wartime service.

After the outbreak of the Second World War the Ministry of Pensions was made responsible for pensions and allowances on account of disablement or death arising out of wartime service from September, 1939. The Ministry also administered the new Personal Injuries (Civilians) Scheme.

The Ministry of National Insurance was established in 1945 to administer health insurance, contributory old-age, widows', and orphans' pensions, unemployment insurance, workmen's compensation, to determine non-contributory pension appeals, and to issue regulations governing the administration of national assistance. Later in the year it was given additional functions under the Family Allowances Act.

In 1953 the two Ministries were merged to form the Ministry of Pensions and National Insurance, except that certain powers concerning medical treatment were transferred to the Ministry of Health and the Secretary of State for Scotland. In 1966 the ministry became part of the Ministry of Social Security.

PIN 1   COMMITTEES.
         1919–1931.   5 pieces.   [III 102]

1   1922–1923. Interdepartmental Committee on Health and Unemployment Insurance (Watson): Ministry papers on the Committee and copies of 1st, 2nd, and 3rd interim reports. For the records of the Committee, *see* PIN 4.

2–5   1923–1931. Committee on Insurance and other Social Services, (Anderson), 1923–25: incomplete set of papers concerning the work of the Committee and copies of the 1st, 2nd, and 3rd interim reports.

PIN 2   NATIONAL HEALTH INSURANCE COMMISSIONS AND JOINT COMMITTEE.
         1911–1948.   49 pieces.   [III 103]

Four National Health Insurance Commissions (for England, Scotland, Wales, and Ireland) were set up under the National Insurance Act, 1911. They were supervised by a Joint Committee. The Ministry of Health in 1919 took over the powers and duties of the English and Welsh Insurance Commissioners and a new Joint Committee was formed consisting of the Minister of Health, (chairman), and representatives of Wales, Scotland, and Ireland (later Northern Ireland). The Committee was dissolved in 1948.

1–14   1911–1948. Minute books of the Joint Committee, indexed.

42   1918–1919. Advisory Committees: draft revised model rules for approved societies.

44   1919. Revision of conditions of medical service: memorandum and report.

45   1921. Insurance committee elections, 1921: forms and procedure.

49   1916–1919. Summaries of legal branch opinions: indexed.

Other records of the Commissions and the Joint Committee are to be found in a number of other classes:

Minutes of a sub-committee of the Joint Committee on Excessive Sickness Claims in 1930, union statistical tables, are in PIN 4.

Minutes and correspondence of the Welsh Insurance Commission are in MH 49.

Correspondence of the English Commission and Secretariat of the Joint Committee with other government departments, local insurance committees, and approved societies, is in MH 62 and MH 81.

Records of London Insurance Committee are in MH 65.

Records of selected local insurance committees for Bedfordshire, Merioneth, and Middlesex, and for the county boroughs of Birmingham, Kingston-upon-Hull, Newcastle-upon-Tyne, and Salford, are in MH 69.

Records of the Consultative Council on National Health Insurance are in PIN 5, and of the Welsh Consultative Council in MH 73 and PIN 5/48.

PIN 3   NATIONAL INSURANCE, PENSIONS, AND UNEMPLOYMENT INSURANCE ACTS:
         BILL PAPERS.
         1907–1966.   111 pieces.   [III 103]

These are bound volumes which include memoranda, correspondence, draft
bills, proposed amendments, etc. on above Acts. The class includes a volume on the
poor law 1934. There are references to bills to be found in other classes also.

PIN 4   PENSIONS AND INSURANCE.
         1911–1958.   182 pieces.   [III 103]

These are Ministry of Health records which passed to the Ministry of National
Insurance in 1945. The files are arranged in sections, an alphabetical key to which is
given at the head of the class.

6	1938. Committee on Inter-County Migration.
11	1932. National Health Insurance Bill, proposed amendments.
13	1935. Widows', Orphans', Old Age Pensions Amendment Bill: Ministry proposals on.
14	1921–1931. Nursing Service for Insured Persons: negotiations with Queen Victoria's Jubilee Institute for Nurses, and approved societies.
15–16	1921–1934. Reading scheme for provision of nursing services for insured persons.
18–25	1922–1923. Interdepartmental Committee on Health and Unemployment Insurance (Watson): records of the Committee. For Ministry comments, *see* PIN 1.
26	1923. Financial sources of National Health Insurance Scheme: statistics, reports by financial advisers.
27–44	1925–1932. Approved societies administration: returns of references to regional medical officers for each society, minutes and statistics from sub-committee of National Health Insurance Joint Committee on excessive sickness claims, 1930; Scottish morbidity statistics, 1930–32; statistics for sickness claims during coal strike in South Wales, 1930–31; disease in the cotton industry.
45–47	1927–1931. Insurability: miscellaneous papers.
49–51	1919–1939. Insurability: regulations.
53–57	1918–1938. Collection of contributions: regulations.
58	1936. Investigation into expenditure by societies on disablement benefits.
59–66	1936–1937. Widows', Orphans', and Old Age Contributory Pensions, Special Voluntary Contributions Bill, 1937; interpretations.
67–89	1925–1939. Contributory pensions: regulations, general papers, reciprocal arrangements in Ireland.
91–92	1929–1932. Committee on Ministers' Powers (Donoughmore): minutes and correspondence. *See also* MH 71/1–3 *and* LCO 2.
93	1937. Pension plan of National Council of Labour.
94	1920–1924. Pensions Increase Act, 1925.

95–110; 119–122	1925–1935. Widows' Orphans' and Old Age Contributory Pensions Act, 1925: bill papers, interpretations, application to Northern Ireland.
112	1927–1928. Old Age Pensions Bill, 1927.
113	1926–1930. National Health and Pensions Insurance: reciprocal arrangements with Dominions.
114	1922–1927. National Health Insurance Fund: Irish Free State, transfer of balance.
115–116	1924–1929. Old Age Pensions: patients in poor law institutions who contributed to their cost of maintenance.
117–118	1928–1930. National Health Insurance Bill, 1928; papers.
123–124	1927–1934. National Insurance and Pensions Insurance: non-compliance, registration of trustees for investments.
125–126	1925–1938. Old Age Pensions Acts, 1908–1924: administration.
127–129	1925–1937. Circulars issued by Ministry of Health to outside staff relating to pensions and insurance.
130–131	1929–1937. Health and Pensions: collection of contributions, age verification.
132–137	1928–1937. Widows' Orphans' and Old Age Pensions Bill, 1929: amendments, interpretations.
138	1932–1937. Royal Commission on Unemployment Insurance: increase of remuneration limit for non-manual workers.
141–142	1934–1935. Health and Pensions legislation: observations by outside staff, questions arising from certain Scottish decisions.
143	1932–1935. International Labour Office: preparations of 'International Year Book of Social Services' for 1930 and 1933.
144–152	1925–1944. Contributions: refunds, non-compliance, interdepartmental committee on irregular stamping.
162–169	1925–1940. Insurability: voluntary contributions and exceptions.
178–182	1911–1941. Miscellaneous: medical benefits review, offences, Unemployment Insurance Bill, 1938–1939, disqualification of patients in mental hospitals from old-age pensions.

PIN 5   CONSULTATIVE COUNCIL ON NATIONAL HEALTH INSURANCE (APPROVED SOCIETIES' WORK).
1919–1940.   48 pieces.   [III 103]

The Consultative Council was an advisory body and was empowered not only to consider proposals submitted to it but also to initiate them.

1–2	1919. Composition of Council.
3	1919. Ministry of Health Act, 1919: draft regulations.
4	1919. Approved Societies: administration allowance.
5–6	1919–1925. Composition of Council.
7–17	1925–1937. Sick visiting, memoranda on medical benefit, etc., and sub-committees on maternity benefit, dental benefit, workmen's compensation, capitation fees for doctors.

| 18–43 | 1919–1940. Minutes of meetings, including appointment of sub-committees on Central Index Register, 1925, to record membership of insurance scheme. |

44   1919–1920. Insurance Medical Records Committee: minutes, memoranda, and draft report.

45–46   1922–1925. Central Index Committee: minutes, organisation.

47   1922–1927. Finance Sub-Committee: minutes.

48   1922–1924. Welsh Consultative Council: proposal for Committee on National Health Insurance. *See also* MH 73 *and* note to PIN 2.

PIN 6   ROYAL COMMISSION ON UNEMPLOYMENT INSURANCE.
1930–1934.   97 pieces.   [III 103]

These records were taken over from the Ministry of Labour in 1944: they include correspondence, working papers, and evidence to the Commission. The final report of the Commission (Cmd. 4185) was published in 1932.

PIN 7   LABOUR EXCHANGES AND UNEMPLOYMENT INSURANCE.
1912–1950.   2,267 pieces.   [III 104]

These are general policy files on unemployment insurance, being records trans-ferred from the Ministry of Labour to the Ministry of National Insurance in 1944. The pieces are grouped under a few general headings, but the subject matter of each overlaps considerably.

6–12   1917–1918. Munitions Workers Act, 1916: amendments, interpreta-tions, draft unemployment insurance scheme by W. H. Beveridge.

13   1918. Proposed universal scheme for contributory unemployment insurance.

14–46   1918–1920. Out-of-Work Donation, benefits under, special groups; Labour Resettlement Committee; Home Affairs Committee circulars to labour exchanges.

47–108   1920–1930. Unemployment Insurance Acts: interpretation and working of the Acts. The files concern applications to special groups, deputations to ministers, Unemployed Workers Committee Move-ment, relation between unemployment benefit and poor law relief, and reports from Ministry of Labour divisional controllers during the General Strike. Also included are references to the following committees:

69   1923. Trade Dispute Disqualification committee: minutes.
71   1923. Departmental Committee on Outworkers.
92   1927–1928. Committee on Blanesborough Report: ad-ministrative allowances made to associations.

109–200   1920–1948. Employment and Training Department: schemes for the unemployed, policy towards deputations and hunger marches, transitional payments, trade union levies, dependants' allowances, reports on unemployment, Orders in Council arising out of National Economy Act, 1931. The following committees and commissions are mentioned:

111   1929–1930. Departmental Committee on the Administration of Unemployment Insurance.

118   1928–1931. Workmen's Compensation Committee Report.

178   1939–1944. Royal Commission on Workmen's Compensation: report by Ministry of Labour.

179,   1939. Unemployment Insurance Statutory Committee.
181

192   1927–1930. Interdepartmental committee to consider payment of contributions by means of impressed stamps.

199   1931. Transitional Payments Committee, minutes.

212–226   1934–1940. Unemployment Insurance Statutory Committee: financial position of unemployment fund, reports, correspondence, papers.

PIN 9   WAR PENSION COMMITTEES.
        1923–1961.   54 pieces.   [III 104]

Records of selected areas; all files extend beyond 1940, some will be open in 1972.

PIN 10   NATIONAL INSURANCE STAMPS.
         1912–1948.   23 pieces.   [III 104]

Samples of stamps and correspondence on their design and production. *See also* PIN 4/181.

PIN 11   WORKMEN'S COMPENSATION: BILL PAPERS.
         1906–1941.   16 pieces.

This class contains papers on Workmen's Compensation Bills, 1906–31, and notes on the Workmen's Compensation Conference, 1922. Also included are papers on the Silicosis and Asbestosis Bill, 1930, and the Adoption of Children Bill, 1934.

PIN 12   WORKMEN'S COMPENSATION: CORRESPONDENCE.
         1900–1956.   120 pieces.

Former Home Office files of correspondence relating to various workmen's compensation schemes, appointment and fees of medical referees, reports on various industries. Also included are references to the following committees.

78   1936–1938. Departmental Committee on Workmen's Compensation (Stewart): publication of evidence and observations on report.

85   1938–1945. Departmental Committee on Alternative Remedies: terms of reference, minutes, reports, etc.

PIN 13   DETERMINATIONS UNDER NATIONAL HEALTH INSURANCE ACTS.
         1912–1949.   947 pieces.   Closed for 75 years.

PIN 14   CODES AND INSTRUCTIONS.
         1918–1955.   15 pieces.

Manuals of codes sent to local offices outlining conditions on which a pension may be granted. Before 1948 they deal only with pensions arising out of war service.

PIN 15 WAR DISABILITY PENSIONS.
   1907–1956.   2,173 pieces.

These files deal with the award and administration of war pensions from 1916.

MINISTRY OF EDUCATION

In 1899 the Board of Education was established, consisting of a President and the chief Ministers of State, to supervise educational matters in England and Wales. The Education Acts of 1902 and 1918 while greatly developing the local educational organisation made no further change in the constitution of the central authority. The reform of the public education system by the Education Act of 1944, however, abolished the Board, whose powers had always been exercised by the President alone, and gave the head of the department the title and authority of a Minister. In 1964, the Ministry of Education and the office of Minister of Science were merged to form the new Department of Education and Science, which also took over certain residuary functions of the Lord President of the Council.

School administration has remained primarily a local government service carried out subject to certain supervisory powers of the central departments. Responsibility for university finance was transferred in 1919 to the Treasury which acts through the University Grants Committee (*see* UGC group). Responsibility for the provision of, and financial assistance to, agricultural education below the university level is shared between the education and agricultural departments.

Transfers of functions since 1918 are set out below, except those between the Ministry and the other social service departments which are listed at the beginning of this section:

1919   From the Paymaster General, payment of teachers' pensions.
        To the Department of Scientific and Industrial Research, the Geological Survey.

1923   To the Ministry of Labour, oversight and grant aid of classes and centres provided by local education authorities for unemployed youth.

1926   To the Paymaster General, payment of teachers' pensions.

1927   To the Ministry of Labour, responsibility for youth employment work.

1945   To the Ministry of Labour and National Service, training of blind and physically handicapped persons not under 16 years.

1949   From the Charity Commissioners, jurisdiction over quasi-educational trusts, (charitable trusts, whose purpose was wholly educational had been handled by the Board of Education since its inception.)
        From the Board of Trade, responsibility for the Imperial Institute except for its scientific and technical work which was transferred to the Colonial Office.

1953   To the Prison Commission, financial responsibility for education in prisons and borstals.

1957   Registration of independent schools begins.

1959	Minister of Science appointed taking over responsibility for five research committees of the Privy Council.
1965	To newly formed Ministry of Overseas Development, some functions concerning the aid and development work of the United Nations.

1965   The Department of Education and Science became responsible for the Medical Research Council, the Agricultural Research Council, and two new research councils, the Science Research Council and the Natural Environment Research Council.

The Science Research Council took over the functions of the Department of Scientific and Industrial Research in relation to research grants and postgraduate training awards not within the fields of other Councils. It took over responsibility for the Radio Research Station, the National Institute for Research into Nuclear Science, the Royal Observatories, the Scientific Space Research Programme, and advises on relations with international organisations for nuclear and space research.

The Natural Environment Research Council took over the Nature Conservancy, the Geological Survey and Museum, the Hydrology Research Unit, the National Institute of Oceanography, and the functions of the Development Commission in relation to marine and freshwater biology and fishery research.

The Secretary of State appointed a Council for Scientific Policy to advise him on the allocation of resources to the four Research Councils. The Social Science Research Council was formed at the end of 1965 under the direction and financial control of the Department of Education and Science. The Council supports social science research, advises the government, and maintains general liaison throughout the field.

1970	Welsh education transferred to Welsh Office.
1971	From the Ministry of Health, education of mentally handicapped children.

The class lists to this group are very comprehensive, giving much historical information as an introduction to each set of records. In the Round Room are 'Notes on the Ministry of Education Records'. Written in 1955 this contains notes on records then at the P.R.O. and in the Ministry, and also records concerning education transferred to the P.R.O. by other departments.

ED 5   COMPULSORY PURCHASE FILES.
        1873–1922.   201 pieces.

Until 1915 local education authorities wanting land presented petitions to the Board of Education. In 1919 a new procedure was adopted and papers relating to compulsory purchase since then have been put on the files for the schools concerned. This class contains only two pieces in the inter-war period relating to the London County Council.

ED 7   ELEMENTARY EDUCATION: PUBLIC ELEMENTARY SCHOOLS, PRELIMINARY STATEMENTS.
        1846–1924.   172 pieces.   [II 112]

Preliminary statements were required by the Board of Education before a school was placed on the list of schools in receipt of annual grant. The form called for details of the tenure of the school, when established, accommodation and staffing, and the school's income and expenditure. Modified statements are still required for new schools; since 1924 they have been placed on school files. Correspondence in connection with preliminary statements may be found in ED 16, 20, 21. Preliminary statements for special schools are in ED 32. The pieces are undated and listed by counties.

ED 8   VARIOUS: SPECIMEN FORMS.
        1846–1924.   101 pieces.   [II 116]

A chronological series of specimens of obsolete forms.

ED 10   GENERAL EDUCATION: GENERAL FILES.
        1872–1945.   311 pieces.   [II 110]

These general files relate to educational subjects common to, or of a nature not restricted within the limits of, elementary and secondary education. The subjects covered include papers defining the internal arrangements of the Board's administration; the Board's relation to, and co-operation with, local government; draft schemes relating to educational charities, and various regulations and parliamentary documents; the Board's spheres of function regarding educational matters also within the scope of other government departments; financial matters, the formation and growth of certain educational and semi-educational bodies; and the effect of non-educational legislation upon the work of the Board. The series has been heavily weeded.

The class list is preceded by an alphabetical list of subject headings; those which contain inter-war material are given below. Many of these have sub-headings which are given where of particular interest:

Accounts and finance.
Acts: Unemployment Insurance, Pensions, Town Planning.
Air raid precautions.
Approved schools.
Board of Trade: granting of licences under Companies Act.
Church of England.
Clothes rationing.
Committees.
Defence, general regulations.
Education policy.
Educational charities.
Equipment.
Evacuation.
Grants.
Land.
League of Nations.
Local education authorities.
Local government.
National Fitness Council (1937–39).
National Service.
Northern Ireland.

Parliamentary bills, orders, and municipal charters of incorporation. *See also* PC 1.

Play centres.

Post-primary education.

Procedure.

Regulations.

Road safety.

Royal charters.

Royal Commission on Historical Monuments.

School journeys.

Social and physical training.

Statistics.

Teachers.

University constituencies.

War, 1914–18.

War, 1939–45.

ED 11   ELEMENTARY EDUCATION: GENERAL FILES.
          1848–1945.   315 pieces.   [II 112]

This, like other 'General' series of files throughout the group, is concerned with the consideration and formation of the Board's policy under various acts and regulations; the series also takes in aspects of procedure and organisation. The class list is preceded by an alphabetical list of subject headings, those containing inter-war material are given below. Many have several sub-headings which are given where of special interest.

Accounts and finance.

Act on summer time.

Broadcasting.

Census.

Cinematographs.

Code of regulations for public elementary schools.

Committees: cost of school buildings, 1934; unemployment grants, 1924–1932.

Education.

Educational endowments.

Examinations.

Homecraft movement.

Illiteracy.

Inspection.

Managers.

Meals.

Mutual service method.

National Society.

Procedure.

Public enquiries.

Pupils: school leaving age, canal boat acts, employment, institution schools.

Rural education.

Safety first.

Schools: administration, etc.

Statistics.

Syllabuses.
Teachers.
See also ED 92.

ED 12   SECONDARY EDUCATION: GENERAL FILES.
        1878–1946.   530 pieces.   [II 113]

The topics covered here include: regulations for secondary schools 1902–4 and subsequently; memoranda and reports concerning the teaching of specific subjects; and conditions for the payment of grants and the provision of advanced courses. There are also papers on the Board's policy on examinations, and the use made by local authorities of powers under Education Act, 1921. Many papers were destroyed; some of particular interest which survived concern the protests evoked against restrictions imposed by the regulations of 1922–23 and 1933–34 (listed under Regulations). Again the class list is preceded by a similar type of alphabetical index as in ED 10 and 11:

Accounts.
Acts, education.
Courses.
Endowments.
Examinations.
Inspection.
Miscellaneous: homework, esperanto, school libraries, theatre visits.
Procedure.
Pupils.
Regulations.
Religious instruction.
Schools.
Teachers.
Timetable and curricula.
War, 1914–18.

ED 13   GENERAL EDUCATION: SCHEMES UNDER THE 1918 AND 1921 ACTS:
        GENERAL FILES.
        1918–1943.   19 pieces.   [II 110]

These are concerned with the general policy governing the preparation and submission by local education authorities for approval by the Board of Education of schemes showing how local education authorities proposed to discharge their responsibilities under the Education Acts. Administrative memoranda to local education authorities and a series of internal procedure instructions were issued, covering the approval of schemes, sites and building, loan sanction, the cost of secondary school equipment, and the recognition of private schools as efficient but not for the payment of grant. The files in the list are fully described. *See also* ED 120.

ED 14   ELEMENTARY EDUCATION: LONDON GENERAL FILES.
        1870–1923.   106 pieces.   [II 112]

The general files are concerned with the problems which confronted the London School Board on assuming the powers and carrying out the duties of the Elementary

Education Act, 1870, and subsequent education acts. The series is unique. Comparable papers for other authorities appear on the general files and the local education authorities series of files. The files are grouped under subject headings and cover many aspects of school administration and finance, but only a few files extend into the inter-war period.

ED 15   INDEPENDENT AND PRIVATE SCHOOLS: PRIVATE SCHOOLS NOT
          RECOGNISED FOR GRANTS OR EFFICIENCY: RETURNS.
          1919–1944.   56 pieces.   [II 114]

Returns were required under the 1918 and 1921 Acts, as an attempt to obtain a census of private schools. This excluded: schools in receipt of grants from the Board of Education or Ministry of Agriculture and Fisheries; elementary schools certified and secondary schools recognised as efficient; universities and university colleges; poor law schools; schools certified under the Children Act, 1908; and educational establishments administered by the Army Council or Admiralty. The information available is uneven. Most of the forms for institutions concerned with art, commerce, or professional training have survived; those for elementary or secondary schools have been destroyed. Some authorities added accommodation figures, age-range, etc. The returns are arranged by county for England and Wales. Few returns survive for Wales before 1930.

ED 16   ELEMENTARY EDUCATION: LOCAL EDUCATION AUTHORITY: SUPPLY
          FILES.
          1870–1945.   837 pieces.   [II 112]

This class contains correspondence with local education authorities about the provision of schooling. Before 1921 the papers are concerned with industrial schools, evening schools, religious instruction, provision for 'half-time' scholars, and the introduction of a Black List of sub-standard schools. After 1921 they cover provision of primary education on an area basis, special category schools, and advanced elementary schools, precedent papers, inspectors' reports, complaints by parents, and alterations and adjustments of boundaries affecting public elementary schools. The files are not described. From 1903–1921 the files are arranged by English and Welsh counties, including Part III authorities which were boroughs of over 10,000 people and urban district councils of over 20,000 recognised as the local education authority for elementary education under Part III of the 1902 Education Act. The Isle of Man and the Channel Islands are also listed. After 1921 the arrangement is by counties (including Part III authorities) and county boroughs for England and Wales.

ED 18   ELEMENTARY EDUCATION: LOCAL EDUCATION AUTHORITY:
          ATTENDANCE FILES.
          1871–1945.   747 pieces.   [II 113]

This class contains papers on enforcement and other aspects of school attendance dealt with by school boards and local education authorities. Aspects of attendance dealt with include bye-laws authorised under the Elementary Education Act, 1870, the restrictions of the 1918 Education Act on the employment of children, the duty expressed in the 1921 Education Act to cause every child to receive education between the ages of 5 and 14 years, and subsequent proposals by local education authorities to raise the school leaving age to 15.

The contents of the files are not described in the list. Before 1927 they are arranged in county order for England and Wales; and subsequent files are in county and county borough order. No papers have been retained for a number of minor authorities. Some aspects of attendance are dealt with in ED 19.

ED 19   ELEMENTARY EDUCATION: LOCAL EDUCATION AUTHORITY CODE FILES.
1903–1935.   568 pieces.   [II 113]

These relate to administration of the codes of regulations of 1903 to 1935, in particular staffing, approval for the purposes of a grant, and some aspects of school attendance. There are also some inspectors' general reports. Many papers have a precedent value beyond the area concerned. The files are again listed only by name of local authority. They are arranged by counties in England, Wales and the Isle of Man up to 1921, and by county and county borough from 1922 to 1935.

ED 20   ELEMENTARY EDUCATION: HIGHER ELEMENTARY SCHOOL FILES.
1896–1926.   174 pieces.   [II 113]

These relate to schools recognised or proposed for recognition as higher elementary schools, following the Board of Education's minute of April 1900 recognising a class of public elementary schools providing a graduated course of elementary science and receiving higher rate of grant. When the Education Act of 1918 came in, the Board withdrew its regulations for higher elementary schools and most of those then in existence sought recognition as central or secondary schools. Preliminary statements for higher elementary schools are in ED 7. The files are for named schools arranged under counties.

ED 21   ELEMENTARY EDUCATION: PUBLIC ELEMENTARY SCHOOL FILES.
1857–1946.   61,214 pieces.   [II 113]

These are files of individual public elementary schools, proposed elementary schools, and schools given temporary approval. Some files deal with important national issues, others with matters relating only to the individual school such as adequacy of accommodation, etc. The files also contain reports of inspectors and correspondence between the Board of Education and the bodies responsible for the schools. The pieces are listed by name of school and arranged alphabetically under counties for England and Wales and the Isle of Man. There are so far four chronological series as follows:

1–754   Schools closed prior to 1906, a few files stretch beyond 1918.
755–23,465   1857–1918.
23,466–47,226   1919–1935.
47,227–61,214   1936–1946.

ED 22   INSPECTORATE: MEMORANDA.
1878–1941.   233 pieces.   [II 114]

These are memoranda to inspectors on a wide range of subjects to give them background information. The class is divided into three series: 1878–1921, 1922–1936, and 1937–1941. Within each series the pieces are fully described and listed in chronological order under the following headings: elementary schools, schools of art, secondary schools, technical colleges, training colleges, Welsh Department, junior instruction centres, and a general section. Not all the headings appear in each series.

ED 23   ESTABLISHMENT FILES.
     1835–1946.   814 pieces.   [II 114]

These papers portray the Board of Education's policy in applying Treasury regulations and Civil Service Commission rules regarding the appointment, pay, promotion, grading, general conditions of service, and superannuation of staff. Covered also are financial arrangements and internal organisation. The papers are fully described and there is a key to arrangement.

ED 24   PRIVATE OFFICE AND PARLIAMENTARY: PRIVATE OFFICE PAPERS:
     SERIES I.
     1,851–1936.   2,141 pieces.   [II 116]

These consist of confidential minutes, memoranda, and correspondence, of the President of the Board of Education. They contain also draft bills, departmental committee reports, and House of Commons returns. The draft bill papers are supplemented by those in ED 31. The class is preceded by an alphabetical index which covers the whole range of education policy and administration.

ED 25   EXTERNAL RELATIONS: UNIVERSITIES BUREAU OF THE BRITISH EMPIRE
     AND BRITISH NATIONAL COMMITTEE ON INTELLECTUAL CO-OPERATION:
     PAPERS.
     1922–1946.   95 pieces.   [II 114]

In 1921 the International Committee on Intellectual Co-operation was established under the auspices of the League of Nations; and individual member nations were encouraged to form National Committees from which delegates could be sent to conferences of the International Committee. Before 1928, Great Britain was represented by the Universities Bureau of the British Empire but in that year a British National Committee was formed which acted as an advisory body to the Government and administered a small grant made to facilitate the exchange of teachers with other countries. In 1931 an executive committee of the International Committee was formed and the status of the National Committees raised but the British National Committee failed to get enough funds from the Government and ended in 1939. The class consists of minutes and papers including those of the International Committee on Intellectual Co-operation, the International Conference on Higher Education, 1937, the International Institute of Intellectual Co-operation, Paris, the International Student Organisations' Representatives Committee, and the National Committees' Conference of 1937. There is correspondence with Professor Gilbert Murray and papers relating to research and educational institutes in Great Britain.

ED 26   EXTERNAL RELATIONS: IMPERIAL INSTITUTE FILES.
     1904–1948.   285 pieces.   [II 115]

The purpose of the Institute, established in 1888, was to act as a centre for information and investigation concerning trade, industry, and emigration, and to promote their development throughout the Empire, both overseas and in the United

Kingdom. From 1902, the Institute was administered by the Board of Trade; in 1907 control was transferred to the Secretary of State for the Colonies. This position was regularised by the Imperial Institute Act, 1916. The work of the Institute developed along three main lines; laboratory and workshop research by the Scientific and Technical Department into the uses of raw materials; the collecting and issuing of information on the uses of raw materials; and the illustration of the resources and potentialities of the Empire by the arrangement of exhibition galleries for the general public and school parties. In 1925, the Institute was transferred to the Department of Overseas Trade (of the Board of Trade). In 1949, the Institute was transferred to the Ministry of Education, and its scientific and technical work was transferred to the Colonial Office. In 1958 it was renamed the Commonwealth Institute.

This class contains the records of the Institute arranged chronologically except for the period 1907–1925 when it was administered by the Colonial Office, see CO 323.

ED 27   LEGAL AND ENDOWMENTS: ENDOWMENT FILES: SECONDARY EDUCATION.
   1850–1935. 9,267 pieces. [III 46]

Under the provisions of the Board of Education Act, 1899, the Board of Education took over powers of the Charity Commissioners in matters relating to purely educational charities. The records are concerned mainly with endowments for secondary education at grammar schools, but also for elementary education, education associated with a religious faith, and trusts for scholarships and prize funds.

The files for named schools and general files are arranged by counties in two series. The first contained in two volumes is mainly for files up to 1903, though a few extend into the inter-war period. The third volume contains the second series up to 1935. Some records of the administration of these charities before 1921 can be found in ED 35, and records of management of property belonging to the charities are in ED 43. ED 49 covers endowments for elementary education.

ED 30   ELEMENTARY EDUCATION: INSTITUTION SCHOOL FILES.
   1873–1935. 153 pieces. [II 113]

This series consists of files for schools held in institutions, mainly orphanages. They are arranged by name of school under counties.

ED 31   LEGAL AND ENDOWMENT: BILL FILES.
   1869–1939. 457 pieces. [II 115]

The files are arranged under four headings: General; Local Government; Charitable Foundations and Institutions; and Provisional Orders Confirmation.

Bill files in the general section deal with education bills, bills concerned with universities, and bills for the Channel Islands and the Isle of Man. There are also files on those bills which affect the administration of the Department directly or indirectly, for example, the Unemployment Insurance Bill and the Ministry of Health Miscellaneous Provisions Bill. Each piece contains memoranda on the drafting of the bill, and resolutions reflecting current opinion.

The files in the local government section relate to corporation charters, improvement bills, provisional orders (extension of boundaries) made under the Local

Governments Acts, 1888 and 1894, review orders and the like, affecting the provision of education in a local government area.

The files in the charitable foundations and institutions section concern bills promoting or relating to charitable institutions subject to the provisions of the Board of Education Act, 1899, and bills relating to institutions not within the jurisdiction of the Board of Education which included educational provisions.

Schemes for educational charities approved by the Board of Education which required confirmation by Act of Parliament are listed under the heading of provisional orders confirmation.

The pieces are arranged chronologically under these headings. *See also* ED 24.

ED 32   SPECIAL SERVICES: SPECIAL SCHOOL FILES.
         1894–1945.   1,038 pieces.   [II 114]

This series contains applications for recognition as special schools; these originally were for blind, deaf, defective, and epileptic children though other categories have since been added. Also included are inspection reports and administrative correspondence. Files are arranged by counties under England and Wales.

ED 33   INDEPENDENT AND PRIVATE SCHOOLS: CERTIFIED EFFICIENT SCHOOL
         FILES.
         1871–1936.   137 pieces.   [II 114]

These are files of schools recognised as 'efficient' which did not wish to become public elementary schools. They are listed by name of school and arranged by county in two series up to and after 1921.

ED 35   SECONDARY EDUCATION: INSTITUTION FILES.
         1818–1946.   7,149 pieces.   [III 39]

The Education Act, 1902, empowered local education authorities to 'supply or aid the supply of education other than elementary'. Any institution providing secondary education could apply for recognition. Endowed and voluntary schools sought approval for the purpose of parliamentary grant, others not eligible or not desiring a grant applied to be recognised by the Board as efficient. The files deal with inspection, recognition, approval, drafting of schemes regulating endowments, etc., and also length of school life, premises, and number of free places. Some files contain statistics on the social class from which pupils were drawn.

The files are in two series. Pieces 1–3455 are files opened early this century and extending to around 1921 in England and 1923 in Wales. Pieces 3456–7149 are files opened after the First World War. The files are arranged by schools in counties and as general files in England and Wales, followed by schools in the Channel Islands and the Isle of Man.

The Welsh general files contain papers of the Central Welsh Intermediate Education Fund and Welsh school files contain inspection reports carried out by both the Board of Education and the Central Welsh Board. Welsh files also contain papers on teaching of Welsh and lodging of children during term time because of difficulty of travel.

ED 37   LEGAL AND ENDOWMENTS: ENDOWMENT FILES: FURTHER EDUCATION.
         1854–1944.   1,067 pieces.   [III 46]

The files relate to endowments of institutions providing instruction in vocational, domestic, art, and general subjects in the field of further education, and of exhibitions and scholarships. They contain papers and correspondence relevant to the administration of these endowments under the Charitable Trusts Acts and the Endowed School Acts. The files are arranged in three series; the second series, pieces 347–953, contains files opened since 1900 which were closed before 1936, and the third series, pieces 954–1067, contains files opened in or after 1936. Within each series the files are of schools arranged by county and general files for England and files of schools arranged by county for Wales.

ED 38   LEGAL AND ENDOWMENTS: ENDOWMENT FILES: SPECIAL SERIES.
         1859–1944.   75 pieces.   [III 46]

These relate to endowments for the education of mentally and physically handicapped children and in some cases adults. The files are for individual institutions arranged by county, in three series, the last two, starting at piece 21 and piece 61, contain inter-war material.

ED 39   LEGAL AND ENDOWMENTS: ENDOWMENT FILES: UNIVERSITIES AND
         COLLEGES.
         1854–1944.   1,377 pieces.   [III 46]

The files in this class are concerned with endowments for scholarships and prizes at universities and colleges and contain papers and correspondence relevant to the administration of these endowments under the Charitable Trusts Acts. The files are arranged in three series: the files for individual institutions and funds are listed under counties in England and Wales; followed by a general section including overseas and religious scholarships and foundations; a section at the end contains Charity Commission papers for Battersea Polytechnic and the City Polytechnic, Northampton Institute.

ED 40   LEGAL AND ENDOWMENTS: ENDOWMENT FILES: TEACHERS' TRAINING
         COLLEGES.
         1858–1938.   99 pieces.   [III 46]

These files are concerned with individual training colleges, but a few are of exhibitions and scholarships. They are arranged by counties in England and Wales in two series, the second of which contains inter-war material.

ED 41   FURTHER EDUCATION: EVENING INSTITUTE FILES.
         1901–1954.   687 pieces.   [III 40]

These files contain applications for recognition of courses, details of staffing arrangements, inspectors' reports, accounts, etc. The files are for individual institutes arranged by counties in England and Wales and in the Isle of Man. There are two series which overlap chronologically.

ED 43   SECONDARY EDUCATION: ESTATE MANAGEMENT FILES.
         1894–1924.   1,252 pieces.   [III 46]

7

The Board of Education in 1899 took over from the Charity Commissioners responsibility for educational charities. This class contains records of the management of property of schools other than that in school use. The records are concerned with purchase or sale of land, redemption of rentcharges, leases, etc. From 1922 for England and 1924 for Wales, these records will be found in ED 27. The files are listed by name of the school or charity under counties for England and Wales, with a separate grouping of general files.

ED 44   TEACHERS' REGISTRATION COUNCIL: MINUTE BOOKS.
            1902–1950.   14 pieces.   [III 47]

This class contains a complete set of bound and printed minutes of the Teachers' Registration Council, also a volume of newspaper cuttings 1932–50. The Council was superseded in 1949 by the National Advisory Council on the Training and Supply of Teachers.

ED 45   FURTHER EDUCATION: LOCAL EDUCATION AUTHORITY: JUVENILE
            UNEMPLOYMENT CENTRES: FILES.
            1918–1946.   146 pieces.   [III 42]

These centres were established to mitigate the effects of unemployment after 1918. They provided education and instruction of an informal character for young persons between 14 and 18 years old. Initially the cost was borne by the Exchequer, but after 1919 grant aid was substituted. In 1927, the Ministry of Labour took over responsibility for this service and under the Unemployment Insurance Acts of 1930 and 1934 education authorities concerned with higher education had to provide centres under the control of the Ministry of Labour. Following the transfer of duties to the Ministry of Labour the files contain correspondence between the two departments concerning the establishment of new centres and the disposal of existing centres. The files also contain the Board's policy concerning the provision, administration, and financial aid to local authorities for the establishment of the centres and their organisation and curricula; and there are inspectors' reports.

The pieces are listed alphabetically by counties in England and Wales and the Isle of Man.

ED 46   FURTHER EDUCATION: GENERAL FILES.
            1904–1945.   294 pieces.   [III 40]

This class of records is formed from a series of general files concerned with the policy and administration of schemes relating to the provision of further education by local education authorities in accordance with the terms of the Education Acts, 1918, and 1921. Most papers relating to provisions under the Technical Instruction Act, 1889 have been destroyed. Welsh files relating to the period 1936–44 were (with one exception) destroyed by flood.

The problems of supply, finance, and organisation, of further education services are reflected in the files which also indicate the relationship between the Board of Education, other government departments, and representative educational, professional, and industrial bodies.

The files, each of which is fully described, are arranged under subject headings, a list of which precedes the class list.

ED 47   AWARDS: SCHEMES FOR HIGHER EDUCATION OF EX-SERVICE
        STUDENTS.
        1918–1925.   20 pieces.   [III 43]

A description of this government scheme heads the class list.

ED 49   LEGAL AND ENDOWMENTS: ENDOWMENT FILES: ELEMENTARY
        EDUCATION.
        1853–1935.   10,430 pieces.   [III 46]

This class contains papers relating to elementary educational endowments. In the case of charities which provide for both elementary and secondary education only the correspondence and papers relating to elementary education will be found in this class, those relating to secondary education and to the charity as a whole will be found in ED 27. Some files have been deposited with the Charity Commission, and these are indicated. The pieces are listed by name of the foundation in county order for England and Wales with a general section at the end.

ED 50   SPECIAL SERVICES: GENERAL FILES.
        1872–1946.   172 pieces.   [III 44]

This class contains files dealing with the school health service, the school meals service, and special educational treatment for mentally and physically handicapped children. There is a detailed key to arrangement at the beginning of the class list.

ED 51   FURTHER EDUCATION: LOCAL EDUCATION AUTHORITY FILES.
        1921–1935.   144 pieces.   [III 43]

These records cover a wide field of local authority administration and include the submission by authorities, before 1933, of annual proposals and estimates for part-time day and evening provision in schools and institutes. The papers contain inspectors' interviews and full inspection reports on the adequacy of provision for further education in each authority's area, problems of reorganisation, and reports on particular schools or institutions. The pieces are listed by the name of the county and county borough for England and Wales and the Isle of Man.

ED 53   SECONDARY EDUCATION: LOCAL EDUCATION AUTHORITY FILES.
        1895–1945.   727 pieces.   [III 39]

Under the Education Act of 1918 education authorities had to submit schemes for the organisation of education other than elementary. Schemes were submitted to the Board in draft form and the correspondence, minutes, and interview memoranda show the significance of, and the varying local reactions to, the Board's insistence on amendments which were considered necessary before the authorities' proposals were accepted. The Board needed complete information about the areas concerned and area records were compiled for that purpose. This class contains correspondence and papers concerned with the local education authorities' schemes for post-elementary education, including the development of the free place requirement scheme for teacher training, and proposals for acquisition of land for school buildings. The files are listed by county and county boroughs in England and Wales and there are some files for the Channel Islands and the Isle of Man; there is a key to arrangement at the beginning of the class list.

ED 54   AWARDS AND SCHOLARSHIPS: GENERAL FILES.
         1879–1944.   62 pieces.   [III 44]

The papers are concerned with financial assistance for higher education at universities and similar institutions, by way of Exchequer grant to institutions and awards to students from public and non-public funds. The series also includes papers on the early history of the state scholarship scheme, instituted in 1920.

ED 55   FURTHER EDUCATION: LOCAL EDUCATION AUTHORITY: FEES AND
         SCHOLARSHIP FILES.
         1931–1935.   143 pieces.   [III 43]

As a result of the 1931 financial crisis the Board was required to look into the scholarships and remission of fees local authorities awarded to further education students. The Board's review showed the lack of uniformity in the system and a system of graduated fees for full time students was introduced. These records deal with the Board's examination of the various schemes submitted by education authorities. References to evening institutes are included. The files are arranged by county and county borough in England and Wales.

ED 56   FURTHER EDUCATION: LOCAL EDUCATION AUTHORITY: PHYSICAL
         TRAINING AND RECREATION FILES.
         1935–1940.   67 pieces.   [III 43]

The Physical Training and Recreation Act, 1937, empowered local authorities to provide recreational centres, swimming baths, playing fields, etc, for young persons and adults not in full time education. These files record the provisions made from 1937 until the outbreak of the Second World War. The files are arranged in county and county borough order in England and Wales. *See also* ED 101.

ED 58   FURTHER EDUCATION: LOCAL EDUCATION AUTHORITY: CLASSES FOR
         UNEMPLOYED ADULTS: FILES.
         1931–1939.   87 pieces.   [III 43]

Files of correspondence and papers relate to the provision by local education authorities of supplementary education facilities, mainly classes of a practical nature, for unemployed adults during a period of extensive unemployment. The papers include reports by inspectors. The files are arranged by county and county borough in England and Wales.

ED 59   SECONDARY EDUCATION: LOCAL EDUCATION AUTHORITY: GRANTS
         FILES.
         1921–1934.   141 pieces.   [III 40]

These papers concern the administration of grant aid to non-provided secondary schools by local authorities and arrangements whereby the Board paid direct to certain schools. There are files covering the local education authorities' reactions to government economies, and the refusal of grants for expenditure deemed to be extravagant under the Economy (Miscellaneous Provisions) Act, 1926. Once the policy of paying a deficiency grant was established it evoked little protest from education authorities and after 1934 the files, consisting largely of standard application forms, were not preserved. The files are listed by name of county and county borough, in England and Wales.

ED 60   ELEMENTARY EDUCATION: LOCAL EDUCATION AUTHORITY: STAFFING FILES.
       1922–1945.   630 pieces.   [III 38]

These relate to a system of approved establishments of teachers ('staffing quotas') introduced in 1927, and include annual returns from local education authorities of numbers of children on the registers and teaching staff. Early material includes questions relating to employment of unqualified supplementary teachers, etc. After 1933 the desire for economy and the anticipated reduction in the number of pupils led to stricter control over the number of teachers employed by local education authorities. The files are listed by name of the local authority under counties and county boroughs in England and Wales in two series, up to 1935 and 1936–1945.

ED 61   FURTHER EDUCATION: LOCAL EDUCATION AUTHORITY: TEACHERS' SHORT COURSES.
       1934–1935.   40 pieces.   [III 43]

This series covers the provision of short courses at further education colleges, art schools, evening institutes, etc. maintained or assisted by local education authorities. These courses were provided for teachers by local education authorities under the further education grant regulations. The papers include syllabuses, handbooks, and inspectors' reports. Earlier records have been destroyed.

The files are listed by names of counties and county boroughs in England.

ED 62   SPECIAL SERVICES: TRAINING ESTABLISHMENTS FOR HANDICAPPED PERSONS: FILES.
       1902–1949.   164 pieces.   [III 44]

These files relate to institutions providing facilities for the further training of handicapped persons in continuation of instruction received at special schools. They contain material relating to organisation, curricula, and fees, and include inspectors' reports and applications for recognition. The pieces are listed by the name of the institution within counties in England and Wales.

ED 63   GENERAL EDUCATION: LOCAL EDUCATION AUTHORITY: AID TO PUPILS.
       1919–1935.   142 pieces.   [III 36]

These files relate to the provision by local education authorities of maintenance and other allowances to children and young persons undertaking post-elementary education who were in need of financial assistance. The files contain details of schemes for assistance to pupils and annual returns and estimates of expenditure submitted to the Board by local education authorities. The files are arranged by counties and county boroughs in England and Wales, and the Isle of Man. Some of the Welsh records were destroyed by floods. *See also* ED 107.

ED 64   FURTHER EDUCATION: PUBLIC LIBRARY FILES.
       1919–1935.   307 pieces.   [III 41]

These files deal with the adoption by county councils of areas not included within the limits of library authorities, the relinquishment of powers by existing library authorities, other than county borough councils, and the delegation of powers by local education authorities to education committees under the Public Libraries Act, 1919. The files include material on the acquisition and disposal of sites, reports by inspectors, approval of bye-laws, etc. They are listed alphabetically by the name of the county authority for England and Wales.

ED 65   SPECIAL SERVICES: EVENING PLAY CENTRES.
        1917–1938.   37 pieces.   [III 44]

These records relate to the grant aided provision by local education authorities and voluntary bodies, under the Regulations for Evening Play Centres, 1917, and subsequent regulations, of facilities for recreation after school hours. The records of individual centres are arranged under English counties and are followed by general policy papers.

ED 66   ELEMENTARY EDUCATION: NURSERY EDUCATION: LOCAL EDUCATION
        AUTHORITY FILES.
        1918–1944.   58 pieces.   [III 37]

This class relates to the provision of nursery education in local authority areas, and is complementary to ED 69. The papers include proposals by local education authorities and voluntary bodies to establish nursery schools and classes for children between the ages of 2 and 5; memoranda on nursery school provision in particular areas; and the results of a survey made by local authorities at the request of the Board, 1936. The files are arranged under counties and county boroughs in England and Wales. *See also* ED 102.

ED 67   TEACHERS: LOCAL EDUCATION AUTHORITY: SUPPLY FILES.
        1912–1915; 1924–1949.   150 pieces.   [III 47]

These records are concerned with the approval of arrangements made by local education authorities for the preliminary education and training of intending teachers, with reports on training and supply provisions. The files also contain material connected with the continued recognition of pupil teacher centres and with the special problems of pupil teachers in rural areas. Papers earlier than 1924 have not survived except for some staff returns of teachers and teachers under training in public elementary schools in Wales, 1912–1915. The files are arranged by counties and county boroughs in England and Wales.

ED 68   FURTHER EDUCATION: ADULT EDUCATION: RESIDENTIAL COLLEGES
        FILES.
        1911–1935.   7 pieces.   [III 42]

Following the establishment of Ruskin College in 1899 a number of residential colleges for adults were founded. This class contains records of the Catholic Workers College, Oxford; Fircroft College, Birmingham; Hillcroft College, Surbiton; Ruskin College, Oxford; and Coleg Harlech, Merioneth.

ED 69   ELEMENTARY EDUCATION: NURSERY SCHOOL FILES.
        1918–1935.   81 pieces.   [III 37]

These are of individual nursery schools, covering recognition for the purpose of
grant, notes of visits made by officers of the Board, and annual summaries of school
accounts. The records are listed by the name of the school, under counties, for
England and Wales. *See also* ED 102.

ED 70   ELEMENTARY EDUCATION: PRACTICAL INSTRUCTION CENTRES: FILES.
        1906–1935.   4,786 pieces.   [III 37]

These relate to the provision of courses of practical instruction in special subjects,
for example domestic economy and handicraft, in elementary and secondary schools
and centres serving a number of schools. The papers include material on the acquisition of land and buildings, inspectors' reports, and applications for the Board of
Education's approval of courses. The pieces are listed by the name of the centre
under English and Welsh counties and county boroughs, and Part III authorities
(*see* ED 16 for definition). *See also* ED 96.

ED 71   AWARDS: STATE SCHOLARSHIP UNIVERSITY COMMITTEE: FILES.
        1920–1944.   16 pieces.   [III 44]

These records deal with the arrangements made between the Board of Education
and Committees of Universities for the assessment of the amount of financial
assistance to be awarded to state scholars.

ED 72   AWARDS: UNIVERSITY EXAMINING BODIES: FILES.
        1920–1944.   14 pieces.   [III 44]

These records are concerned with the administration by the Board of Education
and university examining bodies of the state scholarship scheme set up in 1920.
The files include annual reports by examining bodies on the selection of state
scholars, statistics of successful and unsuccessful candidates, arrangements for the
nomination of candidates, and the allocation of state scholarships.
   The files are listed by the name of the university examining body in two series:
1920–1935 and 1936–1944.

ED 73   FURTHER EDUCATION: ADULT EDUCATION: TUTORIAL CLASSES FILES.
        1921–1935.   51 pieces.   [III 42]

These files concern the provision of tutorial classes for adults by universities
and by voluntary bodies, such as the Workers Education Association, recognised
under the Board of Education (Adult Education) Regulations, 1924. Most files
before 1924 have been destroyed. The pieces are arranged alphabetically under the
name of the university or voluntary body concerned.

ED 74   FURTHER EDUCATION: PRIVATE EDUCATIONAL INSTITUTIONS: FILES.
        1928–1940.   15 pieces.   [III 41]

These records deal with the applications of the institutions which were successful
in obtaining recognition. They include interview memoranda, correspondence,

inspectors' reports and prospectuses. The pieces are listed by name of the school in county order in England and Wales.

ED 75   FURTHER EDUCATION: DAY CONTINUATION SCHOOLS: FILES.
         1919–1947.   79 pieces.   [III 41]

Day continuation schools were established in 1918 to provide for the compulsory part-time attendance of school-leavers 14 to 16 years of age. The papers cover the provision, organisation, and curriculum of the schools, together with correspondence and minutes dealing with various local aspects. The files are listed by the name of the school in counties for England and Wales. *See also* ED 120.

ED 76   FURTHER EDUCATION: ADULT EDUCATION: VACATION COURSE FILES.
         1928–1955.   29 pieces.   [III 42]

These files relate to the recognition and approval for the purposes of grant of vacation courses sponsored by universities and other bodies, *see* ED 73. Papers relating to the earlier provision of vacation courses have not survived. The files are listed by the name of the university or voluntary body concerned, and only one file is open.

ED 77   INSPECTORATE: COLLECTED SPECIAL REPORTS.
         1909–1948.   226 pieces.   [III 45]

A collection of printed reports on diverse subjects of special interest at the time. These reports had restricted circulation and are of particular importance because of the destruction of original drafts. The reports are fully described and are grouped as follows:

17–137	1923–1938. Free place reports dealing with the implementation by local education authorities of the free place system in secondary schools.
138–146	1938–1939. General reports: elementary education in three areas, housecraft, etc.
192–199	1920–1935. Miscellaneous reports on elementary and secondary schools and teacher training.
219–226	1919–1937. Selected reports: handicraft; Labour Examination in London schools; advanced elementary education in Scotland; education week in Northampton, 1921; School Journey Movement in Gateshead, 1921; mental testing in West Suffolk, 1926; and education in two rural schools.

ED 78   TEACHERS: TRAINING COLLEGE FILES.
         1924–1935.   80 pieces.   [III 47]

The records cover the provision, maintenance, and administration of these colleges including those maintained by voluntary bodies and local education authorities, and of university colleges providing similar courses. The pieces are listed by the name of the college under counties in England and Wales. *See also* ED 86.

ED 79   SCIENCE MUSEUM: GENERAL FILES.
        1856–1935.   33 pieces.   [III 47]

Donations from the 1851 Exhibition formed the nucleus of the collection which in 1857 was styled the South Kensington Museum. It expanded to include both art and science material. Other sources of acquisitions were the Patent Office Museum and the Geological Museum. A well stocked library was also established. In 1909 the art collection was moved to a new building and called the Victoria and Albert Museum. Thereafter the science collection was renamed the Science Museum. The files trace the history and administration of the Museum and are arranged under subject headings. Some cover the Bethnal Green Museum which housed the overflow from the Science Museum. *See also* ED 84.

ED 80   FURTHER EDUCATION: ADULT EDUCATION: GENERAL FILES.
        1923–1937.   19 pieces.   [III 42]

These are policy files concerned with the provision of further education for adults. The topics covered include the Board of Education's co-operation with voluntary bodies and local education authorities in this field. Also included are public library schemes, the National Central Library, and the National Museum of Wales. Of particular interest is piece 14, which gives detailed statistics of classes conducted in the school years 1935–1937 and programmes for 1936–1938.

ED 81   TEACHERS: UNIVERSITY TRAINING DEPARTMENT FILES.
        1931–1935.   15 pieces.   [III 47]

University Training Departments provided a four year course enabling students to become certificated teachers. The series suffered much destruction and only papers concerned with general matters for 1931 to 1935 have survived. The pieces are listed by the name of the university department.

ED 82   FURTHER EDUCATION: TECHNICAL SCHOOL FILES.
        1912–1947.   363 pieces.   [III 41]

These records concern the provision under the 1904 and subsequent regulations of technical instruction in subjects, such as mechanical engineering, chemistry, building, etc. They include inspectors' reports, memoranda, minutes and papers relating to the need for, and the establishment of, classes, and approval of proposed National Certificate courses. The records overlap somewhat with ED 41, 46, 90, 98, and 114. Files are listed by the name of the institute under counties and county boroughs in England and Wales, and the Isle of Man, in two series 1912–1935 and 1936–1947.

ED 83   FURTHER EDUCATION: ART SCHOOL FILES.
        1897–1949.   337 pieces.   [III 41]

These records are of the provisions made by art schools and classes for the study of fine art and industrial design, with special attention to the needs of local staple industries. They include reports by inspectors, interview and conference memoranda, material dealing with the acquisition of sites and buildings, and with the classification of art schools and art classes. The files are arranged by name of school under counties and county boroughs in England and Wales and the Isle of Man, in two series up to 1935 and 1936–1949.

ED 84 VICTORIA AND ALBERT MUSEUM: RECORDS.
1844–1935. 247 pieces. [III 47]

This class contains files relating to the formation, building, history, and administration of the Museum, books of correspondence, miscellaneous minutes, papers, and plans. Some papers relate to the Bethnal Green Museum. The records are fully described and arranged chronologically under subject headings. *See also* ED 24 and 79.

ED 86 TEACHERS: GENERAL FILES.
1903–1935. 63 pieces. [III 48]

These general policy files cover the drafting and revision of the Training of Teachers Regulations, the supply of trained teachers, the provision of training colleges, and the introduction of building grants-in-aid of the establishment of training colleges. The files are fully described and listed under subject headings. The class also contains papers and minutes of the Central Advisory Committee on the Certification of Teachers, 1928–1935, and the Training College Reference Committee, 1927–1935. College files are in ED 78, Joint Examination Board files in ED 105, and salary files in ED 108.

ED 87 TEACHERS' TRAINING COLLEGES: BUILDING GRANTS FILES.
1904–1924. 23 pieces. [III 48]

The records cover applications by local education authorities, universities, and university colleges, for grants-in-aid to meet capital expenditure on the acquisition, erection, or improvement, etc. of premises for teachers' training colleges and hostels. The files are listed by the name of the college, alphabetically for England and Wales.

ED 88 ELEMENTARY EDUCATION: LOCAL EDUCATION AUTHORITY: GRANT SCRUTINIES FILES.
1920–1933. 115 pieces. [III 38]

These are papers concerned with the scrutiny of local education authorities' claims for annual grants. This class is of precedent files which contain inspectors' reports, interview memoranda, and reports to Parliament, and provide examples of the parsimony of some authorities where staffing arrangements were so inadequate as to affect the efficiency of the schools. The pieces are listed under counties and county boroughs for England and Wales, and the Isle of Man.

ED 89 ELEMENTARY EDUCATION: LOCAL EDUCATION AUTHORITY: 'EXTRA DISTRICT' CHILDREN: FILES.
1904–1935. 53 pieces. [III 38]

These records are concerned with the problems arising from the provision of education at public elementary schools maintained by a local education authority in respect of children resident in the area of a neighbouring authority. It includes details of disputes between authorities and reports of public inquiries. The files are listed alphabetically under counties and county boroughs for England and Wales.

ED 90   FURTHER EDUCATION: TECHNICAL COLLEGE FILES.
        1907–1935.   306 pieces.   [III 41]

These files contain applications for the approval of National Certificate courses, inspectors' subject reports, comments and reports on the local aspects of technical education, general correspondence, syllabuses, prospectuses, and papers relating to premises. They are listed in county order for England and Wales by the name of the college or institute. *See also* ED 41 and 114.

ED 91–93   WELSH DEPARTMENT

The Welsh Department was set up in 1907. The records have suffered some war-time destruction and further loss was incurred in 1960 by flooding.

ED 91   GENERAL EDUCATION: GENERAL FILES.
        1880–1935.   58 pieces.   [III 48]

Pieces falling in the inter-war period are:

15   1912–1920. Welsh contributions to the annual reports of the Board of Education.

45   1912–1925. General: a miscellaneous selection of files including school buildings, adoption of metric system, conferences, and the establishment of the National Council of Education for Wales.

46   1923–1928. Application of various Board of Education general instructions to Wales.

47   1933–1935. Reprints of lists of schools, and inspection arrangements.

49   1919–1920. Rural folk lore.

50   1916–1921. St. Deinol's Library, Hawarden.

53–56   1921–1926. Statistics.

57–58   1912–1934. Teaching of Welsh.

ED 92   ELEMENTARY EDUCATION: GENERAL FILES.
        1885–1938.   23 pieces.   [III 49]

These are policy files and cover various aspects of administration, including school camps for children from Special Areas, 1935–1938, and the effect of the Welsh Church Act on Church of England schools in Wales, 1920. *See also* ED 11.

ED 93   SECONDARY EDUCATION: GENERAL FILES.
        1900–1935.   14 pieces.   [III 49]

These files include the recognition of Pupil Teacher Centres in Wales, criticism of the 1919 Regulations for Secondary Schools, and their amendment.

ED 95   ELEMENTARY EDUCATION: LOCAL EDUCATION AUTHORITY: POOR LAW
        CHILDREN: FILES.
        1929–1944.   145 pieces.   [III 38]

When the functions of the poor law authorities were transferred to county and county borough councils in 1930, the councils became responsible for the education of poor law children in certified schools, boarded out with foster parents, or being educated in hospitals and convalescent homes.

This class contains the administrative schemes and amendments submitted by local authorities and related papers connected with the provision of such education. The files are listed by the name of the county council and county borough council in England and Wales.

ED 96   ELEMENTARY EDUCATION: LOCAL EDUCATION AUTHORITY: PRACTICAL
           INSTRUCTION FILES.
           1899–1944.   201 pieces.   [III 38]

These files cover the provision of practical instruction in local authority areas and are a complementary series to ED 70, which deals with the individual practical instruction centres. The records have suffered much destruction. Those that remain cover lists of premises proposed for courses in special subjects, arrangements for instruction, inspectors' general reports, and annual returns of premises. The files are listed alphabetically by county and county borough councils in England and Wales and the Isle of Man.

ED 97   ELEMENTARY EDUCATION: LOCAL EDUCATION AUTHORITY;
           REORGANISATION OF SCHOOLS: FILES.
           1909–1935.   705 pieces.   [III 38]

These records are concerned with the reorganisation of schools necessary to provide a system of advanced elementary education in accordance with the policy laid down in the Board of Education's Circular, January, 1925, and the findings of the Hadow Report, 1926.

The files include reorganisation programmes submitted by local education authorities with related correspondence, reassessment of school accommodation, protests against reorganisation proposals, and replies to questionnaires on provision of advanced education. The files are listed alphabetically under counties and county boroughs in England and Wales.

ED 98   SECONDARY EDUCATION: JUNIOR TECHNICAL SCHOOLS: FILES.
           1913–1946.   311 pieces.   [III 39]

The class contains applications for recognition and various correspondence relating to local and general aspects of technical education for young people. The pieces are listed by the name of the college under counties in England and Wales. *See also* ED 82 and 114.

ED 99   ELEMENTARY EDUCATION: PREMISES SURVEY FILES.
           1919–1942.   223 pieces.   [III 37]

In 1925 a survey of rural schools was carried out and a list of public elementary schools with defective premises was compiled. This became known as the Black List; these records contain area reports by inspectors on unsatisfactory school premises, and minutes and memoranda leading to its compilation. They also show the reaction of authorities and voluntary bodies to proposals for improved provision for elementary education, and record parliamentary questions and answers, relating to 'Black List' schools. The files are listed by county and county borough for England and Wales.

ED 100 ACCOUNTANT GENERAL'S DEPARTMENT: FINANCE: GENERAL FILES.
       1915–1936.   42 pieces.   [III 43]

These papers deal with the financial policy and administration of grants to local
education authorities following the Education Act, 1918. They include material
on the drafting and revision of regulations relating to building grants, maintenance
allowances, necessitous areas grants, teachers' salaries, administration of teachers'
pensions, and junior instruction centres. Each piece has a very full descriptive title.

ED 101 GENERAL EDUCATION: LOCAL EDUCATION AUTHORITY: SOCIAL AND
       PHYSICAL TRAINING: FILES.
       1920–1944.   241 pieces.   [III 36]

Regulations dating from 1918 and revised in 1921 gave local education authorities
the power to promote social and physical training, supplementing the instruction
provided for children attending public elementary schools and for persons over the
age of eighteen attending educational institutions. This class shows the wide range
of provisions made available. The files are listed and grouped under counties and
county boroughs in England and Wales. See also ED 56.

ED 102 ELEMENTARY EDUCATION: NURSERY EDUCATION: GENERAL FILES.
       1917–1944.   31 pieces.   [III 37]

The Education Act, 1918, empowered local education authorities to supply or
aid the supply of nursery schools and classes for children between 2 and 5 years of
age. This class contains policy files. See also ED 66 and 69.

ED 104 TEACHERS' MISCONDUCT: GENERAL FILES.
       1904–1935.   9 pieces.   [III 48].   Closed for 100 years.

ED 105 TEACHERS: JOINT EXAMINATION BOARDS FILES.
       1927–1949.   35 pieces.   [III 48]

In 1929 teacher training colleges, in association with local universities, formed
joint examination boards to conduct the final examination for students in academic
subjects. Previously the examination which qualified students to become certificated
teachers was conducted by the Board of Education. These records relate to syllabuses of instruction and regulations for the examinations as approved by the Board,
examiners' subject reports on the standard of examinations, the analysis of results,
and policy connected with the formation of the individual boards. The pieces are
listed by the name of the examining board.

ED 106 ELEMENTARY EDUCATION: LOCAL EDUCATION AUTHORITY: RELIGIOUS
       INSTRUCTION FILES.
       1919–1944.   45 pieces.   [III 39]

These records include minutes and memoranda, inspectors' reports, and correspondence concerning the administration and interpretation of the provisions
of the Education Act, 1921, and later Acts. The files are listed by the name of the
local authority. The records for Wales were destroyed by flooding in 1960 except for
the file for Denbighshire.

ED 107   ELEMENTARY EDUCATION: LOCAL EDUCATION AUTHORITY:
              MAINTENANCE ALLOWANCES: FILES.
              1921–1944.   76 pieces.   [III 39]

This class includes papers concerning schemes for the payment of maintenance allowances, submitted by local education authorities for the approval of the Board of Education. The papers reflect the policy of the Board and the decisions, related to recurring financial crises, recorded in discussions between the Board and the Treasury. The pieces are grouped alphabetically by local authorities. Maintenance allowances were not awarded by all authorities and this accounts for the gaps in this series. *See also* ED 63.

ED 108   TEACHERS' SALARIES: GENERAL FILES.
              1916–1944.   110 pieces.   [III 48]

The files are arranged in chronological order under the following subject headings:

Burnham Committee:
    constitution.
    minutes.
    general.
Disputes.
Educational economy measures.
Miscellaneous.
Salaries branch procedure.

ED 109   INSPECTORATE: REPORTS ON SECONDARY INSTITUTIONS.
              1900–1944.   8,612 pieces.   [III 45].   Closed for 50 years.

This class consists of a master set of inspectors' reports which vary in frequency, scope, and content, in order to meet the Board's particular administrative requirements. The pieces are named for each school and listed under counties for England and Wales, Channel Islands, and Isle of Man.

ED 110   SECONDARY EDUCATION: LOCAL EDUCATION AUTHORITY: FEES AND
              SPECIAL PLACES: FILES.
              1932–1946.   147 pieces.   [III 40]

The files contain proposals submitted by local education authorities and local reaction to the policy and the financial saving achieved by the replacement of the Free Place system by that of Fees and Special Places. The pieces are listed by counties and county boroughs in England and Wales. *See also* ED 53 *and* ED 77.

ED 111   ELEMENTARY EDUCATION: LOCAL EDUCATION AUTHORITY:
              MISCELLANEOUS FILES.
              1903–1935.   278 pieces.

Many of the files are concerned with particular schemes, proposals, etc., but others are of more than local interest such as those relating to the Cambridgeshire Village College Scheme, the installation of wireless receiving apparatus in schools, and the examination of the cost per child figures for 1922–23. An index of subjects of general interest heads the class list. The files are arranged under counties and county boroughs for England and Wales, and the Channel Islands.

ED 112   EXPIRED COMMISSIONS: DURHAM UNIVERSITY.
          1926–1937.   43 pieces.   [III 49]

A Royal Commission was appointed in 1934 to inquire into the constitution and government of Durham University as a means of resolving the difficulties which had, over a period of years, disrupted it. This class contains papers on the setting up of the Royal Commission, memoranda, evidence, and the report. For commissions on Oxford and London, *see* PC 10.

ED 113   NATIONAL FITNESS COUNCIL: RECORDS.
          1937–1947.   85 pieces.   [III 49]

The Council was formed in 1937, and suspended in 1939. The pieces are fully described and include applications for grants, minutes of meetings of the Advisory Council and Grants Committee, and reports on the work of the area committees. *See also* ED 10/263. The Council was not revived after the war but local projects continued.

ED 114   INSPECTORATE: REPORTS ON INSTITUTES OF FURTHER EDUCATION.
          1909–1944.   1,211 pieces.   [III 45].   Closed for 50 years.

This is a master set of inspectors' reports. They are arranged in chronological order for each school and in alphabetical order of district within counties, with general files after England and Wales.

ED 115   INSPECTORATE: REPORTS ON TEACHER TRAINING COLLEGES.
          1907–1939.   99 pieces.   [III 45].   Closed for 50 years.

A master set of inspectors' reports, listed by name of the college within county headings for England and Wales, and one general file on domestic science colleges.

ED 119   UNIVERSITIES AND UNIVERSITY COLLEGES: FILES.
          1874–1944.   84 pieces.   [III 48]

The Privy Council is responsible for granting charters to universities and colleges and for amendments to charters, and it referred to the Board of Education matters to do with educational foundations. The class contains references from the Privy Council to the Board of Education arranged alphabetically by name of universities. Some files are of property transactions.

ED 120   GENERAL EDUCATION: LOCAL EDUCATION AUTHORITY: EDUCATION
          ACTS 1918 AND 1921: SCHEME FILES.
          1918–1932.   164 pieces.   [III 36]

This class consists of schemes submitted by local education authorities outlining their proposals for the organisation and progressive development of education within their areas together with papers reflecting the reactions of local bodies and the Board of Education to the proposals. Other papers concern the applications submitted by local education authorities for the fixing of Appointed Days for the purpose of implementing the abortive proposals for the compulsory attendance of school leavers between the ages of 14 and 16 years at day continuation schools. Not all authorities submitted schemes. Files are listed under counties and county boroughs for England only. *See also* ED 13.

ED 121   EXTERNAL RELATIONS: GENERAL FILES.
         1871–1949.   271 pieces.   Piece 1 closed for 50 years.

This class has papers dealing with international congresses and committees, foreign schools in England, British institutes abroad, and interchange of teachers. A number of files deal with the teaching of world history, languages, the International Labour Office, and the League of Nations. A subject key heads the list.

ED 125   PRECEDENT FILES.
         1905–1921; 1931–1944.   23 pieces.

These are typed copies of letters and minutes extracted from precedent files originating in the Elementary School Branch and Medical Department (now the Special Services Branch). They relate to the provision of maintained and voluntary schools for the period 1931–1944, and to the duty of local education authorities to provide for the medical inspection and treatment of children in elementary schools.

ED 127   PRECEDENT BOOKS.
         1897–1945.   41 pieces.

Precedent and noting books give briefly official decisions on problems arising from the application of Education Acts and Codes from 1870–1926. The pieces are listed by the relevant act with a miscellaneous section dealing with the supply of schools, building regulations, and the Welsh department.

ED 131   TEACHERS' SUPERANNUATION: GENERAL FILES.
         1899–1945.   103 pieces.   Various pieces closed for 50 years.

There is a key to arrangement at the beginning of the class list; the pieces being grouped by topics.

GENERAL REGISTER OFFICE

The General Register Office was set up following an Act of 1836 to organise the registration of births, deaths, and marriages, and an Act of 1840 made it responsible for the periodic census of population. Census Returns are closed for 100 years. In 1970 the Government Social Survey which had been part of the Central Office of Information was merged with the General Register Office to form the Office of Population Censuses and Surveys.

RG 8   REGISTERS: UNAUTHENTICATED: MISCELLANEOUS SERIES.
        1646–1927.   304 pieces.   [III 77]

The only inter-war material is archives of the Russian Orthodox Church in London, pieces 111–304. This contains records of births, marriages, and deaths, and converts, and parish registers. There are also files of correspondence of E. Smirnov, priest of the Russian Orthodox Church in London, with the Russian Embassy, Russian Relief Committee, Russian Red Cross, Imperial Orthodox Palestine Society, and miscellaneous documents (in Russian).

The following classes will probably be transferred to the P.R.O. during 1971, and each contains some inter-war material. In particular there are papers concerning the formation and subsequent history of each registration district, these are linked to the poor law districts and so have had a lasting effect on the structure of modern local services:

RG 19　　CENSUS RETURNS: CORRESPONDENCE AND PAPERS.

RG 20　　ESTABLISHMENT AND ACCOUNTS: CORRESPONDENCE AND PAPERS.

RG 21　　MARRIAGES, REGISTRATION AND LOCAL SERVICES: CORRESPONDENCE AND PAPERS.

RG 22　　NATIONAL REGISTRATION AND NATIONAL HEALTH SERVICE CENTRAL REGISTER: CORRESPONDENCE AND PAPERS.

GOVERNMENT ACTUARY

Before 1912 departments of the civil service used the services of independent actuaries. The National Insurance Act of 1911 led to the setting up of an actuarial branch of the National Health Insurance Joint Committee with Sir Alfred Watson as Chief Actuary. Other departments not concerned with National Health Insurance increasingly asked his advice. In 1917 the title of Government Actuary was conferred and in 1919 a separate Government Actuary's Department was established. The Department is the consulting actuary to all departments of the British civil service and its services are available to certain public boards and also to Commonwealth Governments.

ACT 1　CORRESPONDENCE AND PAPERS.
　　　　1911–1943.　　61 pieces.

This class includes correspondence, calculations, and reports. Topics covered include: Navy and Army Insurance Fund; Actuarial Advisory Committee; civil servants' superannuation; Local Authorities Superannuation Act, 1922; and the National Debt.

ACT 2　APPROVED SOCIETIES: VALUATIONS: REPRESENTATIVE PAPERS.
　　　　1918–1939.　　20 pieces.　　[III 78]

The valuations are those of selected approved societies, with most types represented. Each file contains the papers of the five valuations made between 1918 and 1939, including the valuer's reports, accounts, and balance sheets. The results of the valuations were included in the reports made by the Government Actuary to the chairman of the National Health Insurance Joint Committee, and these, which were published as command papers, are also included in the class.

MINISTRY OF LABOUR

The Ministry of Labour was established in 1916. Between 1939 and 1959 the Minister of Labour was also Minister of National Service. In 1968 the Ministry of Labour was renamed the Department of Employment and Productivity on taking over responsibility for prices and incomes policy from the Department of Economic Affairs. It became the Department of Employment in 1970. Some transfers of function affecting the Ministry are in the chronological list at the head of this section, other include:

1917   From Board of Trade, administration of Conciliation Act, 1896, Trade Boards Act, 1909, Labour Exchanges Act, 1909, National Insurance (Unemployment) Acts, 1911–1916, and Part I of Munitions of War Act, 1915, and collection of labour statistics.

1919   From Ministry of Munitions, responsibility for placing civilian munition workers in peace-time work.

1920   General responsibility for International Labour Office. Unemployment Grants Committee set up, responsible to the Treasury until 1929.

1921   From Ministry of Transport, labour and wages on railways.

1923   From Board of Education, oversight of classes and centres provided by local education authorities for unemployed young persons, and grant aid.

1925   From Home Office, regulations concerning registry of trade unions under Trades Unions Act, 1871.

1927   From Board of Education, supervisory and grant aiding duties over local authority youth employment service.

1931   Transitional Payments Scheme introduced.

1932   To Ministry of Agriculture and Fisheries, supervision of grant payments to Society of Friends towards provision of allotments for unemployed in England and Wales.

1934   Unemployment Assistance Board established, regulations made by Minister of Labour.

1939   Minister of Labour appointed Minister of National Service, ceased in 1959.

1940   From Home Office, wartime administration of Factories Acts.

1942   First Labour Attaché appointed.

1945   From Ministry of Education, training of blind and physically handicapped persons not under 16 years.
        To Ministry of Agriculture and Fisheries, responsibility for the Land Settlement Association.
        To Board of Trade, general responsibility for distribution of industry and development area policy.

1946   From Home Office, permanent transfer of Factories Act administration.
        To Ministry of Agriculture and Fisheries, Land Settlement Association.

1961   To newly formed Department of Technical Co-operation, some functions relating to technical aid.

LAB 2   CORRESPONDENCE.
         1897–1933.   2,186 pieces.   [II 200]

Most of the surviving general papers of the Ministry of Labour until 1933 are
kept in this class which covers the whole range of ministry business, including
general policy, industrial relations, establishment, and trade boards. The class list
is difficult to use but the index in LAB 7 if used with caution and persistence will
provide references to appropriate documents. A handlist of the categories in this
loose-leaf index is in the search rooms.

LAB 3   INDUSTRIAL COURT.
         1919–1945.   39 pieces.   [II 200]

The Industrial Courts Act, 1919, established the Industrial Court and authorised
the appointment of courts of enquiry. A permanent court of arbitration was created
successor to a war-time body, extending the Ministry of Labour's powers of conciliation to threatened as well as actual disputes. The Act did not include provision
for compulsory arbitration or the enforcement of awards made under it. This class
contains reports, minutes, correspondence, and papers. Topics covered include:

1–2	1919–1922. Committee on Increased Production in Industry, 1920.
3	1924. Police strike 1919: dismissed men.
4	1924. Tramways Tribunal: minutes and report.
6	1927–1928. Trade Boards Acts: application to milk distributive trade.
7–25	1919–1939. Industrial Court, Award 728 (railway shopmen).
26–34	1921–1934. Electricity (Supply) Acts: disputes.
35–39	1930–1941. Coal Mines Act, 1930: disputes and papers of Coal Mines National Industrial Board.

The class has been heavily weeded and there are many gaps in records covering
the Industrial Court.

LAB 4   UNEMPLOYMENT GRANTS COMMITTEE.
         1920–1942.   73 pieces.   [II 200]

This Committee was set up under the authority of the Unemployment Relief
Works Act, 1920, to encourage local authorities and public utility companies by
offers of financial assistance to undertake public works in advance of immediate
need and thus provide employment. In 1929, by the Development (Loan Guarantees
and Grants) Act, the Committee, which was originally responsible to the Treasury,
was reconstituted and made responsible to the Ministry of Labour. The records
selected for preservation include minutes of meetings and the final report of the
Committee, together with papers illustrating the operation of various types of
schemes from selected areas. The Committee was abolished in 1950.

LAB 5   WAR CABINET COMMITTEE ON WOMEN IN INDUSTRY: 1918–1919.
         1917–1919.   4 pieces.   [II 201]

1	1918–1919. Verbatim reports of meetings of the Committee, 4th–45th days. Charts showing comparisons between men and women in

industry, women's welfare organisation at Armstrong, Whitworth
and Co. Ltd., and the working of the block system at the London
Omnibus Co.

2   1918. Verbatim report of meetings of the Physiological sub-
           committee.

3   1919. Report, appendices, summaries of evidence. (Cmd. 135 and
           167.)

LAB 6   MILITARY RECRUITMENT.
        1937–1960.   263 pieces.   [III 93]

Very few of these papers cover 1937–1939; they include records relating to the
Militia Recruiting Department and recruitment in general.

LAB 8   EMPLOYMENT.
        1909–1962.   871 pieces.   [III 93]

1–5;   Miscellaneous: deputation for concessions in distressed areas, King's
8–9   National Roll, Registration and Clearing Committee on national
           circulation of particulars of special applicants, port transport
           industry, dock labour.

10–15;   1934–1939. Special Areas: Land Settlement Association, trading
17–20   companies, housing agreements, Depressed Areas Bill, 1934–36,
           Special Areas Act, 1937.

16   1937–1939. Irish Free State: enquiry on immigration into Great
           Britain.

23–45;   1924–1941. National Joint Council for Dock Labour, meetings of
51–52   Port Labour Advisory Committee and correspondence and papers
           of registration committees; Departmental Committee Report on
           Maintenance and Registration of Port Labour, 1924; history of
           committees and dock schemes.

50   1924. Interpretation of 'days of unemployment' under 1923 Act.

53   1926. Payment of unemployment insurance to miners.

57   Set of forms relating to various aspects of unemployment.

63   1938–1939. Special Areas: expenditure policy of Commissioners.

69   1920–1940. Nationality rules on employment in government
           departments.

71   1934–1938. Special Areas, land settlement.

72–85   1934–1939. Immigrant labour.

182–195   1927–1940. National Joint Council for Dock Labour, minutes and
           reports.

198   1920. Treatment of aliens in war-time.

199–203   1922–1940. King's Roll Committees.

204   1924–1936. Dock Transport Workers' Committee report on regis-
           tration and guaranteed week.

205–206   1936–1940. Commissioner for Special Areas: report on induce-
           ments to attract industries, and scheme for Gateshead.

207	1937. Port transport industry, history of registration schemes.
208–211	1937. Special Areas: tax concessions, etc.
212	1937. Government training centres: facilities for married men.
213	1937–1938. Engineering industry: correspondence with the Committee of Imperial Defence.
214	1938. Universities: organisation for war service.
215	1938. Representation on advisory committees.
216–217	1938. Labour position for R.A.F. building programme.
218	1938. Industrial transference scheme.
219	1938–1939. Special Areas: emergency war time arrangements.
220–222	1938–1939. Advisory committee of Central Register.
223	1938–1939. Employment of university staff in war time.
224	1938–1940. Offer of services of Institution of Production Engineers.
225–235	1938–1946. Central Register policy and application to various professions.
236	1939. Interdepartmental Committee on Earmarking for wartime service.
237–261	1939–1940. Mobilisation for war: Control of Employment Bill.
803–806	1937. Interdepartmental Committee on Building Programme of Government Departments.
827–842	1937–1940. Joint Consultative Committee on the Building Programme of Government Departments; England and Wales, and Scotland.
871	1938. Procedure regulating entry of foreigners for employment.

See also LAB 23 *for* Special Areas.

LAB 9 FINANCE.
1912–1961.   104 pieces.   [III 93]

This class contains files of the Finance Department. The topics covered include Special Areas, training centres, administration of unemployment insurance and assistance, employment and transfer of juveniles, Holidays with Pay Bill, 1938, Military Training Bill, 1939, and general correspondence.

LAB 10 INDUSTRIAL RELATIONS: GENERAL.
1917–1959.   399 pieces.   [III 93]

These records are from the Industrial Relations Department. They cover a very wide field: disputes in many industries particularly the cotton industry; committees, including the Holidays with Pay Committee, 1936–1938, *see also* LAB 31; the Royal Commission on the Distribution of the Industrial Population, 1930–1937, *see also* HLG 27; Chief Conciliation and Industrial Relation Officers' weekly reports for 1939; a set of forms on personnel management; National Joint Industrial Councils, 1937–1939; and Civil Service Industrial Court. Subject list is available in search rooms.

LAB 11   INDUSTRIAL RELATIONS: TRADE BOARDS AND WAGES COUNCILS.
          1910–1968.   1,607 pieces.   [III 93]

These records relate to meetings of trade boards and to questions of scope and rates referred to them, with files on the administration of Wages Councils. The pieces are listed chronologically under the name of the industry concerned.

LAB 12   ESTABLISHMENTS.
          1915–1961.   232 pieces.   [III 93]

Normal establishment matters, including papers on Whitley Councils.

LAB 13   OVERSEAS.
          1923–1961.   87 pieces.   [III 93]

These files of the Overseas Department deal mainly with the International Labour Office.

LAB 14   SAFETY, HEALTH, AND WELFARE: GENERAL.
          1878–1966.   167 pieces.   [III 93]

These records relate to the administration of factory inspection. The majority were transferred from the Home Office when factory inspection was transferred to the Ministry in 1940. They include the following pieces:

18   1931. Depressed areas industrial survey: conference.
27   1925. Royal Commission on Food Prices: Night Baking Committee reports.
57   1924–1936. Factory legislation: deputations from the Trades Union Congress.
99   1936–1937. Report of advisory committee on Employment of Women and Young Persons Act.
113   1938. Debit system in payment of wages, Truck Acts, 1831–1940.

LAB 15   FACTORY INSPECTORATE.
          1836–1923.   9 pieces.

8   1922–1923. Staff instructions and circulars. (Incomplete.)

LAB 16   SOLICITOR'S DEPARTMENT.
          1928–1960.   44 pieces.   [III 93]

This class contains files dealing with various bills, acts, and legal questions. The topics covered include:

5   1930. Hours of Industrial Employment Bill, 1920.
6   1934. Unemployment Insurance Acts; recovery of transitional payments.
7–8   1934. Unemployment Bill, 1933–1934; memoranda on Unemployment Assistance Board.

9	1935. Unemployment Assistance (Temporary Provisions) Bill, 1935.
12; 14–17	1935–1939. Special Areas Act, 1934. *See also* LAB 23.
13	1935. Unemployment Insurance Act, 1935 (Scotland).
18–23	1935–1958. Commissioners for Special Areas: afforestation, trade boards.
27–28	1939. Military Training Act, 1939.
30	1934. Depressed areas: draft of Development and Improvement Bill.
31	1936. Education Bill and Education (Scotland) Bill.
32	1937. Annual Holidays Bill.
33	1937. Special Areas Bill, amendment.
34	1939. Chartered and Other Bodies (Temporary Provisions) Bill.

LAB 17   STATISTICS.
1918–1965.   146 pieces.   [III 93]

1	1918–1919. Cost of Living of the Working Classes Committee.
2	1926–1927. Budget Enquiry Committee: constitution and collection of family budgets.
3	1929–1937. Labour displacement: rationalisation in industry.
5–106	Family Budget Enquiry, 1937–1938; Advisory Committee on Working Class Expenditure. This includes minutes of meetings and the returns of the Enquiry named by areas. Piece 7 containing the memoranda ends in 1951.
108–109	1937–1939. Earnings and Hours Enquiry, 1938.
117	1933–1934. Home Office on policy for inclusion of police pay in Ministry of Labour Statistics.
119	1935–1937. Possibility of producing regular statistical tables of unemployed in Special and Depressed Areas.
120	1936–1939. Local Employment Index: revision of basis of calculating percentages of unemployed.
122	1938. Suggestions for supplementing information published in Ministry of Labour Gazette about trends of pension schemes introduced.
123	1938–1939. Suggestion to group exchanges for the purpose of unemployment percentages.
131	1927–1928. Balfour Committee on Industry and Trade: questionnaire regarding government statistics.
132	1932–1935. Suggested enquiry into wages in connection with Census of Production, 1933.
133	1933–1937. Accuracy of statistics for dock industry.
134	1935–1937. Earnings Enquiry, correspondence with employers' organisations.
136	1938. Enquiry into earnings and hours in rubber industries.

LAB 18   TRAINING.
         1922–1962.   166 pieces.   [III 94]

1–17   1928–1937. Juvenile employment and education.

18–22   1928–1938. Juvenile Transference scheme.

23   1931. Unemployment Insurance Act, 1930; increase in short-time workers.

24–27   1926–1934. Training and work centres for unemployed and Land Settlement training scheme.

28–31   1922–1935. Depressed Areas; general correspondence, including file on unemployment among dock workers.

32–40   1933–1937. Special Areas: including files on Land Settlement, trading estates, the industrial position in Wales, and the employment of ex-servicemen.

44   Complete set of forms relating to various aspects of training.

45   1935–1938. Training scheme for ex-Indian Army personnel.

48–64   Miscellaneous files including training scheme for particular groups of unemployed.

See also LAB 19 *for* juvenile training *and* LAB 23 *for* Special Areas.

LAB 19   YOUTH EMPLOYMENT.
         1913–1969.   192 pieces.   [III 94]

1–3, 7, 1935–1936. Proposals for exercise of local education authorities'
36, 38   choice of employment powers in Blackburn, Bury, Brentford and Chiswick, Merthyr Tydfil, Flintshire, and Stockport.

8–26   1934–1950. Vocational guidance: reports, correspondence, and administration in selected local authorities.

28   Complete set of forms relating to youth employment.

29   1923–1939. Unemployment benefit: Lord Chelmsford's scheme.

30   1937–1938. Residential Home Training Centre at Market Harborough.

31–34   1929–1939. Government training centres.

39   1938. Juvenile advisory committees; areas covered by.

41   1919–1935. Registration of juvenile applicants.

42–43   1934–1937. Special Areas: juvenile transference scheme.

58–82   1929–1969. Miscellaneous files dealing with the National Advisory Council for Juvenile Employment, After-Care Association grants, junior instruction centres, transference of juveniles, vocational guidance, and evacuation of school children.

LAB 20   DISABLED PERSONS.
         1921–1961.   146 pieces.   [III 94]

This class consists of files and a complete set of forms relating to the rehabilitation and employment of disabled persons. Few files cover the inter-war period, and most of these extend beyond 1940. *See also* LAB 18.

LAB 23   SPECIAL AREAS.
            1934–1946.   184 pieces.   [III 94]

The Special Areas (Development and Improvement) Act, 1934, provided for the co-ordination of the efforts of government departments, local authorities, voluntary organisations, etc., in developing particular areas in the country affected by industrial depression. The areas were the Tyneside area of Northumberland, practically all Durham, certain districts in Cumberland, most of South Wales, and parts of Scotland. The Act provided for the appointment of two Commissioners (one for England and Wales, and the other for Scotland). The papers relate to the administration of the special areas, including records of local authorities' schemes, apprenticeships, liaison with the social services, and land settlement schemes. The pieces are arranged under the following headings:

1–19	1934–1945. National Council of Social Service.
20	1934–1935. Army recruitment.
21	1934–1939. Hedingham Scout Training and Employment Scheme.
22	1934–1935. Working days lost through industrial disputes.
23–24	1934–1939. Provision of materials for home decoration by the unemployed.
25	1934–1935. Interdepartmental Committee on Special Areas: reports.
26–27	1934–1937. National Playing Fields Association.
28	1934–1942. Village industries in Durham.
29–30	1934–1938. British Legion.
31–32	1934–1937. Special Areas Bill: powers of Commissioners outside Special Areas, suggested amendment from Jarrow Borough.
33–34	1934–1939. Employment schemes: two cited.
35–48	1935–1939. Committee of Enquiry into Land Settlement Schemes.
49–52	1934–1939. District Nursing Associations.
53–73, 79, 85–89, 91–124, 133–174	1934–1946. Voluntary local amenities schemes: particular schemes named.
74–78, 80–84, 90	1935–1940. Social services; schemes, grants.
125–132	1935–1945. Youth Hostels Association.
175–184	1936–1945. Miscellaneous, including activities of Commissioners on expiry of Special Areas Acts, transfer of measures and functions.

See also CAB 24, BT 55, 14 and 15, BT 56, BT 64/11, BT 104, HLG 30, LAB 8, LAB 17, LAB 18, MH 61, T 172, T 175, T 187.

LAB 27   COAL MINING INDUSTRY DISPUTE AND 1926 GENERAL STRIKE.
            1918–1929.   9 pieces.   [III 94]

1	1918–1927. Diary of events compiled by Government.
2	1920–1926. Memoranda.

3	1925. Negotiations leading to and subsequent to Court of Enquiry.
4	1925–1926. Diary of negotiations.
5	1925–1929. Press cuttings.
6	1925–1929. Suggestions for solution.
7	1926. Miscellaneous papers.
8	1929. Coal marketing scheme.
9	1926. General Strike; memorandum by C. W. K. MacMullen, Principal, Ministry of Labour.

LAB 31   HOLIDAYS WITH PAY.
       1938.   4 pieces.

This class contains minutes, papers, and report of the interdepartmental committee on holidays with pay, draft bill, and regulations for agricultural workers. The interdepartmental committee had representatives from 13 departments for England and Wales, 4 Scottish Offices, and the Commissioners for the Special Areas. *See also* LAB 9.

LAB 900   SPECIMENS OF CLASSES OF DOCUMENTS DESTROYED.

| 10 | 1924. Unemployment in Great Britain: particulars of areas where unemployment was heavy as shown by the 'Live Registers' of employment exchanges, etc. |

PUBLIC TRUSTEE OFFICE

The Public Trustee Act, 1906, led to the establishment of the Public Trustee Office in 1908. The Public Trustee, who is appointed by the Lord Chancellor, can act either solely or jointly with others as executor and trustee under a will, as trustee under a settlement, and in other capacities of a like nature. During the two World Wars the Public Trustee acted as Custodian of Enemy Property.

Records of the Office relating to individual trusts are not public records.

PT 1   CORRESPONDENCE AND PAPERS.
       1906–1959.   52 pieces.

The class contains papers dealing with the administration and staffing of the Office, and its branch office in Manchester, and reorganisation following the report of Sir George Murray's Committee. There are also files dealing with the work of the Office under Trading with the Enemy Acts.

REGISTRY OF FRIENDLY SOCIETIES

A Registry of Friendly Societies was set up in 1846 to approve the rules of friendly societies which had previously been under the jurisdiction of the National Debt Commission. Subsequent legislation extended the functions of the Registry to cover industrial and provident societies, building societies, and trade unions. In

1923 the Chief Registrar of Friendly Societies became also the Industrial Assurance Commissioner controlling collecting friendly societies and the industrial assurance business of assurance companies. The department was renamed the Registry of Friendly Societies and Office of the Industrial Assurance Commissioner.

The Registry is subordinate to the Treasury and various statutory powers relating to its work are vested in the Treasury.

Most classes contain documents of selected societies, which have been removed from the Register. Documents are kept for all societies registered before 1876 and for selected years since, roughly every tenth year:

The years selected for friendly societies are 1885, 1895, 1905, 1913, 1926, 1936, 1944, and 1954.

The years selected for building societies are 1885, 1895, 1905, 1914, 1924, 1934, 1945, and 1956.

The years selected for industrial and provident societies are 1885, 1895, 1905, 1914, 1926, 1934, 1945, and 1958.

The years selected for loan societies are 1885, 1895, 1905, 1914, 1928, and 1939.

Rules, regulations, and annual reports of societies still in operation can be seen at the Office of the Registry of Friendly Societies.

FS 10 FRIENDLY SOCIETIES BRANCHES: RULES AND AMENDMENTS, SERIES II.
1851–1939.   101 pieces.   [III 73].   No restriction on access.

Some friendly societies consist of a central body, called the Order, and branches. This class contains the files of Orders which were removed from the Register after 1912, together with a specimen file of a district and a branch, if such files had not already been retained in FS 5 which ends in 1912. The files are arranged alphabetically by name of Order in two chronological series, 1913–1929 and 1930–1939.

FS 11 TRADE UNIONS: RULES AND AMENDMENTS, SERIES II.
1872–1939.   440 pieces.   [III 74]

This class contains the rules, amendments, annual returns, and various statutory documents of:

(a) trade unions registered under the Trade Union Acts and removed from the Register after 1912;

(b) unregistered trade unions which had political objects as defined in the Trade Union Act, 1913, and which subsequently ceased to have political objects;

(c) unregistered trade unions certified as trade unions within the meaning of the 1913 Act whose certificates were subsequently withdrawn.

The files are arranged alphabetically by name of trade union in two chronological series, 1913–1929 and 1930–1939.

FS 12 TRADE UNIONS: ANNUAL RETURNS.
1872–1950.   504 pieces.   [III 75]

This class consists of annual returns not included in FS 11 submitted by registered and unregistered trade unions still in existence when the returns were made. The returns are arranged alphabetically. The files of registered trade unions are open for inspection without restriction. Those of unregistered trade unions come within the thirty year rule and few are open as most files extend to 1950.

FS 13 BUILDING SOCIETIES: RULES AND AMENDMENTS, ETC., SERIES II.
1837–1939. 181 pieces. [III 73]. No restriction on access.

This class is to contain rules, etc., of selected building societies removed from the Register before 1951. The list is arranged alphabetically by name of society in chronological series; so far it includes those removed from the Register before 1929, and those removed from 1930 to 1939.

FS 14 BUILDING SOCIETIES: ANNUAL RETURNS.
1913–1950. 465 pieces. [III 74]. No restriction on access.

This class contains annual returns submitted by selected building societies removed from the Register after 1950. It also includes returns from all societies removed from the Register whose assets on or after 31st December, 1961, exceeded £30 million.

FS 15 FRIENDLY SOCIETIES: RULES AND AMENDMENTS TO RULES, ETC.
1793–1939. 1,139 pieces. [III 73]. No restriction on access.

This class is to contain rules, amendments to rules, annual returns, and various statutory documents of selected friendly societies removed from the Register before 1951. The list is divided into two sections covering societies removed from the Register before 1930 and those removed from 1930 to 1939. The pieces are arranged alphabetically by name of society within the following groups:

Friendly societies and miscellaneous societies other than those listed below.
Cattle insurance societies.
Benevolent societies.
Working men's clubs.
Specially authorised societies.

FS 16 FRIENDLY SOCIETIES: ANNUAL RETURNS.
1909–1950. 83 pieces. [III 73]. No restriction on access.

This class contains the annual returns of selected friendly societies which were removed from the Register after 1950. They are arranged in the same way as in FS 15.

FS 17 INDUSTRIAL AND PROVIDENT SOCIETIES: RULES AND AMENDMENTS ETC.,
SERIES II.
1853–1939. 359 pieces. [III 74]. No restriction on access.

This class is to contain rules, amendments to rules, annual returns, and various statutory documents of industrial and provident societies removed from the Register before 1951. The files are arranged alphabetically by name of society in two chronological series, those removed from the Register before 1930 and those removed from 1930 to 1939.

FS 18   INDUSTRIAL AND PROVIDENT SOCIETIES: ANNUAL RETURNS.
　　　　1919–1950.　　6 pieces.　　[III 74].　　No restriction on access.

This class consists of annual returns of selected societies which were removed from the Register after 1950. The files at present transferred consist only of annual returns submitted by the Co-operative Wholesale Society.

FS 19   LOAN SOCIETIES: RULES AND AMENDMENTS, SERIES II.
　　　　1841–1939.　　86 pieces.

This class contains rules and amendments to rules of selected loan societies removed from the Register between 1913 and 1939. The files are arranged in alphabetical order of societies.

FS 20   DISPUTE FILES.
　　　　1923–1943.　　56 pieces.

This class contains a representative selection of case papers of disputes. They are arranged in two groups, those between collecting societies or industrial assurance companies and persons making claims on them under or in respect of policies issued by them and those between the Post Office Savings Bank and persons making claims in respect of deposits. Within these two groups the files are arranged in chronological order.

Papers of societies removed from the Register between 1940 and 1950 will be transferred during 1971.

UNIVERSITY GRANTS COMMITTEE

From 1889 to 1911 the majority of grants to universities and colleges were administered by the Treasury. In 1911 the administration of the Universities and Colleges Vote covering a number of universities was transferred to the Board of Education, but separate votes for certain universities continued to be administered by the Treasury. In 1919 all the grants were amalgamated and transferred to the new University Grants Committee appointed by the Chancellor of the Exchequer as a Standing Committee of the Treasury. Although formally the Committee is only an advisory body, in practice the allocation of money has been almost entirely entrusted to it.

In 1948, grants-in-aid to university departments of agriculture in England and Wales were transferred from the Ministry of Agriculture and Fisheries and in 1949 responsibilities for grant-aiding the Glasgow Veterinary College and in 1950 for the Royal Veterinary College were taken from the Secretary of State for Scotland. In 1963 the Treasury handed control over the Committee to the Lord President of the Council. In 1964 the Committee became responsible to the Secretary of State for Education and Science.

UGC 1   MINUTES.
　　　　1919–1956.　　4 pieces.　　[III 127]

Volume I covers 1919–1933; Volume II, covering 1934–1949, is not open.

UGC 2   AGENDA AND PAPERS.
            1919–1957.   39 pieces.   [III 127]

Agenda for Committee meetings, together with supporting papers. They are in bound volumes which are designated only by their year in the class list.

1–20   1919–1939. Records for 1929 are wanting. No meetings were held in 1932.

UGC 3   RETURNS.
            1919–1959.   40 pieces.   [III 127].   No restriction on access.

Returns from universities and university colleges in receipt of grants.

1–20   1919–1939. Each volume covers one year. Returns for 1939–1940 are wanting.

UGC 4   DEPARTMENTAL EXPENDITURE SCHEDULES.
            1921–1938.   17 pieces.   [III 127]

Schedules of the Committee's expenditure on grants, showing amounts allocated to each institution, arranged under the different purposes for which the grants were made.

1–17   1921–1938. Volumes are dated and each covers one academic year.

UGC 5   MISCELLANEA.
            1911–1942.   17 pieces.   [III 127]

7   1911–1919. Board of Education Advisory Committee on University Grants: reports, minutes, etc.

8   1918. Correspondence and papers leading to the deputation to the President of the Board of Education and Chancellor of the Exchequer from University Institutions, November, 1918.

9–12   1919–1938. Papers and accounts relating to Irish universities and colleges.

13   1936. Specimen file of interviews with representatives from provincial institutions

14–15   1938–1939. University organisation and finance in wartime.

UGC 6   REPORTS.
            1935–1960.   8 pieces.   [III 127].   No restriction on access.

1   1935–1947. Printed reports.

LAW AND ORDER

HOME OFFICE

Before 1782 the two principal Secretaries of State for the Northern and Southern Departments shared between them duties concerning domestic and foreign affairs. In that year the Secretary of State for the Southern Department was made Secretary of State for Home Affairs, with exclusive jurisdiction over internal business. The Home Office's present duties concern the maintenance of peace and internal security, and it deals with such internal affairs of England and Wales as are not assigned to other departments. Many of the new departments established during this century have taken over and developed powers first exercised by the Home Office, for example the Ministries of Labour and Health. The Home Office has statutory duties concerning the regulation of aliens, naturalisation, the penal system, the police, child care services (until 1970), parliamentary elections, civil defence, and the fire service.

For a chronological list of some of the changes in the functions of the Home Office during the inter-war period, see the general list under 'Social Services'. Other transfers of function affecting the Home Office include:

1920	To Board of Trade, inspection of mines and quarries, see POWER group.
	Responsibility for State Management Districts under the Licensing Act, on the abolition of the Central Control Board (Liquor Traffic) of the Ministry of Munitions.
1922	Home Office became responsible for relations with the newly formed government of Northern Ireland.
1925	To Ministry of Labour, registration of trade unions.
1935	Air Raid Precautions' Department set up to act on behalf of the various departments concerned with civil defence.
1937	To Ministry of Transport, responsibility for the preparation of annual returns of road accidents.
1939	Ministry of Home Security set up. The Minister of Home Security was also Home Secretary.
1940	To Ministry of Labour, the factory inspectorate.
1945	Ministry of Home Security dissolved, some functions to Home Office.
1946	To Ministry of Labour, permanent transfer of Factories Acts administration.
1951	Home Secretary became Minister of Welsh affairs; a separate Secretary of State for Wales was appointed in 1964.
1960	Charity Commission reconstituted. Henceforth to be represented by Home Secretary and not a Parliamentary Commissioner.

Many of the classes consist of 'entry-books' or bound volumes of out-letters; for nearly all of which the last piece is dated 1921, after that date the records are no longer kept.

HO 5   ENTRY BOOKS: ALIENS.
        1794–1921.   142 pieces.   [II 179].   Closed for 100 years.

HO 38   WARRANT BOOKS: GENERAL SERIES.
        1782–1921.   72 pieces.   [II 191]

Entries of warrants. Indexed.

HO 45   CORRESPONDENCE AND PAPERS: DOMESTIC AND GENERAL: REGISTERED
        PAPERS.
        1841–1939.   18,354 pieces.   [II 186]

This is the main class of Home Office papers. It consists of boxes of files. The class list is in four parts: for the period up to 1919, 1919–1920, 1921–1922, and 1923 onward. The pieces are arranged in these lists under subject headings. To obtain references for the papers before 1921, lists of files in the subject list must be keyed with the box references in the box list to find the piece number. From 1921, box numbers as well as file numbers are given together in the class list. There is no contents list to the headings; they are given below to give an indication of the range of topics covered over the inter-war period and the order of arrangement. Registers of the correspondence are in HO 46.

Accidents in the home (including transfer of responsibility from Board of Trade
    to Home Office, 1924–1928).
Acts (under Bills and acts, and Legislation).
Addresses to the Crown.
Advertisements (*see* Bye-laws).
Agriculture.
Albert Medal.
Aliens.
Animals.
Appointments (general not included elsewhere).
Armorial bearings.
Auctions.
Aviation.
Banks.
Baronets.
Bastardy.
Betting and gambling.
Bills and acts.
Blasphemy.
Borstal.
Building societies, 1894–1920.
Burials.
Bye-Laws; cited individually.
Calendar reform.
Capital punishment; statistics, 1910–30.
Cenotaph; Select Committee on, 1930.
Census of 1911.
Channel Islands and Isle of Man.
Charities.

Charters.
Children.
Chimney sweeps.
Civil defence.
Clerks of the Peace.
Clerks to Justices.

Commissions and committees: includes papers dealing with the following:

1914–1919. Committee on Treatment by Enemy of British Prisoners of War.
1916–1919. War Charities Committee.
1888–1924. Railway and Canal Commission Constitution, rules. *See also* J 75.
1927–1928. Royal Commission on London Squares. *See also* HLG 10.
1927–1930. Royal Commission on National Museum and Galleries. *See also* T 105.
1923–1934. Royal Commission on Local Government, three reports. *See also* HLG 8.
1935–1936. Royal Commission on Merthyr Tydfil. *See also* HLG 12 and HLG 30.
1936–1937. Departmental Committee on Hours of Employment of Young Persons in certain unregistered occupations: Home Office comments on report.
1929–1930. League of Nations: Committee on Communication and Transport.
1929–1938. Royal Commission on Civil Service. *See also* T 169.
1935–1938. Examination of Local Government in Tyneside: appointment of members, reports. *See also* HLG 11 and HLG 30.
1927–1930. Indian Statutory Commission.
1937–1940. Royal Commission on Distribution of Industrial Population: copies of reports, appointments. *See also* HLG 27.
1938–1939. Committee on Imposition of Royalties by Marketing Boards: statement by Home Office.

Commissions of the Peace.
Commissions Rogatoires.
Copyright.
Coroners and inquests.
Corporal punishment.
Courts, general.
Criminal.
Dangerous drugs.
Dangerous substances.
Daylight saving.
Debtors.
Deserters.
Diplomatic privilege.
Disturbances: strikes, General Strike, political meetings, demonstrations, suffragettes, Zinoviev Letter, Trade Disputes and Trade Unions (Amendment) Bill, 1931, International Conference on the Repression of Terrorism, 1937, constitution of the Second International.
Ecclesiastical.
Elections.
Entertainments.
Executions.
Exhibitions.

8

Exhumations.

Explosives.

Extradition.

Factories.

Fairs and markets.

Fines.

Firearms.

Fires.

Fisheries.

Food.

Foreign: titles of foreign aristocrats.

Game.

Home Office: staff and office questions, establishment.

Honours.

Inebriates.

Inflammable goods.

Ireland.

Isle of Man.

Juries.

Law Officers' opinions.

Legislation: some of the subjects covered include:

    1906–1923. Weekly Rest Day Bills.

    1920–1926. Reform of Legitimacy Laws.

    1927. Landlord and Tenant Bill.

    1928–1931. Spiritualism and Psychical Research (Exemption) Bill.

    1930–1937. Hawke Committee on the Law concerning Stopping Up and Diverting Highways, 1930–37.

    1932–1938. Chimney Sweepers Acts.

    1938. Jamaican Indemnity.

    1908–1940. Access to mountains.

    1917–1922. Dentists Bill, 1921.

    (There are also references to bills under topic headings.)

Liquor licensing.

Lords Lieutenant.

Lunacy.

Magistrates.

Maintenance (wife and child).

Marriages.

Mayors.

Medical.

Meetings, processions.

Mental health.

Military.

Moneylenders.

Mortmain, licences in.

Names and Arms, change of.

Nationality and Naturalisation.

Naval.

Noise abatement.

Nuisances (public).

Oaths.

Pardons.
Parks, open spaces.
Passes (Ivory Passes).
Pawnbrokers.
Pedlars Acts.
Peerages.
Petitions of Right.
Petitions to the Crown.
Poisons.
Police.
Post Office.
Precedence.
Press.
Prison and prisoners.
Probation.
Property.
Prosecutions.
Prostitution.
Provisional orders.
Publications (including indecent).
Quarter sessions.
Railways.
Rates.
Recorders.
Records (of H.O.).
Registration of births.
Rewards.
Royal.
St. Patrick, Order of.
Schools.
Sedition: Seditious and Blasphemous Teaching to Children Bills, 1922–1930.
Sewers, Commissioners of, 1919.
Ships.
Shops.
Slaves.
Statistics: creation of peers, 1909–1920; deaths from burns, 1873–1929; parliamentary papers, 1896–1929; betting and gaming; homicide; smallpox, 1903–1937; trade and social conditions (abstracts of labour statistics); crime.
Street trading.
Strikes: 1917–18 railway strike (*see also* Disturbances).
Summary jurisdiction.
Sunday observance.
Trade unions.
Traffic.
Universities.
Vagrancy.
Vivisection.
Wales.
War: anti-recruiting and peace propaganda; aliens; public order; exchange of prisoners of war; conscientious objectors.
Wards.

Warrants.
Wild birds.
Witnesses.

HO 46   DAILY REGISTERS OF DOMESTIC CORRESPONDENCE.
            1841–1945.   358 pieces.   [II 186]

These are registers of correspondence received each day at the Home Office and found in HO 45. The series includes indexes of names and special subjects. The volumes are arranged by years and the subjects are in alphabetical order.

HO 56   PETITIONS: ENTRY BOOKS.
            1784–1922.   31 pieces.   [II 191]

Entry books of out-letters relating to Petitions of Right. Indexed.

HO 57   ADDRESSES: ENTRY BOOKS.
            1829–1921.   23 pieces.   [II 191]

These deal with addresses of various kinds, such as applications for patronage, for permission to make presentations to the sovereign, etc. They contain notes of addresses and entries of the relevant out-letters. Indexed.

HO 65   ENTRY BOOKS: POLICE, SERIES I.
            1795–1921.   126 pieces.   [II 182]

Out-letters relating to county, borough, and Scottish police.

HO 82   ENTRY BOOKS: ACCOUNTS AND ESTIMATES.
            1752–1921.   31 pieces.   [II 187]

Accounts relating to staff appointments. Indexed.

HO 85   ENTRY BOOKS: BURIALS.
            1854–1921.   119 pieces.   [II 187]

Correspondence relating to execution of various Burial Acts.

HO 87   ENTRY BOOKS: FACTORIES.
            1836–1921.   53 pieces.   [II 188]

This class contains copies of orders relating to the administration of the Factories, Mines, Collieries, and Highways Acts, with some relating to exemption from military service.

HO 99   CHANNEL ISLANDS: ENTRY BOOKS.
            1760–1921.   48 pieces.   [II 192]

Out-letters.

HO 115   WARRANT BOOKS: CHURCH BOOKS.
             1828–1921.   9 pieces.   [II 192]

These are entries of royal warrants of ecclesiastical appointments, presentations to livings, congés d'élire, appointments of Almsmen and Poor Knights of Windsor, dispensations, degrees, and relevant correspondence. Each volume is indexed.

HO 116   WARRANT BOOKS: CREATION AND WRITS OF SUMMONS.
         1783–1921.   6 pieces.   [II 192]

These are entry books of warrants for the issue of letters patent for the creation of peers, baronets, and knights. They contain also warrants to the Lord Chancellor for settling the 'precedency' of new creations and for writs of summons to peers to attend Parliament. There is one indexed volume for the period 1906–21.

HO 117   WARRANT BOOKS: LETTER OR DOMESTIC BOOKS.
         1806–1922.   46 pieces.   [II 192]

These are entry books of out-letters to the Treasury, Lord Chancellor, Law Officers, College of Arms, and other officers and departments, and miscellaneous individuals, concerning royal warrants, licences, petitions to the Crown, honours and awards, appointments, etc. Each volume is indexed.

HO 118   WARRANT BOOKS: MISCELLANEOUS BOOKS.
         1750–1934.   5 pieces.   [II 192]

The only relevant piece is the Secretary of State's warrant book, 1888–1934, containing entries of warrants of appointments.

HO 120   ENTRY BOOKS: HORSE GUARDS AND PARK GATES.
         1809–1921.   7 pieces.   [II 188]

Out-letters relating to the granting of 'Ivory Passes' allowing people to ride through the Park Gates.

HO 124   WARRANTS: ROYAL MARRIAGES.
         1791–1965.   58 pieces.   [II 191]

These are original letters patent and sign manual warrants signifying the Sovereign's assent.

HO 125   WARRANTS: ROYAL (VARIOUS).
         1860–1948.   16 pieces.   [II 191]

These are original letters patent and sign manual warrants relating to the styles and titles of members of the Royal Family, authority to the Prince of Wales to confer knighthood, and other matters.

HO 133   ENTRY BOOKS: EXPLOSIVES.
         1873–1921.   41 pieces.   [II 188]

Out-letters, mainly concerning setting up of explosives factories and granting of licences.

HO 134   ENTRY BOOKS: EXTRADITION.
         1873–1921.   41 pieces.   [II 188].   Closed for 100 years.

HO 139   OFFICIAL PRESS BUREAU.
         1914–1919.   55 pieces.   [II 190]

The majority of these records were destroyed and most of the files now preserved have lost much of their original contents. Piece 55 is an index, alphabetically arranged.

HO 140   CALENDARS OF PRISONERS.
         1868–1958.   591 pieces.   [II 179].   Closed for 100 years.

These are lists of the prisoners tried at assizes and quarter sessions, showing the charges, verdicts, sentences, etc.

HO 142   WARRANT BOOKS: CHANGE OF NAME AND ARMS.
         1868–1921.   8 pieces.   [II 192]

One indexed volume covers 1912–21.

HO 144–147, 151 and 156 deal with criminals, criminal lunatics, administration of convicts' property, vivisection, etc. and are closed for 100 years.

HO 152   ENTRY BOOKS: DOMESTIC AND INDUSTRIAL.
         1899–1921.   78 pieces.   [II 187]

These are out-letter books classified under the following headings: Anatomy, Children's Act, Commissions and Committees, Fairs, Income Tax, Ireland, Licensing, Title Royal, Promulgation of Statutes, Verification (of signatures for legal purposes), Truck, and General.

HO 153   ENTRY BOOKS: EXCHEQUER FINES.
         1887–1921.   22 pieces.   [II 188]

Out-letters, mainly to clerks to justices about the payment of fines imposed in cases of summary convictions.

   21–22   1916–1921. Out-letter books.

HO 154   ENTRY BOOKS: MERCHANT SHIPPING.
         1880–1921.   16 pieces.   [II 188]

Out-letters of, or concerning the appointment of, assessors to hold investigations under the Shipping Casualties Investigation Act, 1879, and the Merchant Shipping Act, 1894.

HO 155   ENTRY BOOKS: STATISTICS.
         1856–1921.   14 pieces.   [II 189]

These are out-letters to courts, police, coroners, and others, about the provision of statistics concerning civil proceedings, crime, inquests, etc.

HO 157   ENTRY BOOKS: WORKMEN'S COMPENSATION.
　　　　　1898–1921.　13 pieces.　[II 189]

Out-letters of, or concerning the, appointment of medical referees under the Workmen's Compensation Act, 1897. *See also* PIN 11 and 12.

HO 158   CIRCULARS.
　　　　　1835–1945.　37 pieces.　[III 83]

Circulars on various subjects to police and local authorities.

20–31　1918–1939. Most volumes cover two years and each is indexed.

HO 159   ENTRY BOOKS: SALARIES, FEES, AND BOROUGH FUNDS.
　　　　　1887–1921.　10 pieces.　[II 189]

Bound volumes of out-letters relating to salaries and fees of magistrates, coroners, clerks of the peace, and justices' clerks.

HO 162   ENTRY BOOKS: ALIENS RESTRICTION.
　　　　　1905–1921.　128 pieces.　[II 179].　Closed for 100 years.

Entry books of out-letters relating to various aspects of the working of the Aliens Act, 1905, including the appointment of immigration officers, medical inspectors, and immigration boards, the issue of bonds of exemption for shipping companies, expulsion, etc.

HO 163   ENTRY BOOKS: CRIMINAL CASES.
　　　　　1899–1921.　99 pieces.　[II 180].　Closed for 100 years.

Out-letters relating to petitions from or on behalf of prisoners, confirmation and remission of sentences, medical enquiries, dates of executions and respite of capital sentences, the administration of convicts' property, and the production of prisoners to give evidence at trials.

HO 164   ENTRY BOOKS: BILLS AND PROVISIONAL ORDERS.
　　　　　1899–1921.　6 pieces.　[II 187]

Out-letters relating to the approval of and amendments to bills presented by local authorities, railways, and other bodies.

HO 165   ENTRY BOOKS: BYE-LAWS.
　　　　　1899–1921.　10 pieces.　[II 187]

Out-letters relating to the approval of and amendments to bye-laws passed by local authorities.

HO 167   ENTRY BOOKS: CHILDREN.
　　　　　1905–1921.　48 pieces.　[II 187].　Closed for 100 years.

Out-letters relating to the Employment of Children Act, 1903, and Children's Act, 1908.

HO 168   ENTRY BOOKS: EXEQUATURS AND RECOGNITIONS.
1899–1921.   6 pieces.   [II 188]

Letters to mayors, the Foreign Office, and chief constables, regarding the appointment and recognition of consular officials.

HO 170   ENTRY BOOKS: LIQUOR.
1899–1921.   19 pieces.   [II 188]

Out-letters concerning the administration of the Inebriates Acts, the establishment of state (inebriate) reformatories, and the approval of rules made under the Licensing Act, 1904.

HO 171   ENTRY BOOKS: SHOPS.
1900–1921.   12 pieces.   [II 189]

Out-letters relating to closing orders made by local authorities under the Shop Hours Act, 1904.

HO 172   ENTRY BOOKS: PUBLIC HEALTH.
1909–1921.   4 pieces.   [II 189]

Out-letters relating to orders made under the Public Health Acts Amendment Act, 1907.

HO 173   ENTRY BOOKS: HOME OFFICE.
1899–1921.   3 pieces.   [III 83]

Letters to other departments concerning establishment matters within the Home Office, such as works, records, staff, etc.

HO 174   ENTRY BOOKS: ADVERTISEMENTS.
1908–1921.   2 pieces.   [III 83]

Out-letters relating to the control of advertisements on hoardings, etc.

HO 175   ENTRY BOOKS: BARONETAGE.
1910–1921.   3 pieces.   [III 83]

Out-letters relating to creations and successions, etc.

HO 177   ENTRY BOOKS: DANGEROUS DRUGS.
1920–1921.   4 pieces.   [III 83]

Out-letters.

HO 178   ENTRY BOOKS: EDWARD MEDAL AND KING'S POLICE MEDAL.
1920–1921.   1 piece.   [III 83]

Out-letters.

HO 179   ENTRY BOOKS: ENTERTAINMENTS, THEATRES, ETC.
          1910–1921.   1 piece.   [III 83]

Out-letters relating to licensing, safety precautions, etc.

HO 180   ENTRY BOOKS: IMPERIAL SERVICE ORDER AND ORDER OF THE BRITISH
          EMPIRE.
          1902–1921.   6 pieces.   [III 83]

Out-letters.

HO 181   ENTRY BOOKS: TITLE ROYAL.
          1905–1921.   4 pieces.   [III 83]

Out-letters concerning the use of 'Royal' or similar titles.

HO 182   ENTRY BOOKS: TRAFFIC (AERIAL AND ROAD).
          1910–1921.   4 pieces.   [III 83]

Out-letters.

HO 183   ENTRY BOOKS: WILD BIRDS.
          1899–1921.   2 pieces.   [III 83]

Out-letters relating to the protection of wild birds by orders made by the Secretary
of State.

HO 184   IRELAND: ROYAL IRISH CONSTABULARY.
          1816–1922.   64 pieces.   [III 83]

The records preserved consist of: officers' registers, registers of service, returns
of personnel, journals of the Auxiliary Division (1920–22), and law opinions,
indexed, to 1919.

HO 185   CENTRAL CONTROL BOARD (LIQUOR TRAFFIC) AND STATE MANAGEMENT
          DISTRICTS: CENTRAL OFFICE.
          1915–1950.   273 pieces.

This class contains records of the Central Office and minutes, papers, and reprints
of the Royal Commission on Licensing in England and Wales, 1929–1930.

HO 186   MINISTRY OF HOME SECURITY: AIR RAID PRECAUTIONS, 1939.
          1935–1939.   158 pieces.

This class contains some files dated before 1939, which contain material relating
to civil preparation for war. The files are listed under subject headings.

HO 194   CIVIL DEFENCE GRANTS.
          1938–1959.   34 pieces.

This class contains files of the Finance Division of the Ministry of Home Security
dealing with grants to local authorities.

LAW OFFICERS' DEPARTMENT

The Attorney General and the Solicitor General are the Law Officers for England and Wales. They are responsible for giving legal advice to the government, for the interpretation and application of the law. The Attorney General is responsible for the conduct of important prosecutions and litigation to which the Crown is party.

LO 2 REGISTERED FILES.
      1910–1960.   46 pieces.   [III 94].   Files are closed for 50 or 100 years.

This class contains applications for the Attorney General's Fiat for leave to appeal to the House of Lords in criminal cases, and also papers of enquiries for example into articles in the *Daily Worker* in 1932 and the *Sunday Dispatch* in 1935. Two files for 1919 and 1920 are open.

LORD CHANCELLOR'S OFFICE

In addition to his Parliamentary and judicial functions the Lord Chancellor is responsible for the administration of the Supreme Court, county courts, Pensions Appeal Tribunal, the Public Record Office, the Council on Tribunals, the Land Registry, the Lands Tribunal, the Public Trustee Office, and the Judge Advocate General's Office. He is also concerned with the arrangement of judicial business in the House of Lords, Privy Council, Supreme Court, and county courts, with legislation, the making of statutory instruments, with lunacy, legal aid, and other matters. In addition a considerable and varied patronage is vested in the Lord Chancellor, including judicial appointments, the appointment of justices of the peace and certain ecclesiastical appointments. Since 1885 the Permanent Secretary to the Lord Chancellor has also held the office of Clerk of the Crown in Chancery; and some administrative records of the Crown Office will be found in the LCO classes. Other Crown Office records are in the Chancery group.

   In 1925 the Lord Chancellor's Office took over from the Paymaster General the function of pay office under the Court of Chancery Funds Act, 1872. The office of Accountant General of the Supreme Court was revived and performed by the Clerk of Crown in Chancery.

   In 1949 the Copying and Typing Department which performs the copying work of all departments of the Supreme Court was moved from the Central Office of the Supreme Court to the Lord Chancellor's Office.

   The Lord Chancellor has jurisdiction over certain matters concerning the lower criminal courts in England and Wales and his functions have been extended by the Crown Courts Act of 1971.

   The Lord Chancellor's Office has grown during this century from a small private office to a distinct administrative department.

   Many records deal with the law relating to property, including a Ministry of Reconstruction Committee on the acquisition of land, LCO 3.

LCO 2 REGISTERED FILES.
      1882–1966.   2,955 pieces.   [III 95].   Various files are closed for 50 or 100 years.

These contain correspondence and papers dealing with the various courts and government departments for which the Lord Chancellor is responsible, ecclesiastical matters, the interpretation of bills and acts, with the amendments and rules arising, together with the reports of several committees set up by the Lord Chancellor and papers concerning their work. The files are arranged in roughly chronological order under certain broad headings.

These headings appear more than once and the grouping of files is somewhat erratic; for example there is a heading 'Bills' but many references to parliamentary bills fall outside it. The range of topics covered is very wide, including for example adoption of children, appeals under the Health Insurance, Unemployment Insurance, and Pensions Acts, bankruptcy, constitutional matters, property, and Welsh nationalism. A large number of committees are cited, including the Committee on Ministers' Powers (Donoughmore), 1929–31, *see also* PIN 4/91, 92 *and* MH 71/1–3. A subject index is available in the search rooms.

LCO 3   MINISTRY OF RECONSTRUCTION COMMITTEES.
         1917–1919.   45 pieces.   [III 95]

1–12   1917–1919. Acquisition and Valuation of Land Committee: correspondence and papers, including papers on the setting up of the Committee.

13–27   1917–1919. Acquisition and Valuation of Land Committee: agendas, minutes, documents circulated to members, and reports.

23–33   1918. Acquisition of Land Committee (Compensation): agendas, minutes, and documents.

34–45   1918–1919. Acquisition and Valuation of Land Committee, Mining sub-committee: agendas, minutes, documents, and reports.

LCO 4   ESTABLISHMENT.
         1918–1958.   21 pieces.

The only available inter-war material is:

1–3; 5   1938–1941. Committee on the Official Solicitor's Department: papers and report.

6   1918–1922. Refreshment arrangements at the Law Courts.

LCO 5   RETURNS OF CROWN LIVINGS.
         1793–1940.   3 pieces.

2   1874–1940. Account of livings in the patronage of the Lord Chancellor. Returns arranged in alphabetical order of livings.

LCO 6   CROWN OFFICE: REGISTERED FILES.
         1924–1959.   27 pieces.

This class contains files from a Crown Office series introduced in 1925. Earlier files of the Crown Office are in LCO 2. At present the files relate to the preparation of sign manual warrants for the issue of letters patent for:

The Constitution of High Courts of Judicature for various provinces of India.

The appointment of Indian bishops.

The appointment of Indian judges.

The granting of licences in mortmain to be passed under the Great Seal.

METROPOLITAN POLICE OFFICES

The Metropolitan Police Act 1829 provided for the setting up of the Metropolitan Police Force now under the authority of the Home Secretary. The responsibilities of the force are similar to those of any other local police force, but it has in addition some wider functions, such as responsibility for the physical protection of the Royal Family and some Ministers of the Crown, the maintenance of criminal records for the whole country, and assistance to other police forces in the investigation of crime.

The internal organisation and administration of the force was changed in 1968, and the relationship between the Commissioner and the Receiver redefined. Previously the Commissioner had executive control of the force and the Receiver was responsible for finance, buildings, and supply.

The cost of the Metropolitan Police is shared equally between the rates and the Exchequer.

MEPOL 1   OFFICE OF THE COMMISSIONER: LETTERS BOOKS.
        1829–1919.   63 pieces.   [II 215].   Closed for 100 years.

These are entry books or press copies of the Commissioner's general and confidential out-letters.

MEPOL 2   OFFICE OF THE COMMISSIONER: CORRESPONDENCE AND PAPERS.
        1816–1963.   5,787 pieces.   [III 96]

These files deal with the organisation and duties of the Metropolitan Police. Before 1920 the papers are arranged in order of their former departmental references. The registration system in use from 1921 to 1940 provided for the classification of papers under a large number of subject headings. The pieces 1807 and later, falling after 1920, are therefore grouped under these headings but the headings are not in alphabetical order, may appear more than once, and individual files are not in strict chronological order within these sections. There is an index to the class using these section headings. The range of topics is very wide, of general interest are files on civil unrest, listed under 'Meetings and Processions', and on the Geddes cuts, 1922–23, listed under 'Economies'. Below are the pieces containing inter-war material before piece 1807, which are not included in the index:

1121	1907–1919. Pocket books; style of reporting.
1623–1646	1918. Special Constables.
1676	1915–1926. 'Marriages of Convenience' (Aliens).
1693–5	1918–1919. Commissioner's Office: general registry; pay for local service.
1710	1916–1919. 'Red Star Society', unregistered charity.
1735–1806	1918–1922. Miscellaneous: air raids; pilfering; formation of Metropolitan Police Representative Board; visits of foreign statesmen; women police; white slave traffic; discipline and pay; Desborough Committee Report on Police Service; aliens repatriation.

MEPOL 3   OFFICE OF THE COMMISSIONER: CORRESPONDENCE AND PAPERS, SPECIAL SERIES.
        1830–1962.   1,780 pieces.   [III 96].   Closed for 100 years.
These deal with special police duties, murders, and other matters.

MEPOL 5   OFFICE OF THE RECEIVER: CORRESPONDENCE AND PAPERS.
          1829–1960.   231 pieces.   [II 215]

These papers deal mainly with administration and finance. Pieces 91 onwards, starting in 1907, are fully described but are not in chronological order. Subjects covered include: cost of police duties during strikes including the General Strike; claims under Riot Damages Acts; pensions; the Police Reserve, 1916–1920; the use of aircraft; economies, 1931–1933; and the Metropolitan Police College. There is also a section on war measures, 1938 onwards, starting at piece 151.

MEPOL 6   CRIMINAL RECORDS OFFICE: HABITUAL CRIMINALS REGISTERS, ETC.
          1881–1941.   64 pieces.   [III 96].   Closed for 50 or 100 years.

These are registers of criminals as defined by sections 5–8 of the Prevention of Crime Act, 1871, with examples of Police Gazettes, Supplements 'A' and Informations (London Area).

MEPOL 7   OFFICE OF THE COMMISSIONER: POLICE ORDERS.
          1829–1968.   136 pieces.   Closed for 50 years.

The volumes in this class contain general and confidential notices on the application of the law and on personnel matters. Some of them were later incorporated in General Orders in MEPOL 3.

81–82   1919–1920. One year per volume.

PRISON COMMISSION

The Prison Commission was established by Royal Warrant under the Prisons Act, 1877, as a Statutory Board to administer and inspect prisons subject to the control of the Secretary of State. This responsibility was extended to all prisons, and to borstal institutions, remand centres, and detention centres. In 1963 the Prison Commission was absorbed into the Home Office.

PRICOM 7   REGISTERED PAPERS: SERIES I.
           1838–1928.   738 pieces.   [III 108]

Registered files deal with a wide variety of subjects concerned with the management of prisons and the treatment of prisoners. The papers are arranged in three main divisions:

General administration.
Prisoners (general) and prisoners (special classes).
Staff.

The table of contents precedes the class list. The records contain a history of Director of Convict Prisons (1850–1949) and the Prison Commissioners (1877–1963). The files deal mainly with particular cases. Among the topics of interest are a section on young offenders, and one on international congresses on crime.

DIRECTOR OF PUBLIC PROSECUTIONS

The office of Director of Public Prosecutions was set up under the Prosecution of Offences Act, 1879, and between 1884 and 1908 was held in conjunction with the office of Treasury Solicitor. The Home Secretary appoints the Director of Public Prosecutions and the Assistant Directors, but is not responsible for the work of the office which is under the general supervision of the Attorney General who makes regulations governing the duties of the Director. These duties are outlined in the Prosecution of Offences Regulations, 1946. Since 1908 several Acts have been passed under which certain offences can only be prosecuted by the Director or with his consent.

DPP 1   CASE PAPERS: OLD SERIES.
      1889–1930.   95 pieces.   [II 240].   Closed for 100 years.

Files of case papers consisting of police and other reports, copies of depositions and exhibits, counsels' briefs and papers, correspondence. Original documents are returned to their owners by the Clerk of the Court, or the Director, at the conclusion of a trial.

DPP 2   CASE PAPERS: NEW SERIES.
      1931–1943.   1,192 pieces.   [II 240].   Closed for 100 years.

A continuation of DPP 1 based on a different system of registration.

DPP 3   CASE PAPERS: REGISTERS OF CASES.
      1884–1946.   127 pieces.   [III 108].   Closed for 100 years.

Registers of applications for advice or action and of other communications addressed to the Director by chief constables, town clerks, and others.

DPP 4   TRANSCRIPTS OF PROCEEDINGS.
      1846–1931.   47 pieces.   [III 108]

Transcripts of proceedings in selected criminal trials. The only piece falling into the period is:

47   1931. Kylsant and another, case of fraud.

TREASURY SOLICITOR AND H.M. PROCURATOR GENERAL

The office of Treasury Solicitor was created in the seventeenth century to deal with matters relating to revenue. Other functions were added and in 1876 the office was combined with that of H.M. Procurator General which performed many duties under Admiralty, ecclesiastical, and prerogative law. Between 1884 and 1908 the Treasury Solicitor was also Director of Public Prosecutions.

The Treasury Solicitor can hold real and personal property, can sue and be sued, and acts for the Crown in the administration of estates of deceased intestate persons; he also provides legal services for most government departments. During wartime this department had charge of all prize proceedings in this country.

TS 2   LETTER BOOKS: TREASURY.
      1806–1859; 1899–1919.   80 pieces.   [II 302]

   78–80   1918–1919. Copies of out-letters to the Treasury; each volume is indexed.

TS 3   LETTER BOOKS: MISCELLANEOUS.
      1813–1861; 1898–1924.   44 pieces.   [II 302]

   43–44   1919–1924. Prosecution of German war criminals, under article 227 of the Peace Treaty; each volume is indexed.

TS 5   REPORT BOOK.
      1806–1860; 1899–1919.   88 pieces.   [II 302]

   82–88   1918–1919. Reports and letters to the Treasury and various other departments; each volume is indexed.

TS 12   WEST NEW JERSEY SOCIETY RECORDS.
      1658–1921.   100 pieces.   [II 303]

This Society was formed around 1691 for the development of land in New Jersey. The land was divided into 1,600 parts, forming the shares of the Adventurers who had formed the company. In 1914, 28½ shares remained unclaimed and in 1923 were transferred to the Crown as *bona vacantia,* and the records and papers of the Society were deposited at the P.R.O. The only inter-war material is as follows:

   3   1775–1921. General correspondence.

TS 13   KING'S PROCTOR: PRIZE AND PRIZE BOUNTY CASES, DECREES AND AFFIDAVITS.
      1914–1928.   858 pieces.   [II 303]

Enemy ships and cargoes belonging to enemies of the Crown that were seized during the war were subject to the jurisdiction of the High Court of Justice (Probate, Divorce, and Admiralty Division). Ships and cargoes that the Court decided were good and lawful prize were declared to be droits and perquisites of the Crown; the ships were valued, the cargoes sold, and the proceeds were lodged with the accountant general of the Navy. After the war, prize money was distributed among the officers and men of the Navy and aircraft crews attached to naval stations.

Prize Bounty was a grant to officers and men of ships actually present at the taking or destroying of an armed ship of the enemy. The bounty was calculated at the rate of £5 for each person aboard the enemy ship at the beginning of the engagement.

   1–791   Prize cases: papers include affidavits, copies of ships' papers, bills of lading, briefs, and correspondence. Filed by name of ship alphabetically.

   797–798   Prize Bounty cases: papers include decrees, affidavits, and correspondence. Filed alphabetically by name of ship claiming bounty.

   799–810   Decrees of the Court in prize cases.

   811–850   Affidavits filed by the Crown, including information on cargoes and correspondence.

851	Index to names of traders and of ships referred to in affidavits filed by the Crown.
852–857	Appendices to affidavits filed by the Crown, consisting mainly of copies of intercepted telegrams and radio messages.
858	1923. Report of Procurator General upon the prize work of his department during the War, 1914–1918.

TS 14 KING'S PROCTOR: WAR TRADE INTELLIGENCE DEPARTMENT RECORDS.
1914–1919.   55 pieces.   [II 303]

These records of the War Trade Intelligence Department were transferred to the custody of the Procurator General when the department was abolished. The records relate to the blockade of enemy countries and were used by the Prize Court. *See also* FO 902.

1–20	Contraband Committee papers.
21–32	General Black List Committee.
33–36	Enemy Exports Committee.
37–49	Transit letter bulletins.
50	Transit letter bulletins index of names.
51–55	War trade statistics of imports into the Scandinavian countries, including Iceland, and the Faroes, the Netherlands, and Switzerland.

TS 16 PEERAGE CASES: PETITIONS AND PAPERS.
1795–1949.   144 pieces.   [III 126]

Petitions for the right to peerages are heard before the House of Lords Committee for Privileges. The Crown is represented by the Attorney General briefed by the Treasury Solicitor.

TS 17 BONA VACANTIA DIVISION: PAPERS.
1808–1964.   1,244 pieces.   [III 126]

This division deals with estates which revert to the Crown because the owner either died intestate without lawful heirs, or died testate without disposing of the residue of his estate, or without being survived by a lawful heir. The class also deals with cases where the Crown has an interest in the property of dissolved companies, and with questions relating to people dying intestate overseas.

TS 19 MANORIAL DOCUMENTS.
1483–1936.   61 pieces.

This class contains some documents of four manors; the inter-war material is as follows:

10	1874–1924. Court Book of the manor of Warcop, Westmorland, with entries for the manors of Warcop, Sandford, and Great Ormside.
59–61	1890–1936. Manor of Cleygate in Ash, Surrey: Court Book; compensation agreements between the tenants and the War Department.

TS 21   Deeds and Evidences.
      1539–1923; 1947.   78 pieces.

The few inter-war documents deal with patents, and also with an agreement to supply goods to Denikin in South Russia, and an agreement with Reuters Ltd. on the dissemination and distribution of news.

TS 26   War Crimes: Papers.
      1919–1924; 1941–1946.   903 pieces.

1–23	1919–1923. Papers concerned with Peace Treaty, Article 227, and procedure for the trials at Liepzig, and miscellaneous papers.
24–61	1920–1924. Files on alleged war criminals, arranged alphabetically.

COURTS OF LAW

The legal records of the P.R.O. make up the vast bulk of the mediaeval material. They have their origin in the King's Court (Curia Regis) and its various branches covering administrative, financial, and judicial functions, the Chancery, the Exchequer, and the various courts of common law and equity. Some of the groups described in this section contain records going back to this early period.

The modern system of courts in England is based mainly on the reforms made by the Supreme Court of Judicature Acts, 1873–75. These abolished the historic courts with their separate jurisdiction such as the courts of Chancery, Queen's (or King's) Bench, Exchequer, Common Pleas, Admiralty, and substituted a Court of Appeal and a Court of Justice sitting in three divisions, Chancery, Queen's Bench, and Probate, Divorce, and Admiralty Divisions. Each Division has certain classes of work assigned exclusively to it, but apart from these any Division may deal with any matter and the remedies available in one are available in another.

The assizes and the Central Criminal Court try serious criminal cases. In 1876 England was divided into six circuits, later increased, in each of which the assize court is presided over by an officer of the Supreme Court.

The Central Criminal Court was established in 1834. Its jurisdiction covers the city of London, the counties of London and Middlesex, and parts of the counties of Essex, Kent, and Surrey. Cases can be sent from places outside the ordinary jurisdiction of the Court in order to ensure a fair trial where local prejudice exists, or where the frequent sessions of the Court offer the advantage of an early trial and so avoid the delay involved in waiting for the assizes of a county.

The groups in this section follow the division of legal functions. However, some relate to institutions which no longer have an independent existence; for example, records of the High Court of Admiralty still accrue although this is now part of the Supreme Court of Judicature.

In general, the classes of legal records are made up according to the type of record, not the subject. Therefore, any particular case would have to be traced through a number of classes, such as those containing depositions, pleadings, entry books. Following the report of the Committee on Legal Records, 1968 (Denning Committee, Cmd. 3084), a number of classes are scheduled for destruction.

The following is a brief sketch of classes concerning inter-war material which are relevant. The class lists themselves do not normally give a full description of the pieces, generally only the date and volume number of the series. The class lists for the records of criminal trials, however, usually give the title and nature of the proceedings.

To date no inter-war records for divorce or probate are open.

CENTRAL CRIMINAL COURT

CRIM 1 DEPOSITIONS.
    1839–1922.   107 pieces.   [I 132]

Selected depositions are of trials for murder, sedition, treason, riot, conspiracies to effect political changes, or any other trials of general or historical interest. The class list contains the date of the trial, the name of the defendant, and the charge.

CHANCERY

C 211 COMMISSIONS AND INQUISITIONS OF LUNACY (PETTY BAG OFFICE).
    1627–1932.   75 pieces.   [I 35]

These are reports made to the Masters in Lunacy and deal with the financial circumstances and property of lunatics. They are listed chronologically.

CLERKS OF ASSIZE [I 127]

There are several classes in this group relating to the eight circuits. The depositions preserved are similar to those referred to in CRIM 1. The records are listed by the relevant circuits and consist of indictments, depositions in criminal cases, pleadings, and certificates of judgements.

HIGH COURT OF ADMIRALTY

HCA 20 INSTANCE PAPERS: SERIES V.
    1875–1943.   1,930 pieces.   [I 159]

In the Instance Court, proceedings are taken in relation to commercial disputes, wages, collisions, salvage, and droits. These records contain statements of claims and costs. The pieces are listed chronologically by the number of the case.

HCA 27 INSTANCE PAPERS: MINUTE BOOKS.
    1860–1924.   195 pieces.   [I 159]

These contain brief notes under the reference numbers of the cases. The pieces are listed in the same way as HCA 20.

HCA 52 INSTANCE: MISCELLANEOUS CORRESPONDENCE AND PAPERS.
    1853–1963.   119 pieces.

    115   1919–1929. Correspondence and papers of the Admiralty Registry.

119   1876–1963. Register containing a numerical list of papers with dates, writers, subjects, action taken, cross references to related papers, and an alphabetical index of subjects, ships, writers, and officials. Registers are open to inspection regardless of date.

SUPREME COURT OF JUDICATURE

Many classes in this group consist of purely formal documents, which are mainly useful for reference. Other classes, in particular Entry Books of Decrees and Orders, Chancery Division (J 15) also contain some details which are of social interest. The classes listed below cover some specialised functions of the court.

J 71 WORKMEN'S COMPENSATION APPEALS: MOTIONS.
    1910–1926.   25 pieces.   [I 143]

Copies of notices of appeal in workmen's compensation cases from the county courts. The records contain full details of the background information to each case. The pieces are dated in the class list and the case numbers contained in each volume are given.

J 72 WORKMEN'S COMPENSATION APPEALS: ORDER BOOKS.
    1911–1926.   12 pieces.   [I 143]

Entry books of orders of the Court of Appeal in workmen's compensation cases. They contain a brief statement on the appeal. The pieces are dated in the class list.

J 75 EXPIRED COMMISSIONS: RAILWAY AND CANAL COMMISSION.
    1873–1949.   221 pieces.   [I 144]

This consists mainly of appeals from rating decisions of the Railway Assessment Authority and applications for renewal of orders made under the Defence of the Realm (Acquisitions of Land) Acts 1916 and 1920. The class list gives the date and name of the appealing company, individual, etc. The Commission was given additional powers under various Mining Acts, 1923–1938; and the class includes applications, orders, etc. for variation in the rights, powers, duties, and liabilities, including amalgamation and absorption, of companies in the mining industry. *See also* HO 45 *and* LCO 2.

DEFENCE

ADMIRALTY

Since 1832, the civil administration of the Navy has been carried out by the Board of Admiralty through special departments created for that purpose. During this century a number of transfers of responsibility to and from the Admiralty have taken place:

1918   To Air Ministry, Royal Naval Air Service, except for operational control and the administration of the Airship section.

1919   To Air Ministry, Airship Section.

1921   From Ministry of Pensions, all powers and duties previously transferred to it except those relating to:

(1) disablement or death resulting from service in 1914–18 War.
(2) pensions already awarded in respect of disablement in former wars.

To Ministry of Pensions, certain mercantile marine pensions and officers' wounds pensions.

1923   To Board of Trade, Office of Works, and Board of Customs and Excise, responsibility for coastguards and stations.

1924   From Air Ministry, certain functions relating to the Fleet Air Arm.

1937   From Air Ministry, remaining control of Fleet Air Arm, and functions of Naval Division of Meteorological Office.

1939   To Ministry of Pensions, administration of pensions and grants on account of disablement or death arising out of service after the outbreak of war, 1939. Long service pensions and Greenwich Hospital pensions, not transferred.

1940   From Ministry of Shipping, control of merchant shipbuilding and repairs, and of coastguard services.

1941   From Air Ministry, operational control of R.A.F. Coastal Command.

1945   To Ministry of War Transport, control of coastguard service.

1954   From Civil Service Commission, responsibility for interview and selection test arrangements for Service commissions and cadetships.

1959   To Ministry of Transport, supervision of shipbuilding and repairs.

1963   To Ministry of Public Building and Works, responsibility for the Navy's building and civil engineering work.

The classes on Greenwich Hospital have been taken out of numerical sequence and grouped at the end.

ADM 1   ADMIRALTY AND SECRETARIAT: PAPERS.
         1660–1943.   10,136 pieces.   [II 19–20]

After 1832 the centralised direction of naval affairs resulted in the reference to the Admiralty Board of all matters involving policy decisions, and thus in the creation of papers in the Secretary's Department. Moreover, from the middle of the second half of the nineteenth century, arrangements were made for important papers registered in an increasing number of other departments of the Admiralty to be transferred to the Admiralty Record Office, which was part of the Secretary's Department.

Large groups of papers which might have been included in this class were sometimes made up into 'Cases' and these will be found in ADM 116. Papers used by the official historians of the 1914–18 War will be found in ADM 137.

The subject matter covered is wide, ranging from somewhat trivial questions such as designs of cap badges to high level policy on international affairs. The recurrent topics are predictable Navy subjects including staffing, supplies and armaments, costing, and international trade; and there are a great many references to Admiralty committees. A particularly interesting aspect of the papers is that dealing with conditions of sailors, and of pay, welfare benefits, and pensions of service and civilian workers.

Until 1938 and piece 9443 the papers are arranged in several chronological series; the inter-war material is as follows:

8548–8868	1919–1936
8936–9190	1919–1939
9224–9443	1919–1938

Until piece 8779 each piece is a box containing several files.

The files are in roughly chronological order according to the date given to the file when papers first reached the Admiralty Registry, therefore the file may contain earlier and later material than the date given.

Listed below is a selection of files of probable interest to social scientists giving an indication of some of the topics in this very large class.

8579	1920	Memoranda on channel tunnel.
8595	1920	Shackleton's Expedition, also in 8621.
8604	1921	Coal strike.
8605	1921	Formation of 'N.A.A.F.I.'
8621	1922	Air policy.
8657	1924	Prevention of pollution of navigable water.
8657	1924	Communist propaganda (in the Navy).
8657	1924	Industrial mobilisation.
8658	1924	Oil policy.
8667	1924	Legality of using the Armed Forces for strike-breaking.
8678	1925	Reduction and limit of armaments, preparation for Geneva Conference.
8697	1926	General Strike.
8733	1929	Widows', Orphans', and Old Age Contributory Pensions Bill.
8744	1930	Memorandum on proposed European federal union.
8775	1934	Amendment to regulations on assistance by Navy to the civil power in Great Britain.

8941	1920–1	Crime and punishment in the Royal Navy. Report of 50 years statistical investigation.
9018	1935	General Convention to improve means of preventing war.
9121	1937–39	Comparison of service and civil pensions for widows.

In 1938, piece 9,444, the arrangement was changed and papers were divided into sections, the headings of which are given below in the order in which they appear in the class list. Most pieces are dated 1938–40 but earlier material is included. The same headings are used in the arrangement of case papers in ADM 116, with one exception (Code 30), and are based on those used in the Digest, ADM 12.

Codes:
1. Academy and education.
2. Accidents and casualties.
3. Actions with the enemy.
4. Auxiliary vessels.
5. Admiralty.
6. Assistance to and by the Navy.
7. Complement of ships and establishments.
9. Compensation.
10. Commerce, trade, and economic matters.
11. Armaments.
13. Building and land.
18. Charities and trusts.
19. Civil power and legal matters.
20. Flags and crests.
21. Commonwealth of Nations.
22. Fisheries and fishery protection.
25. Contracts.
27. Convoys.
28. Courts martial.
29. Boards of enquiry and disciplinary courts.
30. Foreign naval vessels, damage and loss (ADM 116, commutation of pensions).
31. H.M. Ships, damage and loss.
32. Defence, United Kingdom.
33. British defences overseas.
34. Discipline.
35. Definition of terms and expressions.
38. Expenses and compensatory allowances.
41. Dockyards and naval establishments.
43. Government departments (in ADM 116 only).
44. Communications.
45. Chemical warfare.
46. Preparation for war.
47. Combined operations.
48. Preparation for war (civil).
49. Industrial organisation, mobilisation, etc.
50. Naval stations.
51. International law.
52. Foreign countries.
54. Naval training.

55.	General regulations.
56.	Medical.
57.	Hydrography.
59.	Inventions and suggestions.
60.	Royal Marines: general matters.
61.	Royal Marines: officers.
62.	Royal Marines: other ranks.
64.	Merchant Navy.
65.	Reserves.
67.	Mutinies.
68–9.	Estimates and finance.
71.	R.N. Officers.
72.	Movements.
73.	Pensions and gratuities to widows and dependants.
74.	Pilots and pilotage other than Trinity House.
76.	Censorship.
78.	Prisons (ADM 1 only).
79.	Prisoners of war and internees.
80.	Scientific and cultural.
81.	Machinery.
82.	Strategy and tactics.
83.	Recruiting and re-engagement generally.
84.	Coastguard.
85.	Honours and awards.
86.	Royalty.
87.	Salvage and divers.
88.	Ceremonial.
89.	Tolls and taxes.
90.	Aviation.
91.	Ships and vessels.
92.	Signalling.
93.	Telecommunications and radio.
96.	Security.
97.	Stationery.
98.	Stores.
101.	War Office.
102.	W.R.N.S.
103.	R.N. Ratings.
104.	Yachts and regattas.

ADM 4   ORIGINAL PATENTS: ADMIRALTY.
1707–1951.   368 pieces.   [II 21]

Letters patent appointing Lords of the Admiralty. Each piece is dated but not described.

ADM 12   INDEXES AND COMPILATIONS: SERIES III.
1660–1934.   1,719 pieces.   [II 23]

This series includes the Admiralty Digest and Indexes, the former being subject indexes and the latter indexes of persons and ships. They refer to ADM 1, ADM 116, and ADM 137, and from 1934 all papers emanating from the Cabinet Office and C.I.D. are noted. The Digest gives a brief description of the files arranged under subject headings similar to those listed under ADM 1. It is difficult to work from the Digests and the Indexes to the original papers, especially since many of them may have been subsequently destroyed.

ADM 53   SHIPS LOGS.
          1799–1938.   107,261 pieces.   [II 23]

These are arranged in alphabetical order by name of ship, in several chronological series. The logbooks are dated.

ADM 64   ROYAL MARINES: GENERAL STANDING ORDERS.
          1888–1936.   34 pieces.   [II 31]

Printed regulations regarding conditions of service, duties, uniform, and general organisational matters. They are bound into volumes which are dated and indexed to 1920.

ADM 116   ADMIRALTY AND SECRETARIAT: CASES.
           1852–1941.   4,093 pieces.   [II 20].   Various files are closed
                                                      for 50 or 60 years.

These were files of the Secretariat which have been made up into 'Cases'. There is very little difference between the subject matter of this class and ADM 1. It includes top level policy files and also records of particular cases, for example, pay awards. Each piece is fully described and there is a very comprehensive index up to 1939, and piece 3624. Thereafter the list is arranged by subjects, and includes earlier material which was transferred after the index was completed. The headings are the same as those used for Admiralty and Secretariat papers in ADM 1, with one exception. Code 30 in ADM 116 is used for Commutation of Pensions. Not all these headings are used in each of the two classes, but in both the sections are arranged in numerical order of the code as given under ADM 1. The index uses the same headings in numerical order, with an alphabetical list at the beginning which acts as a contents list. The files are given a case number which has to be keyed to the piece numbers by using tables at the end of the index.

ADM 121   STATION RECORDS: MEDITERRANEAN: CORRESPONDENCE.
           1843–1913; 1918–1920.   87 pieces.   [II 32]

Correspondence and papers relate to naval bases and fleet activities in the Mediterranean. One piece, 86, covering 1918–20 is called Miscellanea.

ADM 123   STATION RECORDS: AFRICA: CORRESPONDENCE.
           1797–1932.   185 pieces.   [II 31]

The relevant pieces cover St. Helena and Tristan Da Cunha, civil disturbances in the Cape of Good Hope and the West Coast of Africa, copies of Commanders-in-Chief's proceedings and correspondence to 1919.

ADM 125   STATION RECORDS: CHINA: CORRESPONDENCE.
           1828–1936.   148 pieces.   [II 32]

The records are arranged in sections; there is inter-war material in those headed General and British Trade, and Relations with Chinese Governments.

ADM 127 STATION RECORDS: EAST INDIES: CORRESPONDENCE.
         1808–1930.   71 pieces.   [II 32]

Correspondence relates to India, Ceylon, Burma, Aden, the Red Sea, the Persian Gulf, the East Coast of Africa, and islands in the Indian Ocean. Many of the volumes have a list of contents.

ADM 130 STATION RECORDS: PLYMOUTH: ORDERS AND MEMORANDA.
         1859–1928.   45 pieces.   [II 33]

Copies of orders and memoranda issued by the Commander-in-Chief. The volumes are indexed.

ADM 131 STATION RECORDS PLYMOUTH: CORRESPONDENCE.
         1842–1926.   124 pieces.   [II 33]

This class consists of letters from the Admiralty. Pieces 56–62 contain general correspondence covering the period 1910–1926.

ADM 136 MATERIAL DEPARTMENTS: SHIPS' BOOKS: SERIES II.
         1854–1962.   50 pieces.   [II 27]

These consist of reports and other papers giving the history of the maintenance of a ship (hull, machinery, and armament) from construction to disposal. They are in the form of loose leaf albums arranged in chronological order of date of launching.

ADM 137 HISTORICAL SECTION: 1914–1918 WAR HISTORIES.
         1914–1924.   3,839 pieces.   [II 26]

This collection of documents was used for the official history of the 1914–18 War. There are three groups: H.S. Admiralty papers; H.S.A., Commander-in-Chief, Home Fleet and of Bases; and H.S.B., Convoy records and records of certain divisions of the Naval Staff, including the Trade Division. Pieces 1–3056 are dated and have a subject index; there is a key to individual papers noted in the Digest and subsequently transferred to the H.S. Series. The remainder of the class consists of fully described pieces. The records deal with war-time operations but some pieces cover the post-war period and deal with the trading position of various countries, allied blockade policy, loss of ships, and the scuttling of German ships at Scapa Flow.

ADM 151 STATION RECORDS: NORE: CORRESPONDENCE.
         1805–1939.   92 pieces.   [II 32]

This class contains correspondence from the Admiralty and others. Piece 92 deals with the mobilisation of the Reserve Fleet in 1939.

ADM 156 COURTS MARTIAL RECORDS.
         1890–1940.   200 pieces.   Closed for 100 years.

Cases extracted from ADM 1, 116, 137, 167; they include courts martial of Royal Marine officers and men.

ADM 167   ADMIRALTY AND SECRETARIAT: BOARD MINUTES AND MEMORANDA.
           1869–1939.   107 pieces.   [III 7].   Various files are closed for
                                                  50 years.

These contain discussion and conclusions on all aspects of policy, in particular manning and naval strength. From August, 1917, a regular series of numbered minutes and subject indexes began but the indexes were not always printed annually and are not included in each annual volume. There is no index to Board memoranda, but from August, 1917, each memorandum to the Board has a numbered cross-reference to the relevant minute. The pieces consist of dated volumes.

ADM 173   ADMIRALTY AND SECRETARIAT: SUBMARINE LOG BOOKS.
           1914–1939.   16,256 pieces.   [III 7]

The books are arranged in date order under the alphabetically listed submarines.

ADM 175   COASTGUARD: RECORDS OF SERVICE.
           1816–1923.   108 pieces.   [III 7]

This class contains establishment books for southern England 1904–18, indexed by stations; service records of R.N. ratings and Royal Marines, 1900–23, arranged both alphabetically and numerically and indexed; registers of discharges (1919) arranged in indexed volumes; and nominal indexes to chief officers, 1915–22.

ADM 176   MATERIAL DEPARTMENTS: PHOTOGRAPHS OF SHIPS.
           1854–1945.   1,141 pieces.   [III 7].   No restriction on access.

A complete set of photographs of ships, which was formerly held by the Naval Construction Department. The pieces are arranged alphabetically, by name of ship, with date of launching, in two series, mounted and unmounted photographs.

ADM 178   ADMIRALTY: PAPERS AND CASES, SUPPLEMENTARY.
           1892–1941.   204 pieces.   Closed for 100 years.

Sensitive items, including papers extracted from ADM 1, 116 and 167.

ADM 179   STATION RECORDS: PORTSMOUTH: CORRESPONDENCE.
           1880–1947.   71 pieces.

Correspondence on routine naval and dockyard matters, refitting H.M.S. *Victory*, ceremonials and reviews, navy weeks, etc.

ADM 181   NAVY ESTIMATES.
           1708–1937.   133 pieces.

Bound volumes of estimates, and related discussion papers and correspondence. They are listed chronologically.

ADM 182   ADMIRALTY FLEET ORDERS.
        1909–1938.   79 pieces.

Printed routine orders issued to the Fleet, Naval Establishments, and Principal Admiralty Overseers, for information, guidance, and necessary action. The orders are bound into dated volumes listed chronologically.

ADM 183–185   ROYAL MARINE DIVISIONS

Each class contains order books to 1941, weekly returns, letter books, registers of marriages, births and deaths of children, etc. Very few records apart from the order books extend into the inter-war period.

   ADM 183   CHATHAM DIVISION.   1755–1941.   130 pieces.

   ADM 184   PLYMOUTH DIVISION.   1760–1941.   56 pieces.

   ADM 185   PORTSMOUTH DIVISION.   1763–1941.   111 pieces.

ADM 186   PUBLICATIONS.
        1827–1953.   793 pieces.

Internal publications of the Admiralty, including manuals of instruction and handbooks. They are arranged under the following headings:

Administration and training.
Armaments.
Engineering.
Historical and geographical studies.
Navigation.
Photography.
Signals.

ADM 189   TORPEDO ANTI-SUBMARINE SCHOOL: REPORTS.
        1881–1956.   183 pieces.

The school is at Portsmouth. This class includes the annual reports of the school, together with other reports and papers dealing with mines and minesweeping, torpedoes, and anti-submarine defences and weapons.

ADM 190   ROYAL GREENWICH OBSERVATORY: BOARD OF VISITORS.
        1827–1964.   18 pieces.

The Royal Observatory was established in 1675 to promote astronomical and nautical research. In 1710 members of the Royal Society were appointed to superintend its work and to ensure that astronomical observations were published. In 1830 membership of the Board of Visitors was extended to the Professors of Astronomy at Cambridge and Oxford and members of the Astronomical Society; in 1858 the Hydrographer of the Navy was added. In 1965 responsibility for the Observatory was transferred to the Science Research Council, and the Board of Visitors was dissolved. The class includes minutes, warrants of appointments, and correspondence concerning visits to the Observatory.

ADM 195   CIVIL ENGINEER-IN-CHIEF: PHOTOGRAPHS.
              1857–1961.   121 pieces.

The Navy Works Department was known as the Civil Engineer-in-Chief's Department. It was responsible for the construction and extension of dockyards and naval establishments, at home and overseas. In April, 1963 the Ministry of Public Building and Works took over its work and the Navy Works Department ceased to exist. This class consists of photographs of works in dockyards, etc. in Great Britain and overseas, arranged alphabetically.

ADM 197   ADMIRALTY WHITLEY COUNCILS.
              1919–1948.   35 pieces.

The Admiralty Administrative Whitley Council held its first meeting in October, 1919. This class contains the minutes of meetings and associated papers of the Admiralty Staff Conference (formed in January, 1919 to deal with staff questions until the Whitley recommendations were put into effect) and of the Administrative Whitley Council. Also included are papers relating to the formation and constitutions of district and office committees.

ADM 198   PRECEDENT AND PROCEDURE BOOKS.
              1860–1949.   51 pieces.

These consist of:

Military Branch: precedent books, indexed; station procedure books, indexed.
League of Nations: precedent book, indexed; procedure books, indexed
Civil Establishment Branch: precedent books, indexed.
Accountant General's Department: precedent book, indexed.
Naval Pay Branch: precedent books, indexed.
Sales Branch: precedent book, indexed.
Commission and Warrant Branch: procedure book.
Civil Engineer-in-Chief: precedent book.
Victualling Department: precedent books.
Ship Branch: precedent book, indexed.

ADM 204   RESEARCH LABORATORY: REPORTS.
              1921–1938.   156 pieces.

Dated quarterly reports with some additional research papers.

ADM 900   SPECIMENS OF CLASSES OF DOCUMENTS DESTROYED.

69–74   1937–1940. Flying log books of Royal Air Force personnel serving with the Fleet Air Arm.

GREENWICH HOSPITAL [II 24–26, III 7]

Greenwich Hospital was founded by William and Mary to relieve distress among seamen and encourage their recruitment. The charter of 1694 states its purpose is 'the relief and support of seamen serving on board the Navy . . . who by reason of age, wounds, or other disablements, shall be incapable of further service at sea, and be unable to maintain themselves; and for the sustentation of the widows and the maintenance and education of the children of seamen happening to be slain or disabled in such sea service; and also for the further relief and encouragement of seamen and improvement of navigation'. It was endowed with land at Greenwich; and subsequently with the effects of William Kidd, the pirate, and the forfeited estates of the Earl of Derwentwater after the 1715 rebellion. By an Act of 1696 all naval seamen had to pay 6d. a month to Greenwich Hospital; and this payment was extended in 1708 to the merchant seamen who became eligible for benefits if wounded in battle. In 1806 the Chatham Chest with funds from estates and fines imposed by naval courts-martial was transferred to Greenwich and amalgamated with the Hospital.

At first the Hospital was concerned only with in-patients, lodged in the palace begun by Charles II, but in 1762 an Act allowed the Hospital to pay out-pensions to 'seamen worn out and become decrepit in the service of their country', and this was extended to officers of the navy in 1806 and the Hospital was to receive $1\frac{2}{3}\%$ of prize money, droits and bounty. In 1830 the naval 6d. was ended and out-pensions were paid by the Treasurer of the Navy through Greenwich Hospital. In 1834 the merchant seamen's 6d. was also stopped and the Hospital was compensated by the payment of £20,000 from the Consolidated Fund. In 1865 all the property of the Hospital was transferred to the Admiralty which assumed responsibility for payment of age pensions to selected naval life pensioners at the age of 55 years. The hospital at Greenwich was closed soon after, the building being used for the Royal Naval College. In 1919 the Admiralty undertook to pay age pensions at 55 to all naval life pensioners, the Treasury providing the balance of the money needed, Greenwich Hospital continuing to pay what it could manage after meeting its other liabilities.

During the inter-war period Greenwich Hospital continued to be responsible for the following:

1. Pensions to officers as compensation for loss of posts on the Hospital staff which had been given to officers with distinguished service.
2. Educational allowances to officers' children.
3. Contribution to the Naval Vote for age pensions for seamen and mariners.
4. Special pensions awarded on charitable grounds to naval ratings under pre-war regulations.
5. Maintenance of men in naval hospitals and allowances to their families.
6. Pensions to widows of seamen killed or drowned on duty before the 1914 war.
7. Maintenance of necessitous children of seamen and mariners; most boys were educated at the Royal Hospital School which in 1933 moved from Greenwich to new buildings at Holbrook, Suffolk.

The following classes contain records dealing with these various activities and the management of the estates and funds of the Hospital; except that records dealing with age pensions are at present kept by the Navy Department.

ADM 69   TREASURER'S LEDGERS.   1695–1937.   68 pieces.
          Most are indexed.

ADM 71   ESTATES AND OTHER PROPERTIES: LEDGERS.   1810–1930.   17
          pieces.

ADM 73   MISCELLANEOUS REGISTERS.   1704–1966.   464 pieces.

ADM 75   DEEDS.   1340–1931.   236 pieces.
          List preceded by topographical index to the premises and estates.

ADM 79   SURVEYS, RENTALS, ETC. 1547–1928. 72 pieces.
Indexed register of property in the Northern Estates.

ADM 80   VARIOUS. 1639–1919. 181 pieces.
Salaries paid to officers and staff of the hospital.

ADM 161   REGISTERS OF CLAIMS: GREENWICH HOSPITAL SCHOOL.
1865–1930. 19 pieces.
Applications for entry.

ADM 162   REGISTERS OF CLAIMS: ORPHANS. 1882–1961. 9 pieces.
Applications of orphan children of sailors.

ADM 163   REGISTERS OF CLAIMS: SONS AND DAUGHTERS OF COMMISSIONED
OFFICERS. 1883–1922. 2 pieces.
Claims for school admission.

ADM 164   REGISTERS OF PENSIONS: REGISTERS OF GRANTS TOWARDS THE
EDUCATION AND MAINTENANCE OF CHILDREN OF COMMISSIONED
OFFICERS. 1907–1933. 1 piece.

ADM 165   REGISTERS OF PENSIONS: NAVAL AND MARINE OFFICERS:
GREENWICH HOSPITAL STAFF. 1871–1931. 7 pieces.

ADM 166   REGISTERS OF PENSIONS: WIDOWS OF SEAMEN AND MARINES, ETC.
1882–1949. 14 pieces.

ADM 169   REGISTERED FILES. 1870–1967. 830 pieces.
Cover all aspects of the hospital, school, and estates, grouped
under subject headings.

ADM 203   ROYAL NAVAL COLLEGE. 1872–1957. 46 pieces.

AIR MINISTRY

The Admiralty formed an Air Department in 1910, and the War Office created an
Air Battalion of the Royal Engineers in 1911. In 1912, the Royal Flying Corps was
set up with naval and military wings, and a permanent consultative Air Committee
with representatives from the Admiralty and War Office. The naval wing gradually
became independent and in 1914 was reconstituted as the Royal Naval Air Service
under Admiralty control.

In 1916 the first Air Board was formed, with Lord Curzon as president, to co-
ordinate design policy and the supply requirements of the two Services. In 1917 the
Board was given the status of a ministry and was reformed but is usually known
as the Second Air Board. It still had no executive powers.

In 1918 the Air Ministry was established, with an Air Council, and the Royal
Flying Corps and the Royal Naval Air Service combined to form the Royal Air
Force. In 1937 control of the Fleet Air Arm was transferred to the Admiralty.

In 1919 the Air Ministry was given control of civil aviation; this passed to a
separate Ministry of Civil Aviation in 1945.

In 1920 the Air Ministry became responsible for the Meteorological Office which
combined the Meteorological Office which had functioned under the Treasury and
the meteorological services maintained by the three Forces. All meteorological
records are retained by the Meteorological Office. In the same year when the

Ministry of Munitions was dissolved, responsibility for aircraft production passed to the Air Ministry; in 1940 it was transferred to the Ministry of Aircraft Production.

In 1964 the Air Ministry was absorbed by the Ministry of Defence.

AIR 1   AIR HISTORICAL BRANCH RECORDS: SERIES I.
         Mainly 1914–1918.   2,434 pieces.   [III 14].   Piece 29 is closed for 75 years.

AIR 5   AIR HISTORICAL BRANCH RECORDS: SERIES II.
         Mainly 1921–1930.   1,437 pieces.   [III 14].   Various files are closed for 50 or 75 years.

These are documents collected by the Air Historical Branch for use in compiling the official history of the war in the air. AIR 1 contains most of the material dealing with the First World War, and with active operations that continued afterwards, such as those in the Middle East, Russia, and Sudan.

The first volume of each series of lists contains a list of subject headings which can be used as a quick means of reference to groups of files. There is a very detailed 9 volumed index which is in three parts; the first part is an alphabetical index to subjects; the second is a chronological index to particular events, 1903–1918; and the third is an index to the Air Ministry, Admiralty, and War Office, registered files incorporated in these two classes, AIR 1 and 5.

The index consists of pages containing photocopies of index cards, nine to a page, mostly handwritten. In the alphabetical section, the cards are grouped under subject headings, and are numbered serially under each letter of the alphabet that is used. At the beginning of each volume there is a list of main subject headings for most of the letters contained in the volume.

The records have been weeded since the index was made, and some of the papers have not survived. Files with an A.H. or A.H.B. number can be found in AIR 1, volumes 1–4, others may be in AIR 5. There is no quick means of reference from the index to AIR 5; it is necessary to study the list of codes at the beginning of AIR 5, and to look up the various codes under which a particular file might have been placed.

These records cover all aspects of the work of the R.A.F. There are, for example, files on the use of the R.A.F. in civil disturbances, and how R.A.F. establishments were affected by the Cabinet decision in 1921 on short-time working.

The arrangement and numbering of the volumes for these two classes and the index is as follows:

1. AIR 1 Vol. I   Key to subject headings Piece nos. 1–623 (part).
                     A.H. nos. 4/1–16/15/373 Part C.
2. AIR 1 Vol. II   Piece nos. 623 (cont).—856.
                     A.H. nos. 16/15/373 Part D—204/5/411.
3. AIR 1 Vol. III   Piece nos. 857–1,612.
                     A.H. nos. 204/5/412–204/87/40.
4. AIR 1 Vol. IV   Piece nos. 1,613–2,434.
                     A.H. nos. 204/88/4–305/33/1.
5. Index Vol. 1   Alphabetical Index. A.
6. Index Vol. 2   B and C.
7. Index Vol. 3   D–L.

8. Index	Vol. 4	M–Q.
9. Index	Vol. 5	R1–R2395.
10. Index	Vol. 6	R2396–R4694.
11. Index	Vol. 7	S–Z.
12. Index	Vol. 8	Chronological Index.
13. Index	Vol. 9	Index to Air Ministry, Admiralty, and War Office registered files.
22. AIR 5	Vol. I	Key to subject headings, codes 1–42.
23. AIR 5	Vol. II	Codes 43–57/7.

AIR 2 CORRESPONDENCE.

1887–1962. 4,490 pieces. [II 42]. Various files are closed for 50 or 75 years.

The papers in this class deal with all aspects of the work of the Air Ministry and most deal with the period of the First World War. Some of the records originated in the two Air Boards that preceded the Air Ministry, in the Admiralty, the War Office, and the Ministry of Munitions. Many of the papers that would have been in this class were used by the Air Historical Branch and are to be found in AIR 1 and 5.

The papers are arranged by subject, there is a key to arrangement, and the papers are divided into two periods up to and later than 1920. The volumes are as follows:

14. Codes	1–29	Up to 1920.
15. Codes	1–29	1921–1939.
16. Codes	30–45	Up to 1920.
17. Codes	30–45	1921–1939.
18. Codes	46–57	Up to 1920.
19. Codes	46–57	1921–1939.
20. Key to arrangement. The coding used is the same as that for AIR 5.		

AIR 3 AIRSHIP LOG BOOKS.

1910–1930. 64 pieces. [III 14]

This class contains all the airship log books known to have survived.

43–64   1919–1930. Log books for the R.33, 1919–1926; R.36, 1921; R.100, and R.101, 1929–1930.

AIR 4 AIRCREWS' FLYING LOG BOOKS.

1917–1956. 173 pieces. [III 14]

A representative selection of log books, mainly R.A.F. personnel, some Commonwealth and foreign personnel. Arranged alphabetically by name of compiler of log book.

AIR 5 See AIR 1.

AIR 6 RECORDS OF MEETINGS OF THE AIR BOARD AND AIR COUNCIL.

1916–1945. 75 pieces. [III 14]

14–15   1919–1921. Air Council Minutes, meetings 70–155.

19–22   1918–1935. Memoranda submitted to Air Council.

23–40   1935–1939. Secretary of State's progress meetings on R.A.F. expansion measures.

43–58   1935–1949. Memoranda submitted to above meetings.

AIR 8   CHIEF OF THE AIR STAFF.
        1916–1945.   299 pieces.   [III 14].   Three files closed for 50 or 75 years.

Papers deal with all aspects of policy and planning, including many committee papers, papers on R.A.F. action overseas, disarmament, and R.A.F. expansion. Arranged chronologically.

AIR 9   DIRECTOR OF PLANS.
        1914–1941.   131 pieces.   [III 14].   Three files closed for 75 years.

A Director of Plans was appointed in 1939, previously planning had been the responsibility of the Director of Operations and Intelligence. The department was responsible for air strategy, inter-service policy, co-operation with the Dominions and with allies, preparation of war plans, and air defence. There are papers on civil aviation, disarmament, papers submitted by Air Ministry to the Committee on National Expenditure, and reports on various countries, on their air forces, industrial capacity, etc.

AIR 10   AIR PUBLICATIONS.
        1917–1927.   1,335 pieces.

A selection of administrative instructions, regulations, reports, and manuals of instruction in the use and servicing of aircraft and equipment, arranged under the following headings:

Codes: 1. Administration and training.
           2. Armament.
           3. Engineering.
           4. Navigation.
           5. Photography.
           6. Signals.
           7. Works services.

AIR 11   ROYAL AIRSHIP WORKS, CARDINGTON: CORRESPONDENCE AND PAPERS.
        1911–1939.   246 pieces.   [III 14]

AIR 12   ROYAL AIRSHIP WORKS, CARDINGTON: AIRSHIP AND ENGINE DRAWINGS.
        1910–1931.   318 pieces.   [III 14]

The papers are listed by subject, full list at beginning of the class list, and are concerned with airships, balloons, and kite balloons. There is a miscellaneous section on gas, parachutes, telephones, and photographs. There are indexes to some of the series of drawings. *See also* AVIA 24.

9

AIR 14   BOMBER COMMAND.
       1936–1946.   483 pieces.   Piece 310 is closed for 75 years.

AIR 15   COASTAL COMMAND.
       1930–1950.   719 pieces.

The few pre-war files are scattered throughout these two classes and deal with organisation, training, and reports of exercises and trials.

AIR 16   FIGHTER COMMAND.
       1925–1946.   1,011 pieces.   Various files are closed for 50 years.

The many pre-war files deal with training, defence against air attack including papers on the Observer Corps, balloon barrage, and various detection systems. Fighter Command was set up in 1936; earlier records are of the Air Defence of Great Britain Command.

AIR 17   MAINTENANCE COMMAND.
       1936–1962.   13 pieces.

AIR 19   PRIVATE OFFICE PAPERS.
       1917–1945.   144 pieces.

1–22	1935–1945. General, including papers on the Shadow Scheme for aircraft production, and correspondence with the Admiralty.
23–24	1936–1938. Papers of Viscount Swinton, Secretary of State for Air.
25–72	1937–1940. Papers of Sir Kingsley Wood, Secretary of State for Air.
75–83	1923–1939. Papers of Sir James Ross, Deputy Secretary of the Air Ministry, including papers on the Czech crisis, 1938.
84–144	1917–1936. Papers of Sir C. L. Bullock, Secretary of the Air Ministry, including papers on relations with the Navy, Geddes Committee on National Expenditure, Colwyn Committee on Defence Expenditure, civil aviation, and special quarterly reports of the Aeronautical Research Committee.

AIR 20   UNREGISTERED PAPERS.
       1912–1948.   762 pieces.   Various files closed for 50 or 75 years.

Papers deal with all aspects of the work of the R.A.F. They include Air Estimates, 1932–1938, pieces 442–447; papers on civil aviation pieces 394–6 and 414; overseas missions; Committee for Scientific Survey of Air Defence; and on the airship R100 pieces 104–136 and 146–154, and R101 pieces 159–161. Most of the pieces 500–760 are concerned with operations in the Middle East, South Russia, 1915–1922, and the Sudan Defence Force, 1920–1939.

AIR 23   OVERSEAS COMMANDS.
       1916–1945.   807 pieces.   Various files are closed for 50 or 75 years.

1–679; 796–801; 806; 807	1918–1941. Iraq Command, including Air Staff. Intelligence reports on Iraq, Persia, Arabia, Southern Desert, Transjordan, Syria, Kurdistan, Anatolia, Armenia. Iraq War Diaries, 1923–1930.
680–691	1916–1937. India Command, including papers on Afghanistan.
692–713; 802–805	1927–1944. Aden Command.
714–794	1922–1945. Middle East Command, including Egypt, Palestine, and Transjordan.
795	1939. Far East Command.

AIR 30   SUBMISSION PAPERS
         1918–1945.   186 pieces.

Recommendations for appointments, promotions, awards and decorations, and amendment of regulations.

AIR 31   DEPARTMENTAL WHITLEY COUNCIL MINUTES.
         1919–1936.   5 pieces.

Record of proceedings and relevant documents.

MINISTRY OF AVIATION

This Ministry existed from 1959 until 1967. It was formed by the merger of the civil aviation section of the Ministry of Transport and Civil Aviation and the Ministry of Supply which had lost nearly all its functions except those to do with aircraft.

Control of civil aviation was the responsibility of the Air Ministry from 1919 to 1945 when it passed to the new Ministry of Civil Aviation. This was merged with the Ministry of Transport in 1953.

Responsibility for aircraft production rested with the Air Ministry from 1920 to 1940 when it passed to the Ministry of Aircraft Production. When that Ministry was dissolved in 1946, its functions relating to production and supply of aircraft and aircraft equipment, and to research and development, were transferred to the Ministry of Supply.

Before 1959, the Ministry of Supply lost control of non-ferrous metals to the Ministry of Materials in 1951, responsibility for atomic energy to the Atomic Energy Authority and the Lord President of the Council in 1954, and control of iron and steel to the Board of Trade in 1955. In 1959, the powers of supply transferred from the War Office in 1939, returned to the War Office, and those received from the Air Ministry and Ministry of Aircraft Production returned to the Air Ministry, except those relating to aircraft.

The new Ministry in 1959 was responsible for civil aviation, aircraft production, and electronics. Responsibility for electronics was transferred to the Ministry of Technology in 1964.

In 1966, it was decided to abolish the Ministry of Aviation, its functions relating
9*

to civil aviation passed to the Board of Trade, and those to do with aircraft production were transferred to the Ministry of Technology in 1967.

For records of the Aeronautical Research Council, *see* DSIR group.

AVIA 1   ROYAL AIRCRAFT ESTABLISHMENT, FARNBOROUGH: FLIGHT LOG BOOKS.
1914–1948.   20 pieces.   [III 15]

These books are held on long term requisition in the Main Library at the R.A.E., Farnborough.

AVIA 2   AIR MINISTRY: CIVIL AVIATION FILES.
1909–1958.   2,806 pieces.   [III 15].   Various files are closed for 50 years.

This class contains files dealing with all aspects of civil aviation. The few early files originated in the War Office and in the Ministry of Munitions. The files are arranged in sections and there is a detailed key to arrangement at the beginning of the class list.

AVIA 3   AIRCREW LICENCES: REPRESENTATIVE FILES.
1925–1951.   50 pieces.   [III 15]

Selected files illustrate regulations governing issue of licences under the Air Navigation Acts to: aircraft engineers, maintenance, operational, and ground engineers, navigators, operators of radio telephones and wireless telegraphy, and airship pilots, master pilots, private and professional pilots.

AVIA 4   CERTIFICATES OF AIR-WORTHINESS AND AIRCRAFT REGISTRATION: REPRESENTATIVE FILES.
1929–1951.   30 pieces.   [III 15]

Selected files illustrate regulations governing issue of the certificates under the Air Navigation Acts.

1–4   1929–1940. Files of four different types of aircraft.

AVIA 5   AIRCRAFT ACCIDENT REPORTS.
1919–1936.   18 pieces.   [III 16]

Reports of accidents involving civil aircraft, details of aircraft, names of owner, pilots, and passengers, opinions on cause of accident, and recommendations arising.

1–18   1919–1936. Numbered reports, one year per folder; some reports are wanting.

AVIA 6   ROYAL AIRCRAFT ESTABLISHMENT: REPORTS.
1916–1948.   8,641 pieces.

Experiments with observation balloons began in Woolwich in 1878; these grew into a balloon factory which moved to Farnborough in 1905. Dirigibles were designed and built, and in 1912 it was renamed the Royal Aircraft Factory and designed and built different types of aircraft and aircraft engines. In 1916, production work was transferred to industry and the station at Farnborough was used entirely for research and development. It was renamed the Royal Aircraft Establishment in 1918. The reports are divided into sections and there is a key to the arrangement at the beginning of the class list.

AVIA 7   ROYAL RADAR ESTABLISHMENT: FILES.
          1917–1945.   3,607 pieces.

This establishment, formerly called the Radar Research Establishment, was formed in 1953, by the merger of the Radar Research and Development Establishment and the Telecommunication Research Establishment, both at that time under the control of the Ministry of Supply. For the history of R.R.D.E. see AVIA 17. T.R.E. developed from a research station set up by the Air Ministry in Suffolk in 1935, which later was called the Bawdsey Research Station. In 1939, it moved to Dundee and was called the Air Ministry Research Establishment. In 1940, it moved to Worth Matravers, Dorset, and was transferred to the Ministry of Aircraft Production. In 1942 T.R.E. and A.D.R.D.E. moved to Malvern, Worcestershire.

The files are in series according to their place of origin. This is fully explained in the description at the beginning of the class list. There is a glossary of terms at the end of the class list.

For further information on Bawdsey Research Station, *see* AIR 20/195.

AVIA 8   AIR MINISTRY: INVENTIONS AND RESEARCH DEVELOPMENT FILES.
          1915–1960.   530 pieces.   [III 16]

Most files originated in the Air Ministry between 1918 and 1940 during which period the department was responsible for its own research and development. The few files earlier than 1918 came from the Air Department of the Admiralty, the Air Inventions Committee, or the Ministry of Munitions. The files deal with aircraft, engines, equipment, and instruments of all kinds, materials used, navigational systems, and armaments. There is a detailed key to arrangement at the beginning of the class list.

AVIA 13   ROYAL AIRCRAFT ESTABLISHMENT: FILES.
           1918–1957.   616 pieces.

The files are arranged chronologically in the following sections:

1–191	1918–1944. Engines.
279–398	1920–1944. Radio.
399–543	1918–1955. Instruments and electrical engineering.
544–565	1935–1950. Aerodynamics.
566–616	1918–1957. Chemistry, physics, and materials.

AVIA 14   ROYAL AIRCRAFT ESTABLISHMENT, FARNBOROUGH: DRAWINGS.
           1911–1944.   97 pieces.   No restriction on access.

This class contains tracings of aircraft, engines, and equipment designed and built at Farnborough between 1911 and 1918; and also drawings which were of interest to the R.A.E. but which did not originate there. The drawings are grouped to correspond with the catalogue published by R.A.E. in 1964. There is a full description in the class list.

AVIA 15   MINISTRY OF AIRCRAFT PRODUCTION: FILES.
          1925–1967.   3,925 pieces.   Various files are closed for 50 years.

The Ministry of Aircraft Production existed from 1940 to 1946 when its functions were transferred to the Ministry of Supply. Files which are earlier than 1940 were taken over from the Air Ministry. Most files extended beyond 1940. There is a detailed key to arrangement at the beginning of the class list.

AVIA 16   AIRCRAFT TORPEDO DEVELOPMENT UNIT: REPORTS.
          1933–1941.   57 pieces.

This Unit was set up by the Air Ministry after the First World War and was transferred to the Ministry of Aircraft Production in 1942. The reports are arranged chronologically.

AVIA 17   AIR DEFENCE EXPERIMENTAL ESTABLISHMENT: REPORTS.
          1925–1936.   45 pieces.

In 1917 an experimental section of the Royal Engineers was set up at Woolwich to study searchlights. In 1924, it was renamed the Air Defence Experimental Establishment and moved to Biggin Hill, Kent. Later it moved to Christchurch, Hampshire, and was transferred to the Ministry of Supply. It was renamed the Air Defence Research and Development Establishment in 1941, and the Radar Research and Development Establishment in 1944. *See also* AVIA 7 *and* WO 187.

AVIA 18   AEROPLANE AND ARMAMENT EXPERIMENTAL ESTABLISHMENT:
          REPORTS.
          1924–1952.   722 pieces.

This establishment was set up by the Air Ministry in 1917 at Martlesham Heath, Suffolk, to carry out acceptance tests on aircraft. In 1939 it was moved to Boscombe Down, Wiltshire, and was taken over by the Ministry of Aircraft Production. These are reports on instruments, equipment, aircraft armament, and aircraft performance tests and trials.
          Earlier reports are in AIR 1 and 5.

AVIA 19   MARINE AIRCRAFT EXPERIMENTAL ESTABLISHMENT: REPORTS.
          1924–1943.   1,026 pieces.

This establishment was set up by the Air Ministry after the First World War to test performance of water-based aircraft and associated equipment and armaments. It was based at Felixstowe, Suffolk, moved in 1939 to Helensburg, Scotland, and in 1940 was transferred to the Ministry of Aircraft Production. The reports are divided into sections, listed at the beginning of the class list; the first eleven have reports for the inter-war period.

AVIA 20 RESEARCH AND DEVELOPMENT ESTABLISHMENT, CARDINGTON:
         REPORTS.
         1936–1947.   174 pieces.

See AVIA 24.

AVIA 22 MINISTRY OF SUPPLY: REGISTERED FILES.
         1935–1962.   3,298 pieces.

Most of these files are from 1940 onwards. The files that have so far reached
the P.R.O. are divided into the following sections, each of which has one or more files
for the period 1935–1939.

1–3	Central Priority Department.
4–230	M.O.S. headquarters staff, organisation, duties, buildings, etc.
278–280	Arbitration.
281–297	Passive air defence.
298–303	Plant and stores for works services.
304–360	Parliamentary, legislation, legal, etc., including files on Ministry of Supply Bill, and Finance Bill papers relating to armament profit duty.
1023–1158	Civil staffs. (Outstations).
1485–1507	Mobilisation, Home Defence, etc.
1535–1550	Inventions, patents; claims.
1704–1723; 2036–2056	Explosions and chemical defence.
2139–2154	Inspection Department, Research Department.
2159–2177	Scientific Research.

See also WO 185 *and* SUPPLY group.

AVIA 23 SIGNALS RESEARCH AND DEVELOPMENT ESTABLISHMENT: REPORTS.
         1919–1939.   715 pieces.

These reports are from the Signals Experimental Establishment set up in 1916
to develop wireless and line equipment for the army and later included other
electrical and electronic equipment. In 1939 control of this establishment passed
to the Ministry of Supply, and it was given its present name in 1941. The reports are
listed chronologically. *See also* WO 187.

AVIA 24 RESEARCH AND DEVELOPMENT ESTABLISHMENT, CARDINGTON:
         DRAWINGS.
         1917–1940.   780 pieces.

AVIA 25 RESEARCH AND DEVELOPMENT ESTABLISHMENT, CARDINGTON:
         CORRESPONDENCE AND PAPERS.
         1933–1944.   40 pieces.

Cardington station was developed by the Admiralty in 1917 for work on airships.
It was taken over in 1919 by the Air Ministry and became known as the Royal Airship Works. After the R101 disaster in 1930, the station worked on balloon develop-

ment. It was taken over by the Ministry of Aircraft Production, and in 1945 it was given its present name. There is a glossary and key to arrangement at the beginning of the class list. Drawings dating from 1926 were made at Cardington, the origin of earlier ones is obscure. *See also* AIR 11 and 12, *and* AVIA 20.

MINISTRY OF DEFENCE

In 1936 a Minister for the Co-ordination of Defence was appointed. This ceased as a separate office in 1940, and the Prime Minister assumed the additional responsibility of being the Minister of Defence for the duration of the war.

A Ministry of Defence was established in 1947, responsible for formulation and general application of a unified policy for the armed forces. In 1964 this was transformed into a unified Ministry of Defence absorbing the Admiralty, Air Ministry, and War Office.

Records of the Minister for the Co-ordination of Defence are in CAB 64.

DEFENCE 1   POSTAL AND TELEGRAPH CENSORSHIP DEPARTMENT.
              1920–1921; 1938–1948.   334 pieces.   [III 34].   Closed for
                                                                          50 years.

Postal and cable censorship operated during the First World War as part of the Military Operations Directorate of the War Office. The only papers so far open in this class are as follows:

130   Report on Cable Censorship during the Great War, 1914–1919.
131   Report on Postal Censorship during the Great War, 1914–1919.

MINISTRY OF MUNITIONS

The Ministry of Munitions was established in June, 1915; its purpose was 'to ensure such supply of munitions for the present war as may be required by the Army Council or the Admiralty, or may be otherwise found to be necessary'. It worked mainly for the War Office and later for the Air Ministry, the Admiralty supplying most of its own needs but obtaining steel, explosives, and propellant, and, later, aircraft, from the Ministry of Munitions.

In 1916 the Ministry was given the task of supplying mechanised transport and railway material, and in 1917 it became responsible for the manufacture and inspection of aircraft, other than lighter-than-air machines.

The Ministry rapidly became the largest government department that had existed up to that time. It controlled the iron, steel, chemical, and engineering industries. Over 200 factories were built or nationalised for munitions work, and in addition there were over 5000 controlled establishments, and 10,000 other firms engaged on work for the department. At one time it employed nearly 2½ million people.

In 1919 proposals for transforming the Ministry into a permanent Ministry of Supply were abandoned, and the various functions of the Ministry of Munitions were gradually passed to other departments. In 1919, control of design and research was transferred to the War Office, and control of electric power and optical glass to the Board of Trade. In 1920, supply of aircraft passed to the Air Ministry, housing functions to the Office of Works, supply of building materials to the Ministry of Health, and control of ordnance factories and military stores, to the War Office. In 1921, control of petroleum was transferred to the Board of Trade, and the Ministry of Munitions was abolished.

In 1918 the Ministry of Munitions set up the Surplus Government Property Disposal Board to deal with its own surplus property and that of all other government departments. After the abolition of the Ministry, this work was continued by a Disposal and Liquidation Commission appointed by the Treasury. This Commission came to an end in 1924, and the remaining work in connection with disposal of surplus government property and completion of winding-up of contracts was continued by the Surplus Stores, etc. Liquidation Department of the Treasury. This department ended in 1927 and remaining functions were divided between the Treasury and the War Office while responsibility for caring for unsold properties passed to the Office of Works.

At the beginning of the class list there is a 'Note on Systems of Registration of the Ministry of Munitions', by H. L. Durant, Superintendent of Registries, Disposal and Liquidation Commission, 1923. A booklet on 'Records of the Ministry of Munitions, Disposal and Liquidation Commission, and Surplus Stores, etc., Liquidation Department' is available in the Round Room. This describes the records in detail and lists the records and the twenty departments to which they passed. Some records passed to other ministries, but when deposited at the P.R.O. some of these were returned to this group. For example, some records which went to the War Office and hence to the Ministry of Supply are now in MUN 7, but others are to be found in SUPPLY 2, 5, and 6. The records of the Central Control Board (Liquor Traffic) set up under the Ministry of Munitions are in HO 185.

MUN 1   MUNITIONS COUNCIL DAILY REPORTS.
          1917–1919.   24 pieces.   [II 216]

17–24   1919. January to August. Bound copies of daily confidential reports, one volume per month. These were circulated to members of the Munitions Council, and heads of departments; they contain papers of various committees and sub-committees, summaries of labour returns from national factories, and statistics of employment and unemployment.

MUN 2   REQUIREMENTS AND STATISTICS BRANCH: SECRET WEEKLY REPORTS.
          1915–1919.   34 pieces.   [II 216]

18–20   1918–1919. Reports of contracts placed and printed statistical tables showing weekly deliveries of materials, labour returns, etc. Each volume is indexed.

MUN 3   SPECIMENS OF DOCUMENTS DESTROYED.
          1915–1926.   465 pieces.   [II 216]

This class includes a complete set of account books of the Rochdale National Shell factory, supply records, contract records, and various labour records concerning time keeping, dilution, exemptions from military service, release of men from armed forces for munitions work, employment of aliens, part-time and week-end labour, etc.

MUN 4 RECORDS OF THE CENTRAL REGISTRY.

    1909–1937.   7,064 pieces.   [II 216]

This class contains files of the Ministry of Munitions, of the Disposal and Liquidation Commission, and of the Surplus Stocks, etc., Liquidation Department of the Treasury. A new class list arranged by subject is in course of preparation.

Case papers involving litigation conducted by the Treasury Solicitor on behalf of the Ministry of Munitions and succeeding departments have been returned to this class.

MUN 5 HISTORICAL RECORDS BRANCH.

    1907–1923.   393 pieces.   [II 216].

In 1916, it was agreed that a detailed record of the work of the Ministry of Munitions should be made in order to preserve the knowledge and experience gained in the rapid establishment of a large ministry. A 12 volume History of the Ministry of Munitions was produced but not published; it is arranged as follows

Vol. I	Industrial Mobilisation, 1914–1915.
II	General Organisation for Munitions Supply.
III	Finance and Contracts.
IV	Supply and Control of Labour.
V	Wages and Welfare.
VI	Manpower and Dilution.
VII	Control of Materials.
VIII	Control of Industrial Capacity and Equipment.
IX	Review of Munitions Supply.
X–XII	Supply of Munitions.

1–218   These documents formed the main source for the preparation of the history; they include papers acquired from departments or branches, or copied from other records. They are arranged according to their own classificatory system, set out in Appendix A at the beginning of the class list, and are called 'R', 'His. R', or 'His. Rec. R'.

219–320B   Unregistered papers: additional papers collected for the History, but not included in the above classificatory system.

321A   A set of the History of the Ministry of Munitions.

321B–322   Schemes for the History.

323–340   Correspondence with ministers and others concerning the History, with sections on each volume.

341–393   Additional papers, given 'H' 'His. H', or 'His. Rec. H'. numbers, following a classificatory system similar to the 'R' records.

MUN 7 FILES TRANSFERRED TO THE WAR OFFICE.

    1881–1930.   558 pieces.

These files were transferred to the War Office when the Ministry of Munitions was disbanded; the early files had originated there. The files are mainly for the war period and are concerned with contracts, explosives, inventions, and inspection. The post-war files are scattered throughout the class and deal with matters such as disposal of factories, and pay and pensions of munition workers. There are papers on subjects of general interest, for example:

12	1915–1919. Experiments and report on manufacture of smokeless fuel.
292	1917–1919. Hydro-electric power scheme for Scotland.
302	1917–1919. Stereoscopic photography.
536	1917–1920. Cultivation of flax from Japanese seed in Canada.

MUN 8 FILES TRANSFERRED TO THE AIR MINISTRY.
    1916–1923.   56 pieces.

These files were transferred after the disbanding of the Ministry of Munitions; they are concerned with aircraft production and aeronautical supplies. Post-war material includes reports on German aircraft, reports on development of aircraft and equipment, for example:

| 26 | 1918–1923. Invention of helicopter. |
| 35 | 1919. Report on flying-boat development. |

There are papers on disputes over rewards for inventions, and disposal of land, and piece 54 deals with transfer of work on aircraft production from Ministry of Munitions to Air Ministry.

MINISTRY OF SUPPLY

The department was formed in August, 1939, and became responsible for Army and Air Force supplies, other than aircraft, and for supply of 'common war articles', that is those used by more than one government department. Records concerned with these functions were transferred to the new ministry from the War Office and other departments. In 1959, it combined with the civil aviation section of Ministry of Transport and Civil Aviation to form the Ministry of Aviation. *See also* AVIA group, POWER 5, *and* WO 185.

SUPPLY 2 ROYAL ORDNANCE FACTORIES: ACCOUNTS.
    1888–1940.   59 pieces.   [II 263]

| 27–46, 49 | 1918–1940. Balance sheets. |
| 47 | 1924–1939. Public Accounts Committee notes. |

SUPPLY 3 PRINCIPAL SUPPLY OFFICERS COMMITTEE.
    1922–1939.   88 pieces.   [II 264]

This was a committee of the Committee for Imperial Defence which was responsible for the supply of materials and was absorbed into the Ministry of Supply when it was formed in August, 1939.

SUPPLY 4 CONTRACT RECORD BOOKS.
    1922–1958.   370 pieces.   [II 264]

Records incomplete, arrangement haphazard. Most files extend beyond 1940 and are not yet open. The few that are open refer to building materials and electrical stores.

SUPPLY 5   ROYAL ORDNANCE FACTORIES: FACTORY RECORDS.
            1710–1954.   994 pieces.   [II 263]

Most of the files are grouped under factories: Woolwich, Waltham Abbey, and Drigg. Arrangement haphazard.

SUPPLY 6   ORDNANCE BOARD: PROCEEDINGS, REPORTS, AND MEMORANDA.
            1855–1950.   671 pieces.   [III 162]

237–258	1919–1926. Ordnance Committee, minutes.
268–286	1919–1937. Ordnance Committee, annual reports.
290–360	1919–1938. Memoranda.
366–373	1939. Proceedings.
505–507	Indexes to memoranda and proceedings.
510–663	Mainly committee papers.

SUPPLY 10   QUINAN PAPERS.
            1902–1921.   300 pieces.   [II 264]

K. B. Quinan was an American engineer who worked for the British Government, 1914–1918. *See also* MUN 7/26.

1–107	Factories and plants producing chemicals and explosives.
108–221	Techniques and processes used in manufacture of chemicals and explosives.
222–258	Statistics of production.
259–276	Costs of production.
277–279	Correspondence.
280–300	Miscellanea, including reports on factories in Occupied Zone of Germany, 1920–1921, and visits to iron and steel works in America.

WAR OFFICE

By the War Office Act, 1870, the direct control of every branch of Army administration was vested in the Secretary of State for War. In 1964 the War Office was abolished, and its functions transferred to the Ministry of Defence. The following transfers of functions have taken place since 1918:

1919	From Ministry of Munitions, responsibility for design, research, inventions, and technical military stores.
1920	From Ministry of Munitions, remaining Army supply functions.
1921	From Ministry of Pensions, powers previously transferred except those over pensions arising from disablement or death during service in 1914–

1918 War and pensions already awarded in respect of disablement in former wars.

To Ministry of Pensions, officers' wounds pensions.

1922   To Air Ministry, military control of Iraq.

1923   From Ministry of Agriculture, administration of light horse breeding scheme.

1928   To Air Ministry, military security of Aden.

1929   To Air Ministry, control of Observer Corps.

1930   To Air Ministry, acquisition, management, and sale of Air Ministry lands.

1939   Ministry of Supply established. Agreed supply functions taken from War Office.

To Ministry of Pensions, administration of pensions arising out of war service.

1945   From Foreign Office, responsibility for British elements of Control Commission for Germany.

1947   To Foreign Office, Control Office for Germany and Austria.

1948   To Ministry of Defence, Joint Services Staff College.

1949   To Foreign Office, responsibility for former Italian colonies in Africa.

1954   From Civil Service Commission, responsibility for interview and selection test arrangements for service commissions.

1959   From Ministry of Aviation, some supply functions other than supply of aircraft and functions under Gunbarrel Proof Acts. Minister of Aviation to exercise concurrently with War Office and Air Ministry, supply functions previously exercised by Ministry of Aviation alone.

1963   To Ministry of Public Building and Works, most works services.

WO 25   REGISTERS: VARIOUS.
1660–1938.   3,992 pieces.   [II 313]

The inter-war material starts at piece 3578 with embarkation and disembarkation returns to 1938. There are also: pieces 3914–3919, records of service of officers in the Royal Engineers to 1935; piece 3956, recommendations for appointments to the Military Nursing Establishment to 1926; and piece 3991, candidates for ex-soldier clerkships to 1919.

WO 32   REGISTERED PAPERS: GENERAL SERIES.
1855–1964.   10,815 pieces.   [II 306]

These are documents selected for permanent preservation from the series of registered files. They relate to all aspects of the work of the War Office. The range of topics covered is very wide; it includes questions of recruitment, training, finance, conditions of service, defence policy, colonial military administration, and preparation for war, 1939. The files are arranged in 88 sections the code headings of which are set out clearly in alphabetical order at the beginning of the class list followed by a list of code headings in numerical order from o to 87. The sections are arranged in numerical order. For reference to countries see under Overseas, code o.

WO 33   REPORTS AND MISCELLANEOUS PAPERS.
1853–1939.   1,623 pieces.   [III 166].   Various files are closed
for 50 or 75 years.

916–1517   1919–1939. These are papers which had a limited circulation. They
cover the following subjects: armaments, organisation and distribution of military forces, reports of military missions and operations
such as those in Russia and the Middle East, comparative strengths
of foreign armies, the army in India, reports of the Research
Department, Woolwich, preparation of civil emergency schemes,
censorship, and papers of various committees in particular the
Mobilisation Equipment and War Reserves Committee and the
Chemical Defence Committee. Towards the end of the inter-war
period there are papers on air raid precautions, mobilisation, war
exercises, defence schemes for various places, and a conference on
preparation of charcoal from coal. The pieces are fully described
and are roughly chronological; there is no index.

WO 35   MISCELLANEOUS: IRELAND.
1775–1923.   207 pieces.   [II 320].   Various files are closed for
100 years.

The class contains records of the administration of the Army in Ireland, including
the period of 'Troubles', 1914–1922. There are papers on the application of the
Defence of the Realm Act and Restoration of Order in Ireland Regulations, Raid
and Search reports, war diaries, military courts of inquiry in lieu of inquests on
civilians, claims for damage alleged to have been done by military personnel while
raiding premises, evacuation, Irish Settlement, and press cuttings.

WO 55   ORDNANCE OFFICE: MISCELLANEOUS.
1568–1923.   3,038 pieces.   [II 329]

The Board of Ordnance was abolished in 1855. Many of the records of the bodies
which succeeded it were inherited by the Ministry of Supply and are described among
the records of that department. The only piece which extends into the inter-war
period is as follows:

2270   1870–1923. Reports, estimates, contracts, and correspondence, concerning works carried out at a coastguard station in Sussex.

WO 68   MILITIA RECORDS.
1759–1925.   568 pieces.   [II 310]

The only piece falling into the period is:

564   1908–1925. Precedents; extracts from files of rulings, etc., affecting
Militia and Supplementary Reserve.

JUDGE ADVOCATE GENERAL'S OFFICE
WO 71, 83, 84, 90, 93, 213.   [II 330–331].   Closed for 100 years.

The Judge Advocate General is the supreme officer responsible for the conduct
of prosecutions in courts martial. He also acted as Secretary to the Board of General

Officers and upon its abolition remained as legal adviser to the Commander in Chief. In 1948, the Judge Advocate General's office was transferred to the Lord Chancellor's establishment.

WO 73   RETURNS: DISTRIBUTION OF THE ARMY.
      1859–1938.   141 pieces.   [II 310].   Records open after 5 years.

These are the printed summarised returns bound in dated volumes. They give the distribution of the Army month by month (a) by divisions and stations and (b) by regiments in numerical order. They give the station of each battalion or company, the numbers of officers and other ranks present or absent, and other statistical information.

WO 76   RETURNS: RECORDS OF OFFICERS' SERVICES.
      1755–1954.   550 pieces.   [II 311]

These give the different ranks held by the officers and certain personal particulars. This series, supplementary to WO 25, was transferred from regimental record offices. The pieces are dated and listed by area record offices, each gives the name of the regiment or division. Few so far extend beyond 1919.

WO 78   MISCELLANEA: MAPS AND PLANS.
      1627–1953.   5,430 pieces.   [II 320]

The pieces are listed by geographical areas and fully described.

WO 79   PRIVATE COLLECTIONS: VARIOUS.
      1709–1937.   72 pieces.   [II 324]

This class consists of privately owned papers which have been presented to the War Office. There is a digest of service of the Connaught Rangers, 1908–1919 and papers of Field Marshal the Earl of Cavan, 1916–1937.

WO 94   TOWER OF LONDON: CONSTABLE'S OFFICE.
      1610–1936.   73 pieces.   [II 322]

The documents relate to the duties of the Constable and his staff. The pieces are described, and a few extend into the twentieth century.

WO 95   WAR OF 1914–1918: WAR DIARIES.
      1914–1922.   5,487 pieces.   [II 322]

These diaries contain the daily record of events, reports on operations, intelligence summaries, etc., of headquarters, army, corps, divisional, regimental, and other commanders, including those of colonial contingents in all theatres of war during the war 1914–18, and of the armies of occupation, 1919–22. The diaries are arranged by theatres of war and within each theatre by headquarters, armies, corps, divisions, and lines of communication troops. An index to the pieces and a guide on how to use the list appears at the beginning.

WO 101   MERITORIOUS SERVICE AWARDS.
      1846–1923.   7 pieces.   [II 310]

The medal and gratuity were instituted by Royal Warrant in 1845 for award to warrant and non-commissioned officers above the rank of corporal. The class comprises registers of candidates for, and recipients of, the award.

WO 106 DIRECTORATE OF MILITARY OPERATIONS AND INTELLIGENCE: PAPERS.
        1837–1939. 1594 pieces. [II 319]

This class contains correspondence and papers relating to military operations and defence including the following: Army of Occupation to 1930, Abyssinia, China, India, Middle East, Persia, Russia, Singapore, the Spanish Civil War, and Turkey.

WO 107 QUARTERMASTER GENERAL: PAPERS.
        1763–1919. 74 pieces. [II 306]

37   1919. Work of the labour force in France.

71–74   1919. History and organisation of salvage branch.

WO 111 ARMY ORDNANCE CORPS.
        1901–1919. 13 pieces. [II 318]

The relevant piece is a volume covering 1915–1919 which consists of a record of important events, changes, decisions, etc., compiled by the Commanding Officer at Woolwich. There is an index.

WO 113 FINANCE DEPARTMENT: PRECEDENTS.
        1878–1919. 9 pieces. [II 319]

A collection of precedents covering pay, allowances, retirement pensions, uniform, rank, concessions, etc. for officers and men. There is an index.

WO 114 STRENGTH RETURNS OF THE ARMY.
        1890–1920. 55 pieces. [II 317]

Weekly returns of the British Army and Dominion contingent at home including embodied Territorial Force and permanent staff.

WO 115 DIRECTORATE OF MEDICAL SERVICES: REPORTS, RETURNS, AND
        SUMMARIES.
        1921–1935. 47 pieces. [II 318]

These consist of annual statistical returns by commands at home and abroad, of admissions to hospital, deaths, discharges from the Army, periods of treatment, and annual reports of the Deputy Directors of Medical Services on the health of troops, the prevalence of disease, and the work of military hospitals. The pieces consist of dated volumes of reports, unindexed.

WO 137 PRIVATE OFFICE PAPERS: DERBY PAPERS.
        1921–1923. 12 pieces. [II 324]

Correspondence and papers accumulated at the War Office by the Earl of Derby during his term as Secretary of State for War.

WO 140   SCHOOL OF MUSKETRY: HYTHE.
         1853–1928.   15 pieces.   [II 322]

List of instructional prints of arms and ammunition received, 1909–1928.

WO 142   CHEMICAL WARFARE RECORDS.
         1914–1924.   221 pieces.   [III 128]

Reports, minutes of committees, and papers connected with the development, manufacture, and use of poison gases by Britain and her allies during the War, 1914–1918; also drawings and specifications of British respirators.

WO 143   DUKE OF YORK'S SCHOOL AND ROYAL HIBERNIAN SCHOOL.
         1801–1958.   65 pieces.   [III 129]

The records include minutes of General Board meetings, registers of admissions to 1919, and discharges to 1923. *See also* WO 32 (Code 34).

WO 144   WAR OF 1914–1918: INTER-ALLIED ARMISTICE COMMISSION.
         1918–1920.   35 pieces.   [III 128]

The Commission was formed in 1918 to deal with prisoners of war and the handing over of materials, transport, and stores, under the terms of the Armistice. Its duties were increased beyond its original instructions to include a variety of administrative functions. It also acted as a means of communication between the Allied Governments and the German representatives until the ratification of the Peace Treaty. The class consists of a war diary and the despatches of Lieut. General Sir Richard Haking, Chief of the British delegation.

WO 145   RETURNS: MEDALS AND AWARDS: ROYAL RED CROSS.
         1883–1928.   1 piece.   [III 128]

A register of recipients.

WO 153   WAR OF 1914–1918: MAPS AND PLANS.
         1914–1921.   1,215 pieces.

This class contains some post 1918 maps for Europe including France and Belgium road traffic maps, 1918–1919; American dispositions, 1918–1919; and Russian fronts to 1921. There are also maps for Palestine and Syria, including the Sykes-Picot line and suggested post-war spheres of influence, 1919; and for Mesopotamia, Persia, and India.

WO 155   ALLIED MILITARY COMMITTEE OF VERSAILLES.
         1919–1927.   64 pieces.

The class contains minutes of meetings of the Inter-Allied Military Commission in Hungary, and in Bulgaria, the final report of the Inter-Allied Military Commission of Control in Germany, and minutes of the Financial Administration Committee. There are papers on the military situation in Germany, transformation of war factories in Germany and Austria, and illegal manufacture and sale of arms. *See also* FO group for records of Inter-Allied Control Commissions.

WO 156   RETURNS: REGISTERS OF BAPTISM AND BANNS OF MARRIAGE.
         1865–1947.   8 pieces.

A miscellaneous collection of registers kept at several garrisons in the British Isles and Palestine.

WO 157   WAR OF 1914–1918: INTELLIGENCE SUMMARIES.
         1914–1921.   1,307 pieces.   [III 129]

Summaries of information and reports on military, economic, and political matters from various fronts. There is post-1918 material on: France, Belgium, Germany, South Russia and Caucasas, Mesopotamia, North Russia, India, and East Persia.

WO 158   WAR OF 1914–1918: CORRESPONDENCE AND PAPERS OF MILITARY
         HEADQUARTERS.
         1914–1929.   963 pieces.   [III 129]

There is inter-war material on the Army of Occupation to 1923, Mesopotamia including north Persia, Russian fronts, Turkey, and Greece. There is a guide to contents acting as an index at the front of the class.

WO 161   MISCELLANEOUS UNREGISTERED PAPERS.
         1914–1944.   87 pieces.

This class contains files of the Director of Supplies and Transport, Home Forces, Master General of Ordnance, Director of Fortifications and Works, and statistical abstract of armies at home and abroad, 1920.

WO 162   ADJUTANT-GENERAL.
         1847–1937; 1952.   98 pieces.

This class contains papers on organisation, recruitment, hospital and women's services, Royal occasions 1936–37, and of the Committee on Drafts for India.

WO 163   WAR OFFICE COUNCIL AND ARMY COUNCIL.
         1870–1938.   46 pieces.   [III 128]

Minutes and précis, listed in indexed dated volumes.

WO 181   DIRECTORATE OF MILITARY SURVEY: PAPERS.
         1887–1942.   306 pieces.   Various files are closed for 50 or 100
                                      years.

These are registered branch files of the Geographical Section, General Staff, which became the Directorate of Military Survey, 1943. The class includes the minutes of the Colonial Survey and Geophysical Committee, and papers on aerial surveys and mapping of boundaries.

WO 185   MINISTRY OF SUPPLY: WAR OFFICE FILES.
         1934–1962.   224 pieces.

This class contains the files which were opened and closed in the Ministry of Supply; files which were opened in the War Office before September, 1939 and whose life was completed in the Ministry of Supply, are in WO 32. Very few files predate 1939. *See also* AVIA 32 *and* SUPPLY group.

WO 186 PROOF AND EXPERIMENTAL ESTABLISHMENTS, SHOEBURYNESS.
1852–1855; 1914–1924; 1935–1936.   11 pieces.

Reports on Ballistic Range and experimental firings by HMS *Rodney*.

WO 187 ROYAL ENGINEERS AND SIGNALS BOARD PROCEEDINGS.
1919–1937.   30 pieces.

The long established Royal Engineer Committee became the Royal Engineer Board in 1918. It had executive functions, including the direction of various experimental establishments (*see* AVIA 17 and AVIA 23). In 1936 it became the Royal Engineers and Signals Board. The class consists of printed handbooks of extracts relating to equipment and research from the proceedings of the 'A' (Field Engineer), 'B' (Air Defence), and 'C' (Signals) Committees of the Board.

WO 188 CHEMICAL DEFENCE EXPERIMENTAL ESTABLISHMENT (PORTON): CORRESPONDENCE AND PAPERS.
1916–1939.   387 pieces.

These files are mostly records of experiments and trials of chemical weapons and protective devices carried out at this establishment and elsewhere. There are also more general papers on chemical warfare in Britain and other countries and reports of Porton and other research establishments. The class is arranged in file reference order.

WO 190 APPRECIATION FILES.
1922–1939.   890 pieces.

Reports on the military, political, economic, and social situation in Germany and adjacent countries prepared by the Director of Military Operations and Intelligence. Each piece is fully described and the list is in chronological order.

WO 191 WAR DIARIES AND H.Q. RECORDS: MINOR CAMPAIGNS.
1927–1937.   62 pieces.

Headquarters and operational papers of campaigns in Abyssinia, 1935–1936; Egypt, 1935–1936; India, 1930–1937; Palestine, 1936; and Shanghai, 1927–1932.

WO 192 FORT RECORD BOOKS.
1892–1945.   160 pieces.   Various files are closed for 50 or 75 years.

The official records of the operation, administration, and history of forts at home and abroad.

WO 194 FIGHTING VEHICLES RESEARCH AND DEVELOPMENT ESTABLISHMENT.
1921–1950.   154 pieces.

The class contains technical reports of tests undertaken by the Mechanical Warfare Experimental Establishment, which was set up in 1928, and the Wheeled Vehicle Establishment, which was set up in 1931. The class also contains minutes of meetings of the Mechanical Warfare Board, data books, photographs, and drawings of vehicles.

WO 196   DIRECTOR OF ARTILLERY.
    1892–1946. 32 pieces. Various files are closed for 50 years.

Reports on coast defence of British and overseas stations.

WO 197   WAR OF 1939–1945: MILITARY HEADQUARTERS PAPERS: BRITISH
    EXPEDITIONARY FORCE.
    1939–1941. 134 pieces.

This class contains papers dealing with the organisation of the British Expeditionary Force before the outbreak of war.

WO 206   DIRECTORATE OF ARMY MEDICAL SERVICES: ARMY PATHOLOGY
    ADVISORY COMMITTEE.
    1919–1939. 3 pieces.

This Committee was set up in 1919, and in 1923 its services were extended to the Royal Air Force. The class consists of minutes of the Committee, indexed.

WO 207   INDIA DEFENCE EXPENDITURE TRIBUNAL.
    1932–1933. 14 pieces.

This was set up in 1932 under Sir Robert Garran to consider questions of expenditure which were in dispute between the Government of India and the War Office and Air Ministry. The class consists of the War Office's set of circulated papers of the Tribunal and also of notes for the War Office Counsel not submitted to the Tribunal.

COMMON SERVICES

CENTRAL OFFICE OF INFORMATION

The Ministry of Information which existed from March to November, 1918, dealt with overseas propaganda and was the first separate information department. In the inter-war period the development of information services both external and domestic was left to individual departments, apart from the Empire Service of the British Broadcasting Corporation and the work of the British Council. Some departments, notably the Home Office, Ministry of Health, and the Post Office, established public relations divisions.

In September, 1939, a Ministry of Information was set up in accordance with pre-war plans, taking over some functions from the Foreign Office and the Home Office. The Ministry was responsible for press censorship, for facilitating the collection and transmission of war news, for all overseas publicity except to enemy and enemy-occupied territories, and for providing publicity services for most of the domestic departments.

At the end of the war the duties of the Ministry in connection with censorship and the press ceased and the Ministry was abolished in 1946. Responsibility for overseas publicity reverted to the Foreign, Colonial, and Dominions Offices. The common service and production sections of the Ministry of Information became the nucleus of a new Central Office of Information responsible for producing publicity material. The Government Social Survey was part of the Central Office of Information until 1970 when it merged with the General Register Office to form the Office of Population Censuses and Surveys.

Most of the records in this group relate to the Second World War and there is very little inter-war material.

INF 1   FILES OF CORRESPONDENCE.
      1936–1946.   435 pieces.   [II 196].   Closed for 50 years.

INF 4   WAR OF 1914–1918: INFORMATION SERVICE.
      1915–1943.   11 pieces.

Enquiries and reports on methods employed by various departments in distributing information to neutral and allied countries during the First World War. Most papers deal with 1917–18 and were assembled during the preparation of an official history of the Ministry of Information. The papers were accumulated from various sources but relate mainly to the enquiries conducted by Sir Robert Donald, then editor of the *Daily Chronicle*, into the methods employed by various departments in distributing propaganda to neutral and allied countries during the First World War. His reports and recommendations resulted in the formation of the Ministry of Information in 1918.

INF 5   CROWN FILM UNIT: FILES.
      1936–1954.   112 pieces.

Government-financed films were first made by the Empire Marketing Board in 1929. This film unit moved to the General Post Office in 1933 and was renamed the

Crown Film Unit in 1940 when it came under the direction of the Ministry of Information. A few of the studio files are open.

CIVIL SERVICE COMMISSION

The Civil Service Commission was established in 1855 following the Northcote-Trevelyan report. Its main purpose is to test the qualifications of candidates applying for appointment to the civil service or for transfer to another grade within the civil service. The Commissioners are appointed by Order in Council, and the regulations they lay down for the qualifications needed were approved by the Treasury and since 1968 by the new Civil Service Department.

The Civil Service Commission is also responsible for examination of candidates applying for Service commissions and cadetships, but since 1954 the interviewing of candidates has been done by the Service departments.

For papers of the Royal Commission on the Civil Service, 1929–1931, *see* T 169 *and* HO 45.

CSC 3   COLLECTIONS: FILES, SERIES I.
      1875–1953.   374 pieces.   [II 51]

This class contains files of correspondence on all aspects of the work of the Commission; the files were opened in 1908 or before but many contain later material. There is an index for the papers up to 1944; this is divided into six parts to which there is an alphabetical index.

CSC 4   ANNUAL REPORTS.
      1855–1967.   53 pieces.   [II 51]

CSC 5   COLLECTIONS: FILES, SERIES II.
      1908–1958.   310 pieces.   [III 24]

This is a continuation of CSC 3 with files opened in 1908 or later. The order is roughly chronological; there is no index.

CSC 6   REGULATIONS, RULES, AND MEMORANDA (INDEXED): OPEN AND LIMITED COMPETITIONS.
      1863–1939.   44 pieces.   [III 24].   No restriction on access.

CSC 7   ABSTRACTS.
      1860–1939.   23 pieces.   [III 24]

23   1939 edition contains brief information on conditions for entry attaching to competitions. Other volumes for the inter-war period are bound with annual reports in CSC 4.

CSC 10   EXAMINATIONS: TABLES OF MARKS AND RESULTS.
      1876–1943.   4,835 pieces.   [III 24]

ROYAL COMMISSION ON ANCIENT MONUMENTS IN WALES AND MONMOUTHSHIRE

This Royal Commission was set up in 1908 to survey the ancient and historical monuments in Wales and Monmouthshire and to make recommendations on those which should be preserved. Originally set up as a temporary commission, it has been renewed periodically.

MONWAL 1 RECORDS.
          1908–1944.   5 pieces.   [III 96]

  2–3   1908–1944. Record of proceedings at meetings of the Commission and various reports.
  5   1928–1930. Proposals for reorganisation.

MINISTRY OF PUBLIC BUILDING AND WORKS

An Office of Works has existed since the sixteenth century, its principal officers meeting together as a Board. In 1782 a single surveyor was appointed who was to be an architect or builder. In 1832 the Office was combined with that of the Commissioners of Woods, Forests, and Land Revenues. A new Office of Works was formed in 1852 which took over all the duties previously exercised by the Surveyor of Works, and in addition responsibility for metropolitan improvements from the Office of Woods.

In 1882, the Board was given responsibility for the protection of Ancient Monuments. Its functions connected with metropolitan improvements were taken over by the Metropolitan Board of Works and its successor, the London County Council. The Ordnance Survey and Kew Gardens were transferred to the Board of Agriculture in 1889 and 1903 respectively.

In the inter-war period, the Board was responsible for the design, building, and furnishing of government offices and embassies, and for buildings for the Armed Forces at home and abroad. It also maintained the Houses of Parliament, palaces, and royal parks. During the two world wars, the Board erected ordnance factories. In 1920, it took over the Housing Department of the Ministry of Munitions (WORKS 6). It became the Ministry of Works and Buildings in 1940. In 1942 it was given control and supervision of the building and civil engineering industries for wartime purposes. It became the Ministry of Works and Planning when it took over the planning functions of the Ministry of Health; but these were transferred to a separate Ministry of Town and Country Planning, and the ministry was renamed the Ministry of Works in 1943. In 1963 it became the Ministry of Public Building and Works, when it was given a general surveillance over the building industry. In 1966 functions relating to the National Building Agency, building regulations, production of housing statistics, and protection of historic buildings, were transferred to the Ministry of Housing and Local Government. In 1967 the Building Research Station was transferred to the Ministry of Public Building and Works from the Ministry of Technology.

In 1970 the Ministry became the Housing and Construction side of the new Department of the Environment.

WORKS 5   ACCOUNTS.
           1638–1924.   210 pieces.   [II 336]

204/1   1914–1924. Accounts of Queen Victoria Memorial Fund, and Victoria Tower Garden.

WORKS 6   MISCELLANEA.
           1609–1956.   423 pieces.   [II 336–337]

The following pieces contain inter-war material:

135/1–137/10	1920–1927. Housing schemes undertaken by the Office of Works on behalf of local authorities.
187/1–187/10	1920–1932. National Shipyards.
187/11–191/7	1917–1928. Farm buildings and factories.
351/1–352/1	1921–1922. De Bartolomé's Committee on Decentralisation of Government Staff.
362/8	1919. Memorandum on problems of reconstruction in Belgium.
362/9	1917–1930. Silvertown explosion, reconstruction of area destroyed.
362/10	1921. Louth flood, expenditure on temporary measures.
363/1	1917–1923. Ministry of Shipping grain stores.
364/1–367/3	1921–1945. Buildings at Cranwell, Rosyth, Botleys Park, and in London.
368/8	1922–1931. Reports on dry rot, Professor Percy Groom, consultant.
394/1–399/3	1920–1947. Housing Schemes (Ministry of Munitions).
403–405	1928–1940. River Thames flooding.
407–409	1937–1942. Central Register policy, co-ordination of accommodation.
415–419	1913–1953. Kew Observatory.
421	1922–1941. Isle of Man.

WORKS 7   DEEDS: SERIES I.
           18th–20th centuries.   84 pieces.   [II 337]

The only deeds relating to inter-war transactions are:

60/8–60/26   1919–1928. Ministry of Pensions; hospitals and convalescent centres.

WORKS 10   PUBLIC BUILDINGS: OVERSEAS.
           1834–1959.   126 pieces.   [II 338]

Papers deal with the acquisition, alteration, and maintenance of public buildings overseas, mainly legations, embassies, and consulates. Pieces 31/1–32/13 are concerned with accommodation of the British delegation to the Peace Conference in Paris, 1919.

WORKS 11   HOUSES OF PARLIAMENT.
1709–1952.   408 pieces.   [II 338]

Papers deal with the maintenance of the Houses of Parliament; inter-war material can be found in 29/2–29/13 and in most files from 194 to 396.

WORKS 12   PUBLIC BUILDINGS: ENGLAND.
1731–1952.   276 pieces.   [II 338]

Papers concerning the management of public buildings in England and Wales. There is some inter-war material; the arrangement is haphazard.

WORKS 13   DEEDS: SERIES III.
1844–1951.   1,395 pieces.   [II 337]

These are original contracts for erection and maintenance of various public buildings, with specifications of works and materials, and architects' drawings.

696–1389   1919–1943. Contract Rolls and Flats.
1390–1395   1938–1940. Contract bound volumes. (Royal Ordnance Factories).

WORKS 14   ANCIENT MONUMENTS AND HISTORIC BUILDINGS.
1699–1957.   1,385 pieces.   [II 338]

Papers relating to the preservation of the monuments and buildings for which the Ministry is responsible are arranged in several alphabetical lists, interspersed with files on general topics and London buildings. Properties near the Roman Wall are to be found under that name.

WORKS 15   OSBORNE ESTATE.
1902–1956.   111 pieces.   [II 338]

The files are described and dated and the arrangement is roughly chronological.

WORKS 16   ROYAL PARKS.
1736–1952.   1,528 pieces.   [II 338]

There is inter-war material in the following pieces:

484–494   1913–1942. Regulations made under Parks Regulation Acts, 1872 and 1926.
523–570   1909–1941. General.
574–587   1916–1941. Wild life.
588   1889–1938. Brompton Cemetery.
773–787   1910–1948. Wild life; annual reports by Bird Sanctuaries Committees, 1924–1947.
819–863;   General.
994–1062

Subsequent files are arranged alphabetically under the name of the park, followed by general and miscellaneous.

WORKS 17   ART AND SCIENCE BUILDINGS.
          1794–1958.   251 pieces.   [II 338]

Papers are arranged under the name of the building in several alphabetical series, as the material reached the P.R.O. The class covers London museums, galleries, and research stations.

WORKS 19   ROYAL PALACES.
          1689–1955.   1,051 pieces.   [II 338]

Correspondence and papers concerning royal palaces; arrangement is roughly alphabetical, followed by miscellaneous. There are also entries for Longford River, a canal made in the seventeenth century to take water from the River Colne to Hampton Court.

WORKS 20   STATUES AND MEMORIALS.
          1810–1954.   232 pieces.   [II 338]

The inter-war material is after piece 94; the arrangement is haphazard.

WORKS 21   CEREMONIALS.
          1727–1953.   112 pieces.   [II 358]

Most inter-war material is from piece number 52 onwards, but 36/2–3 deal with state visits, 1918–20.

WORKS 22   ADMINISTRATION (GENERAL) AND ESTABLISHMENT.
          1802–1961.   174 pieces.   [II 338]

Apart from establishment matters, the class contains the following:

4/4	1928. Thames flood, emergency services.
30	1914–1936. History, powers, and duties of the Commissioner of Works.
36–37	1919–1921. Reorganisation of Office of Works.
120	Electricity Supply Acts, 1882–1936.

WORKS 23   MINISTRY OF LABOUR TRAINING CENTRES.
          1919–1923.   1 piece.   [II 339]

Papers relating to a training centre for the building trade at Haydn Park Works, Shepherds Bush, London.

WORKS 24   DEEDS: SERIES II.
          1614–1929.   8 pieces.   [II 337]

The following refer to inter-war transactions:

1/1–1/9	1913–1920. Flax factories.
1/10–1/14	1922–1925. National shipyards.
6/14–6/17	1923–1929. Millbank prison site.

8/1–8/8   1920–1925. Birtles housing estate.

8/9–8/17   1915–1928. Coventry housing estate.

WORKS 26   ROYAL ORDNANCE FACTORIES.
                    1936–1951.   19 pieces.   [II 339]

Contracts for work at R.O.F.s arranged alphabetically by name of factory. Most
files extend beyond 1940.

WORKS 27   PUBLIC BUILDINGS: NORTHERN IRELAND.
                    1921–1954.   17 pieces.   [II 389]

Papers relate to Parliament Buildings, Law Courts, Stormont Castle, and Hills-
borough Castle.

WORKS 28   AIR RAID PRECAUTIONS AND CIVIL DEFENCE.
                    1935–1951.   35 pieces.   [II 389]

Most files extend beyond 1940.

WORKS 29–38, 40–44   MAPS AND PLANS   [III 130]

The following contain maps and plans drawn in the inter-war period. The class
lists give full particulars.

29   HOUSES OF PARLIAMENT. 1698–1927. 3,400 pieces.

30   PUBLIC BUILDINGS, ENGLAND. 1738–1939. 6,088 pieces.

31   ANCIENT MONUMENTS AND HISTORIC BUILDINGS. 1668–1932. 820 pieces.

32   ROYAL PARKS AND PLEASURE GARDENS. 1701–1930. 658 pieces.

33   ART AND SCIENCE BUILDINGS. 1815–1934. 2,958 pieces.

34   ROYAL PALACES. 1662–1929; 1935. 1,550 pieces.

36   CEREMONIAL. 1685–1919. 98 pieces.

38   MISCELLANEOUS. 1702–1927. 297 pieces.
       Ontario Military Hospital, Orpington, and Southampton dockyard.

40   PUBLIC BUILDINGS: OVERSEAS. 1850–1937. 411 pieces.

41   NAVAL ESTABLISHMENTS. 1820–1936. 70 pieces.

42   PUBLIC BUILDINGS: NORTHERN IRELAND. 1920–1929. 25 pieces.

43   ARMY ESTABLISHMENTS. 1713–1935. 412 pieces.

44   AIR FORCE ESTABLISHMENTS. 1914–1936. 18 pieces.

WORKS 46   OFFICIAL HISTORY OF THE SECOND WORLD WAR: WORKS AND
                    BUILDINGS: UNPUBLISHED SOURCES.
                    1919–1945.   10 pieces.

PUBLIC RECORD OFFICE

The Public Record Office was set up under an Act of 1838 which placed the Public
Records under the charge of the Master of the Rolls. In 1851 work began on a new

repository on the Rolls estate in Chancery Lane. During this century, the enlarged P.R.O. in Chancery Lane was inadequate, and various provincial repositories have been used, the main one at present being at Ashridge, Hertfordshire.

A Committee on Departmental Records under the chairmanship of Sir James Grigg was appointed to review the arrangements for the preservation of departmental records. It reported in 1954, (Cmd. 9163), and its recommendations formed the basis of the Public Records Act, 1958, which governs the administration of the P.R.O., the selection and preservation of public records, their availability for public access, etc. The administration of the P.R.O. was entrusted to a Keeper responsible to the Lord Chancellor. There is an Advisory Council under the chairmanship of the Master of the Rolls, responsible for advising the Lord Chancellor on the Public Records.

Apart from records of the work of the P.R.O., this group contains papers acquired by gift, deposit, or purchase (PRO 30).

PRO 1   GENERAL CORRESPONDENCE.
      1819–1945.   461 pieces.   [II 241]

This class contains correspondence dealing with all aspects of the work of the P.R.O., including transfers of records, staffing, and accommodation. Indexes are in PRO 34.

PRO 5   REGISTERS: LEGAL SEARCH ROOM.
      1871–1950.   168 pieces.   [II 242]

PRO 6   REGISTERS: LITERARY SEARCH ROOM.
      1871–1960.   326 pieces.   [II 242]

These two classes contain records of documents produced to searchers.

PRO 8   VARIOUS: MISCELLANEA.
      1772–1955.   42 pieces.

The inter-war material in this class consists of papers on the organisation of the P.R.O. Museum, registers of students' tickets, and returns from colonial governments giving details of their archives in 1936–1938.

PRO 12   REGISTERS: REPAIR.
      1882–1961.   9 pieces.   [II 242]

PRO 13   VARIOUS: SUMMARIES OF RECORDS.
      1863–1963.   21 pieces.   [II 243]

PRO 15   INSPECTING OFFICERS' COMMITTEE: MINUTE BOOKS.
      1881–1958.   25 pieces.   [II 242]

PRO 17   INSPECTING OFFICERS' COMMITTEE: CORRESPONDENCE AND PAPERS.
      1861–1929.   7 pieces.   [II 242]

PRO 30   DOCUMENTS ACQUIRED BY GIFT, DEPOSIT, OR PURCHASE.

PRO 30/9   COLCHESTER PAPERS.
           1613–1919.   104 pieces.   [II 246]
    103   1918–1919. Journal of the 3rd Lord Colchester.

PRO 30/30 MILNER PAPERS.
           1915–1920.   25 pieces.

Lord Milner was Secretary of State for the Colonies, 1918–1921.

PRO 30/33 SATOW PAPERS.
           1856–1927.   23 pieces.   [II 251]

   The private and diplomatic papers of Sir Ernest Satow deal with the pre-war
period, but his diary continues up to 1926.

PRO 30/52 LEAGUE OF NATIONS ASSEMBLY AND COUNCIL DOCUMENTS.
           1920–1946.   768 pieces.   [II 248].   No restriction on
                                                  access.

Records of the London Office of the League of Nations.

PRO 30/59 STURGIS DIARY.
           1920–1922.   5 pieces.   [III 109].   Closed for 50 years.

Sir Mark Sturgis was Joint Assistant Under-Secretary for Ireland, 1920–1922.

PRO 30/63 QUEEN'S INSTITUTE OF DISTRICT NURSING: RECORDS.
           1890–1948.   597 pieces.   [III 110].   No restriction on
                                                   access.

   The Institute supervised county and district nursing associations.

PRO 30/66 MANCE PAPERS.
           1899–1924.   33 pieces.

   Sir Osborne Mance, after a career in the army, advised the British Delegation to
the 1919–1920 Peace Conference on communications. He subsequently served
on League of Nations' committees and conventions dealing with transport
problems.

PRO 30/67 MIDLETON PAPERS.
           1885–1941.   57 pieces.

   Lord Midleton was leader of the Southern Unionists in Ireland after the First
World War, and was instrumental in arranging the discussions with the Sinn
Fein which led to the 1921 truce.

PRO 30/68 ANDERSON PAPERS.
           1915–1936.   29 pieces.

   Sir Alan Garrett Anderson was Vice-Chairman of the Royal Commission on
Wheat Supplies during the First World War, and served on various trade missions
and committees during the period 1923–1936.

PRO 30/69 RAMSAY MACDONALD PAPERS.
           1793–1937.   1679 pieces.

   These papers are expected to reach the Public Record Office during 1971. The class will contain the official and private papers of Ramsay MacDonald who was the first Labour Prime Minister in 1924, an office he then combined with that of Foreign Secretary. He was Prime Minister again in 1929 until 1935, heading first a Labour and then a coalition ministry; from 1935–37 he was Lord President of the Council. The class also contains family papers, and those of his wife, Margaret MacDonald, who died in 1911. The class list is very detailed, and there is a description of the papers and their arrangement in the introduction. The papers are arranged as follows:

1. *Official*

    1/1–1/9.   1924–1937.   Correspondence.
    1/10–1/242.   1924.   Government papers.
    1/243–1/479.   1929–1935.   Government papers.
    1/555–1/656.   1929–1937.   Various official papers.

2. *Official–Private*

    2/1–2/18.   Correspondence.
    2/19–1/46.   General.

3. *Personal*

    3/1–3/46.   Correspondence.
    3/47–3/133.   General.
    3/134–3/210.   Family and personal papers of Margaret MacDonald.
    3/211–3/231.   Photographs.

3A. *Personal–Literary*

    3A/1–3A/131.   Articles, reviews, correspondence, etc.

4. *Indexes*—original indexes to collections of official papers.

5. *Political—Party*

    5/1–5/230.   1883–1937.   Articles, pamphlets, newspapers, and correspondence.
    5/231–5/247.   1883–1911.   Correspondence and papers of Margaret MacDonald.

6. *Political—Public*

    6/1–6/266.   1888–1937.   Correspondence, speeches, lectures, press cuttings, etc.

7. *Political—Constituency*

    7/1–7/66.   1892–1937.   Correspondence and general.

8. *Miscellaneous*

    8/1–8/21.   1892–1937.   Diaries, note books, general.

PRO 34   INDEXES TO GENERAL CORRESPONDENCE.
    1838–1938.   26 pieces.   [II 241]

There are two indexes, one chronological, and the other alphabetical, to the general correspondence in PRO 1.

PRO 39 COMMISSIONS AND COMMITTEES: COMMITTEES.
1859–1957.   9 pieces.   [II 243]

Papers of committees in the inter-war period are as follows:

4   1912–1930. Advisory Council on Publications.

5   1919–1922. Records Accommodation Committee.

6   1920–1922. War Memorial Committee.

7   1929–1933. Committee on Make-up and Materials of Departmental Records.

PRO 40 REGISTERS: TRANSFER REGISTERS, ETC.
1840–1967.   18 pieces.   [III 109]

Registers of transfers of records to and from the department, and warrants for transfer of records to the department.

STATIONERY OFFICE

The Stationery Office was established in 1786 as a central agency for the purchase of printing and stationery supplies for government offices. It is now responsible for the supply of stationery, printing, binding, office machinery and equipment other than furniture, and printed books for the public service. It also publishes Parliamentary Debates, the London and Edinburgh Gazettes, and other government publications; and it prints all reports laid before Parliament. The copyright of government publications is vested in the Controller of the Stationery Office.

The Stationery Office has its own printing presses and binderies and provides a central duplicating and distributing service for government departments. It has a regional organisation including a number of book-shops. It acts as agent for the publications of the United Nations and other international bodies.

STAT 2 REGISTERS OF IN-LETTERS.
1855–1955.   69 pieces.   [II 260]

Registers of in-letters found in STAT 12 and STAT 14.

STAT 3 OUT-LETTERS.
1785–1920; 1937–1955.   237 pieces.   [II 260]

STAT 4 COPYRIGHT OUT-LETTERS.
1888–1920.   13 pieces.   [II 260]

STAT 5 REGISTERS OF COPYRIGHT IN-LETTERS.
1888–1920.   4 pieces.   [II 260]

The in-letters to which these registers refer have not been preserved.

STAT 6 CONTROLLER'S PRIVATE LETTER BOOKS.
1846–1961.   13 pieces.   [II 260]

11   1916–1925. Entry books and copies of official and semi-official out-letters.

STAT 7   MISCELLANEOUS.
       1792–1954; 1961.   23 pieces.   [II 260]

7–14   1919–1940. Registry circulars.

22   1929, 1930, 1937. Guide to the supply and control of printing, stationery, etc.

TENDER BOOKS [II 260–261]

STAT 8   MISCELLANEOUS SUPPLIES. 1833–1951. 46 pieces.

STAT 9   PAPER. 1876–1955. 30 pieces.

STAT 10   PRINTING AND BINDING. 1873–1944. 26 pieces.

STAT 12   FILES OF CORRESPONDENCE: SERIES I
       1858–1920.   44 pieces.   [II 260]

This correspondence is arranged in two series General and Treasury, L and LT. The class list gives the L and LT numbers for each piece number; and a subject index gives the L and LT numbers. The class list in the Round Room contains the subject index and a digest for this class.

STAT 13   ESTABLISHMENT AND ACCOUNTING RECORDS.
       1786–1954.   42 pieces.   [II 261]

STAT 14   FILES OF CORRESPONDENCE: SERIES II.
       1871–1964.   1,486 pieces.   [III 114]

A new system was started in 1921 whereby the L and LT series were superseded by four series, E, C, K, G; to which D was added later. Under this system files remained 'live' for many years. There is a digest to the files which were closed in the period 1921–1934. Pieces 1–26 have references to file numbers and can only be used in conjunction with the digest; in pieces 27 onwards the files are described. The papers are arranged as follows:

1–16; 284–801	E	Establishment files, includes annual reports and papers of the Committee of Enquiry into the Government Printing Works (Gretton Committee), reported 1927.
17; 27–255	C	Copyright files.
18–20; 1358–1486	K	Contracts files.
21–26; 802–1357	G	General files.
256–283	D	Duplicating files: most files were closed in the 1950's and are not open, and the series is not in the digest.

BIBLIOGRAPHY

D. N. Chester and F. M. G. Wilson: *The Organisation of British Central Government, 1914–1964.* A survey by a Study Group of the Royal Institute of Public Administration, 1957. Second edition 1968.

Whitehall Series, edited by Sir James Marchant, volumes written between 1925 and 1935 describing various government departments.

New Whitehall Series, edited by Sir Robert Frazer, for the Royal Institute of Public Administration.

ANNUAL PUBLICATIONS

The British Imperial Calendar and Civil Service List.
Whitaker's Almanack.

The first bulletin each year of the Organisation and Methods Division of the Civil Service Department contains an account of the main changes in government machinery that occurred during the preceding year.

P.R.O. PUBLICATIONS

Guide to the Contents of the Public Record Office

Part I. *Legal Records.* (1963)
Part II. *State Papers and Departmental Records.* (1963)
Part III. *Documents Transferred 1960–1966.* (1968)

Handbooks

3. *The Records of the Colonial and Dominions Offices.* (1964)
11. *The Records of the Cabinet Office to 1922.* (1966)
13. *The Records of the Foreign Office, 1782–1939.* (1969)

LISTS AND INDEXES

The P.R.O. between 1892 and 1936 began the publication of some of the more important means of reference to the national archives as a series of lists and indexes. This series is now being continued by the Kraus-Thomson Organisation. The relevant volumes produced by Kraus-Thomson for the inter-war period are in the Supplementary Series.

The List and Index Society, formed in 1965, issues certain class lists of records not covered by the agreement with the Kraus-Thomson Organisation.

GLOSSARY

Establishment: the staffing and organisation of a department. Establishment classes contain material on Whitley Councils and staff associations, and may include other records such as histories of the departments, transfers of functions, records of departmental committees, etc.

Handlist: list of documents in numerical order, with names or summaries of contents.

In-Letters and *Out-Letters:* letters received or copies of letters sent by a department, often in bound volumes; these can be useful in checking whether a particular subject was dealt with by the department.

Private Office Papers: papers kept in the office of a minister or senior civil servant.

Registered Files: files which pass through the registry and are given a registry number.

Unregistered Files: files which have not passed through the registry for various reasons; for example some private office papers or some papers from out-stations may not be registered.

Wanting: either no evidence for the existence of the document or document was lost before it reached the P.R.O.; as opposed to 'missing' which means mislaid.

Weeding: term used for destruction of papers considered unsuitable for permanent preservation; carried out before 1959 under destruction schedules made under the Public Record Office Acts, 1877 and 1898.

Printed in England for Her Majesty's Stationery Office
by William Clowes & Sons Limited, London, Colchester and Beccles
Dd 500013 K 16 10/71 WmC 3307